"As a Global South leader committed to community-led structural change, I highly recommend this book to my colleagues as well as to anyone seeking a comprehensive understanding of the humanitarian sector. The historical background, the contextual framework and the strategic planning tools that it provides are invaluable to practitioners interested in making a meaningful and systemic impact."

Marie-Rose Romain Murphy, *Co-Founder of ESPWA and The Haiti Community Foundation*; and *President of RMC-Romain Murphy Consulting, USA*

"The authors artfully combine foresight theory and practical tools for designing and implementing effective aid programmes. Fundamental reading for both aid theorists and practitioners interested in innovation and transformative change, and an essential playbook for making humanitarian aid both immediately impactful and future-ready."

Christina Bennett, *CEO Start Network, UK*

"I welcome this new book by Michel Maietta and Eilidh Kennedy. It is truly easy to understand and follow, and, more importantly, use. They give a gift of relevance and accessibility. Clearly, a text and process all can benefit from that can help create a transformed tomorrow."

Sohail Inayatullah, *Unesco Chair in Futures Studies, IIUM, Malaysia; and Professor, Tamkang University, Taiwan*

"The humanitarian ecosystem faces a period of real disruption. To help humanitarian actors succeed and seize the opportunity for transformation, the authors offer a pioneering and exciting toolbox mixing structural analysis, scenarios and strategic planning. For the humanitarian sector, this book will become a key reference for both practitioners and researchers."

Philippe Ryfman, *Honorary Professor, Pantheon-Sorbonne University, France; and researcher and lawyer specialising on the humanitarian sector and NGOs*

"The flexibility of the approaches outlined in this book ensure its relevance for all actors involved in development work, particularly LGBTI – often left behind. The guidance for how to implement strategic foresight projects virtually makes it all the more pertinent in a post-Covid 19 world."

Vincent Kyabayinze, *Director, East Africa Visual Artists (EAVA Artists); and LGBTI activist, Uganda*

"Thoughtful, insightful and practical book; essential reading for aid and development professionals in the ever-changing world."

Anika Krstic, *Country Director, Plan International, Sudan*

"The manual you have in your hands gives you the keys to foundational strategic foresight approaches and methods adapted for humanitarian actors. Using these approaches you can create transformative narratives and build resilient strategies with communities. Eilidh and Michel have tested, piloted and implemented these tools in multiple settings, combining high professional standards with accessibility and commitment."

François Bourse, *Director of studies, Futuribles, France*

"The use of foresight methodology for strategic planning involving our local partners was instrumental for us as an ecosystem of actors to be impactful in a very dynamic operational context! I am really happy to see the toolkit is coming to the public domain for wider use and adoption in the humanitarian sector."

Nipin Gangadharan, *Country Director, Action Against Hunger Bangladesh*

Strategic Planning in the Humanitarian Sector

This book provides humanitarian practitioners and policy makers with a manual for how to apply foresight and strategy in their work.

Drawing on extensive research, the book demonstrates in practical terms how embedding futures-focused thinking into practice can help humanitarian actors to enhance their impact and fit for the future. The book provides readers with a step-by-step guide to an innovative combination of tools and methods tested and refined over the course of several years. However, it also goes beyond this, by grounding the approach within the broader ambition of making humanitarian action more effective. Overall, the analytical and strategic processes outlined in this book will accompany a decision maker through every stage of creating a robust, agile and impactful long-term strategy.

This accessible guide will be an essential point of reference for practitioners and decision makers in the humanitarian ecosystem, as well as students studying humanitarian affairs, global development, conflict studies and international relations.

Eilidh Kennedy is Co-Founder and Director of the Inter-Agency Research and Analysis Network (IARAN). She has more than ten years' experience working with humanitarian actors providing trainings, research, foresight analysis and supporting strategic development.

Michel Maietta is Co-Founder and Director of the Inter-Agency Research and Analysis Network (IARAN). He has two decades of experience in high-profile, strategic leadership, and has developed and turned around multiple start-ups, programmes and operations in the humanitarian and development sector.

Strategic Planning in the Humanitarian Sector

A Manual to Foresight and Futures-Focused Thinking

Eilidh Kennedy and Michel Maietta

LONDON AND NEW YORK

First published 2022
by Routledge
2 Park Square, Milton Park, Abingdon, Oxon OX14 4RN

and by Routledge
605 Third Avenue, New York, NY 10158

Routledge is an imprint of the Taylor & Francis Group, an informa business

© 2022 Eilidh Kennedy and Michel Maietta

The right of Eilidh Kennedy and Michel Maietta to be identified as authors of this work has been asserted by them in accordance with sections 77 and 78 of the Copyright, Designs and Patents Act 1988.

All rights reserved. No part of this book may be reprinted or reproduced or utilised in any form or by any electronic, mechanical, or other means, now known or hereafter invented, including photocopying and recording, or in any information storage or retrieval system, without permission in writing from the publishers.

Trademark notice: Product or corporate names may be trademarks or registered trademarks, and are used only for identification and explanation without intent to infringe.

British Library Cataloguing-in-Publication Data
A catalogue record for this book is available from the British Library

Library of Congress Cataloging-in-Publication Data
A catalog record has been requested for this book

ISBN: 978-0-367-55697-6 (hbk)
ISBN: 978-0-367-55696-9 (pbk)
ISBN: 978-1-003-09475-3 (ebk)

DOI: 10.4324/9781003094753

Typeset in Bembo
by Deanta Global Publishing Services, Chennai, India

This book is dedicated to all the jellyfish

Contents

List of figures	xi
List of tables	xiii
Foreword	xv
Preface	xvii
Acknowledgements	xix
Abbreviations	xx

1 Strategic foresight for transformation — 1

2 Embracing uncertainty with foresight — 20

3 Developing a strategy for effective change — 47

4 A toolkit for humanitarian action — 79

Scoping Workshop 82
PESTLE 94
Architecture 100
Importance/Uncertainty Matrix (MIU) 107
Morphological Scenarios 117
Matrix Scenarios 126
Driver Files 137
Actors File 141
Influence/Dependency Matrix (MID) 146
Writing scenarios 163
The Strategy Tree 170
Actor/Objective Matrix (MAO) 181
Testing 195

x   *Contents*

Annex 1: Glossary   207
Annex 2: Platforms for virtual facilitation/engagement   212
Index   215

Figures

1.1	Possible, probable and preferable futures as subsets of possibility space (Candy 2010, p. 35)	10
1.2	Toolkit contents and flow	16
2.1	Foresight toolkit contents and flow	25
2.2	Matrix Scenarios, 2025: Agri-food systems in a plus COVID-19 world (CIMMYT 2021)	33
2.3	The CLA iceberg image with layers (Inayatuallah 2017, p. 5)	42
3.1	Strategy, plan and the subsets of the strategic, tactical and operational dimensions	53
3.2	MID chart of the study North-Central South Sudan 2018, with MAO-selected actors in black	63
3.3	Optimisation chart flow	75
4.1	Flow of the toolkit	81
4.2	Optimised list of changes for a Scoping Workshop	85
4.3	Impact–Readiness chart	86
4.4	X–Impact chart with changes ranked by impact	87
4.5	Readiness–Impact chart with ranked changes by impact and readiness	88
4.6	Readiness–Impact chart with ranked changes by impact and readiness plus interpretation	89
4.7	An Architecture template	101
4.8	Example of an organisational Architecture, 2025: Agri-food systems in a plus COVID-19 world – Global perspective (CIMMYT 2021)	103
4.9	Example of a contextual Architecture, Food insecurity in Yemen: an outlook to 2020	104
4.10	Empty Importance/Uncertainty Matrix	108

xii *Figures*

4.11 Abbreviated example of a completed Importance/
Uncertainty Matrix used for a study on counterterrorism 109
4.12 Interpretation factors in an Importance/Uncertainty Matrix 110
4.13 Interpretation actors in an Importance/Uncertainty Matrix 112
4.14 Selecting scenario drivers from the MIU –
Morphological Scenarios 118
4.15 Abbreviated and adapted MIU for Matrix Scenarios,
2025: Agri-food systems in a plus COVID-19 world –
Global perspective (CIMMYT 2021) 127
4.16 Abbreviated and adapted MIU (actors removed
for clarity) for a system of study with a contextual
viewpoint to build Matrix Scenarios examining the
future of counterterrorism 129
4.17 Frame for Matrix Scenarios for a system of study with
an organisational viewpoint, 2025: Agri-food systems
in a plus COVID-19 world – Global perspective'
(CIMMYT 2021) 132
4.18 Matrix Scenarios for a system of study with an
organisational viewpoint, 2025: Agri-food systems in a
plus COVID-19 world (CIMMYT 2021) 133
4.19 Example of am MID chart 155
4.20 Example of an MID chart with nine areas and two
diagonal lines 155
4.21 Example of an MID chart with all the roles and behaviours 156
4.22 Example of an MID chart with game of actors analysis 158
4.23 Case study for MID chart Sudan 2027 158
4.24 Example of diagram of causality (problems are in grey
textboxes) 172
4.25 Example of diagram of objectives 174
4.26 Example of diagram of objectives with strategic options
(in black textboxes) 175
4.27 Example of outlined strategy draft 175
4.28 Use of a triangle tip to identify a strategic option 178
4.29 Case study for MID chart Sudan 2027, with actors
selection (bolded icons) 183

Tables

3.1	MAO for the draft strategy 'Reaching the Unreachable'	64
3.2	MAO for the draft strategy 'Feeding the Markets'	65
3.3	MAO for the draft strategy 'Communities are Key'	66
3.4	The robustness test and the most robust strategy (in grey)	71
3.5	The relevancy test and the most relevant strategy (in grey)	72
4.1	Example of a PESTLE table	95
4.2	Example of a filled in PESTLE table	96
4.3	Sample of a PESTLE table for a completed Importance/ Uncertainty Matrix used for a study on counterterrorism (components in top-right box of Figure 4.11)	109
4.4	Example of a spreadsheet with combined inputs from an Importance/Uncertainty survey	114
4.5	Example of a hypothesis grid using selected drivers looking at the future of financial assistance – multiple scenario paths	122
4.6	Example of indicators for a Driver File	140
4.7	Example of an Actors File	143
4.8	Example of an MID table with actors' agenda cases	148
4.9	Example of an MID table with Actor × Actor cases	150
4.10	Example of an MID table with directions of influence	152
4.11	Example of an MID table with filled Actor × Actor cases	154
4.12	Examples of indicators for the sample scenario in Step 5	167
4.13	Empty MAO table	185
4.14	Example of a MAO table with cells filled with relevant signs, figures and sense of the analysis	186
4.15	Example of a MAO table with filled in cells and interpretation	189

xiv *Tables*

4.16 Example of robustness matrix, empty 197
4.17 Example of Relevancy matrix, empty 197
4.18 Example of filled robustness matrix 198
4.19 Example of filled relevancy matrix 200

Foreword

I was delighted to be asked to contribute to this book because not only have I known Eilidh and Michel for many years, but I, and my organisation, have benefitted from the work that they do via the Inter-Agency Research and Analysis Network (IARAN). It is clear to me, after decades of working as an activist for the rights of people infected by HIV/AIDS that short-term thinking disenfranchises communities by robbing them of the right to have hope and plan for their own future. Humanitarian actors must do better.

As the president of the National Association of Support for Seropositive and AIDS Patients (ANSS), which I founded in 1993, I am keenly aware of the need to think about complexity and to consider the long term. As the first civil society organisation dedicated to the prevention of HIV transmission and improving the well-being of people infected with HIV in Burundi, we have seen how it can take many years if not decades to see system-wide change. My work has centred on challenging the structures which underpin the prejudice against those living with HIV/AIDS. It is only by unpacking and better understanding the systems in place that we can find opportunities for transformation and leverage our influence and resources to achieve change for the people we serve. It takes commitment, a deep understanding of the context in which you are working and a robust, flexible strategy to truly be able to have a lasting impact.

As a leader I am constantly faced with questions of how to best deploy our resources, to find alternative avenues of funds and to consider the big picture as I make decisions about how to structure our organisation to achieve our stated goals. I believe deeply in the value that foresight and strategic development bring to these processes. I know that I am not alone in the challenges I face; as a member of the board of numerous international non-governmental organisation (INGOs), such as Coalition Plus and Sidaction, I have clearly seen the need for greater xvi *Foreword*

strategic thinking in order to be more impactful with limited resources among many organisations.

The authors have dedicated the better part of a decade to testing and exploring the tools and methods outlined in this book. Drawing on their practical experience of delivering strategic foresight support to humanitarian actors from governments to local civil society organisations, large INGOs and global research institutions, they have curated a series of tools which are easy to use while delivering robust outputs. They have cultivated an approach to strategic foresight which is adapted to the needs and decision-making culture of humanitarian organisations while providing an avenue through which to challenge the inertias that have stalled progress towards a more representative and inclusive aid sector. Not only do Eilidh and Michel have the real-world experience to understand where the challenges lie in implementing strategic foresight projects, they have crafted ways to overcome them and have clearly demonstrated the value of futures thinking for finding new ways of working in the sector, pushing all humanitarian actors to think more collaboratively about how to achieve their missions.

After years of designing courses for both academic and professional settings, this book is the culmination of their practical and academic experience. In these pages they have demonstrated that they have the skills to communicate what they have learned effectively, creating an entry point for anyone interested in applying futures thinking to their work and building on their skills of strategic development. The pedagogic approach they employ to craft a narrative that is easy to follow while introducing the reader to complex tools is what makes this book so valuable for practitioners such as myself. By including notes for facilitation, particularly virtual facilitation, they have given readers the information they need to run a project by themselves, from start to finish.

This is exactly the kind of support that my team and so many others like us need to ensure our long-term impact. Reading this book, other leaders like myself can learn how to employ strategic foresight to help us pursue the transformation we seek.

I hope you find this text as illuminating as I have and that you use the tools it explores with your communities and partners to do your work more effectively. We do not have the time or resources to waste. We must begin to think more strategically and this book is an important step in the right direction.

Jeanne Gapiya-Niyonzima
President of National Association of Support for
Seropositive and AIDS Patients (ANSS)

Preface

This book is the culmination of nearly a decade of research into the uses of strategic foresight in the humanitarian ecosystem by the Inter-Agency Research and Analysis Network (IARAN). The work that has comprised this experience has mostly been in the practical application of strategic foresight for operational humanitarian actors, though it has also included support to governments and academic institutions. Since its inception, and in every version of its structure, the IARAN has been working towards a vision to create a more equitable and effective humanitarian ecosystem where every actor leverages their particular skills and experiences to contribute to the achievement of the Sustainable Development Goals.

The IARAN was conceived of as an operational research project at the French think tank IRIS (Institut des Relations Internationales et Strategiques) in 2012. Between 2013 and 2015 the test phase of the project was implemented with Save the Children International as the operating partner. During this time, a small team was embedded within the humanitarian department of Save the Children International with up to three analysts covering the Middle East, East and Southern Africa, and West Africa. In 2015, the project graduated to a pilot phase where it moved to Action Against Hunger and scaled up to have over ten staff members covering four regions, producing more than 50 foresight reports per year. The IARAN initiative has always worked in partnership with other academic and operational organisations, such as Futuribles in Paris, collaborations which contributed significantly to the development of the project. At the end of 2018, the operational research project was concluded and the IARAN became an independent initiative.

Now, we operate as a collaborative network of humanitarian professionals with decades of experience working for a multitude of different

xviii *Preface*

organisations. IARAN is a think tank with an active fellowship and a consultancy wing through which we provide training, foresight research and strategic development support to a wide range of humanitarian actors.

For more information about the IARAN, please see our website www.iaran.org.

Acknowledgements

The learnings in this book are built on the tireless work of IARAN staff over many years. We would like to thank the following people for all their efforts, patience and good humour throughout our time together: David Africa, Marie-Jeanne Berger, Sterling Carter, Maria Di Loreto, Ana Arribas Gil, Leonie Le Borgne, Jade Le Grand, Caelum Moffatt, Tyler Rundel, Adam Rybo, Chloe Schmitt and Victoria Watt-Smith. We would also like to thank the leadership at IRIS, Futuribles, Save the Children International and Action Against Hunger for their support of the IARAN initiative.

In addition, we are continually indebted to the IARAN fellows and supporters; many of them have challenged our thinking, helped develop our approaches and contributed to the review of this book. We would especially like to recognise Amara Bains, François Bourse, Juan Sebastian Brizneda, Giulio Coppi, Miguel Leroy, Mariana Merelo Lobo, Eva Molt, Luana Moussallem, Isabelle Pelly, Matt Thomas and Matt Twilley.

Without this community this book would not have been possible.

Abbreviations

DAC	Development Assistance Committee
EC	European Commission
IASC	Inter-Agency Standing Committee
INGOS	international non-governmental organisations
LFA	Logical Framework Approach
LMIC	low- and middle-income countries
MAO	Actor/Objective Matrix
MICMAC	Matrix-Based Multiplication Applied to a Classification
MID	Influence/Dependency Matrix
MIU	Importance/Uncertainty Matrix
NGOS	non-governmental organisations
ODA	official development assistance
ODI	Overseas Development Institute
OECD	Organization for Economic Cooperation and Development
PCM	Project Cycle Management
PESTLE	political, economic, social, technological, legal and economic
SDGS	Sustainable Development Goals
TOC	theory of change
UN	United Nations

1 Strategic foresight for transformation

Introduction

Strategic foresight is about creating a narrative and pathways for sustainable change and transformation. We believe it is a critical approach for anyone seeking to build resilience among people affected by crises in a rapidly changing world. This book has been written to provide an entry point for humanitarian actors to improve their futures literacy and exploit strategic foresight tools in their work. In order to use these tools in a transformative way you need to accept that you do not know everything, centre the lived experience of people affected by crises and be open to challenging your worldview (Bhagat et al. 2021). The ethos of our work is founded on creating flexible ways to mainstream collaboration between humanitarian actors and encouraging them to adopt systems-based approaches to build better futures.

The humanitarian ecosystem

Before we can begin to discuss strategic foresight and its uses in humanitarian action, we must first define what we mean by the term 'humanitarian'. In aid work the term 'humanitarian' is often used synonymously with emergency responses; however, for the purpose of this book we have extended its definition to include all activities which are undertaken to improve the human condition. In short, we use the term 'humanitarian' to refer to all activities along the humanitarian–development–peace nexus, as we believe that the common thread linking these areas of work must be placing humans at the centre of the system.

Building on this broad definition of humanitarian action, we consider the actors who provide humanitarian assistance at every level (locally, nationally and internationally) to be very diverse. They include people affected by crises, religious or secular movements, non-governmental

DOI: 10.4324/9781003094753-1

2 *Strategic foresight for transformation*

organisations, multilateral organisations, networks, state actors (including their militaries) and, increasingly, the business sector.

Within the broader group of humanitarian actors we distinguish two categories: formal and non-formal actors. The first includes actors for whom the provision of humanitarian assistance is their primary role and who have significant decision-making power in the ecosystem, namely the United Nations (UN), the International Red Cross and Red Crescent Movement, international non-governmental organisations (INGOs) and traditional donor governments such as those in the Organization for Economic Cooperation and Development (OECD) Development Assistance Committee (IARAN 2016). The second cohort, which is not new to the ecosystem but is playing an increasingly important role in the decision-making space, includes people affected by crises, local authorities and national governments in areas of humanitarian operations, local NGOs, military actors, the business sector and new donors (IARAN 2016).

All of these actors, their complex interconnections, the power dynamics between them, and the rules and norms that govern humanitarian action constitute the humanitarian ecosystem. The humanitarian ecosystem is an incredibly politicised space where norms, power and resources are contested.

The economy of the humanitarian ecosystem and the potential for transformation

The most significant dynamic that defines the relationship between actors in the humanitarian ecosystem is the flow of money. There are a multitude of financial flows funding the humanitarian ecosystem. Each of these distinct flows creates a different power dynamic depending on which actors in the system amass and control these funds. It is difficult to get a comprehensive picture of all of the funding streams which reach actors in the humanitarian ecosystem. We have tried to categorise the main flows of funding by their sources:

1. Official development assistance (ODA)
2. Private donations to humanitarian organisations
3. Remittances

The best tracked flow of money into the humanitarian ecosystem's economy is the funding provided through ODA for international humanitarian assistance.[1] In 2019, this totalled US$23.2 billion (Thomas and Urquhart 2020, p. 30). The vast majority of this funding is allocated to multilateral institutions, INGOs, and the International Red Cross and Red Crescent Movement (Thomas and Urquhart 2020, p. 30). While this figure represents the funding that is dedicated to specifically 'humanitarian' considerations, a broader look at ODA demonstrates that there is a substantial pot of resources which complements these funds through bilateral support to governments (in the form of grants or debt relief) and to a more diverse group of multilateral institutions investing in development pursuant to the Sustainable Development Goals (SDGs). While international humanitarian assistance from ODA is often represented as being the core of the humanitarian ecosystem's economy, in reality it is only a small proportion of its resources.

The funding stream of private donations is not tracked comprehensively at the global level. The primary source of private donations is individuals. However, figures tracking private funding streams also include the money channelled into the humanitarian ecosystem by foundations or trusts, companies, and national societies (Thomas and Urquhart 2020, p. 39). The funds from private donations are primarily streamed through INGOs and NGOs. While it is difficult to create a full picture of how much money private donors bring into the ecosystem, it was estimated to be around US\$6.4 billion in 2019 (Thomas and Urquhart 2020, p. 30).

Though it is not often acknowledged by many humanitarian actors (especially formal actors), people affected by crises engage in their own crisis response, orchestrating support from within their communities both near and far, and appealing to other humanitarian actors within the humanitarian ecosystem when it is beneficial (Brown et al. 2014). Remittances sent by diaspora communities to friends and family in low- and middle-income countries (LMIC) of origin is an increasing source of support leveraged by people affected by crises, especially as transmitting money virtually becomes easier through increased global connectivity. The volume of remittances dwarfs the funds provided through ODA, reaching a record of US\$554 billion in 2019 alone (Ratha 2020). However, unlike ODA, which is channelled through a small group of powerful formal actors, remittances are dispersed in relatively small amounts to billions of people. This means that while the overall amount of remittances is much greater than ODA funds, it does not translate into power.

While they do not represent the majority of actors nor do they control the majority of the resources flowing into the humanitarian ecosystem's economy, formal humanitarian actors persistently dominate decision-making in key international fora, dictate the norms and standards to which most actors in the humanitarian ecosystem must adhere and craft the narrative which defines how the humanitarian ecosystem

4 *Strategic foresight for transformation*

is perceived. The behaviours of these formal actors are defined by their history and as such it is critical to understand how they evolved to address the cultural challenges which exist today.

A brief history of how formal humanitarian actors have developed

The history of modern humanitarianism has been broken down into several distinct time periods, each depicting a different stage of its evolution.[2] While there are several interpretations of where each period begins and ends, we find Barnett's suggested three 'ages of humanitarianism' where he delineates periods of *imperial humanitarianism, neo-humanitarianism* and *liberal humanitarianism* (Barnett 2013, p. 29) to be the most compelling. In the following we present and adapt his categorisations by focusing on the evolution of the formal humanitarian system, a subset of the humanitarian ecosystem. With each shift that we identify there was a major evolution in the ways of working of the actors and the norms that govern the formal humanitarian system. Each period will be named Formal Humanitarian System 1.0, 2.0, etc. We focus on this small area of the humanitarian ecosystem to draw attention to its outsized power in shaping the culture of international humanitarianism and governing the resources which flow through ODA. Understanding how dominance of the formal humanitarian actors in many spaces evolved is critical to understanding the power dynamics at play in the humanitarian ecosystem at large.

"Caring for the sick, the poor and those in need, and easing their suffering are gestures of solidarity as old as humanity" (Maietta 2015, p. 53). However, the foundation of the Formal Humanitarian System, defined as organised interactions between actors operating internationally with the aim of alleviating suffering, can be traced to Europe in the 19th century and the signing of the first Geneva Convention in 1864. The Geneva Convention of 1864 was first signed by 12 Western states and the newly founded International Committee of the Red Cross (ICRC); it set a body of rules for the treatment and care of the wounded and prisoners of war (ICRC n.d.).

The rules that governed the Formal Humanitarian System 1.0 mainly focused on the laws of war. This system would continue to evolve and adapt from the end of the American Civil War (1861–1865) to World War I (1914–1918). The Formal Humanitarian System 1.0 reached its maturity in the aftermath of WWI when the first secular INGO was founded in 1919, Save the Children – formerly the Save the Children Fund. The Save the Children Fund would soon be joined by other humanitarian INGOs from both religious and secular traditions such as Norwegian People's Aid, the humanitarian wing of the Norwegian

Strategic foresight for transformation 5

labour movement, created to respond to the humanitarian crisis caused by the Spanish Civil War. In addition to the new actors joining the space, other legal initiatives would be formalised in this period, building on the body of rules of the Geneva Convention (revised in 1906) and the League of Nations, such as the Nansen Passport in 1922, that set the base for refugees' security and protection.

The first iteration of the Formal Humanitarian System was conceived and matured during what Barnett (2013) defines as the age of 'imperial humanitarianism'. At its apogee, it was a dynamic interaction between state actors, the International Red Cross and Red Crescent Movement, and INGOs, navigating a set of international treaties protecting prisoners of war and the victims of war or natural disasters such as refugees. During this time, INGOs were game changers, leading the evolution of the Formal Humanitarian System itself by securing and protecting communities which fell outside the existing body of rules or supporting those that were not serviced by other actors. INGOs were critical in pushing the other actors in the Formal Humanitarian System to consider new ways of working and an ever-increasing number of people for humanitarian support. For example, in 1942 Oxfam began campaigning to force the British government to reconsider its blockade on Greece, which was creating intolerable living conditions and pushing vulnerable communities into famine (Oxfam International n.d.).

The Formal Humanitarian System 1.0 evolved into its second iteration in the second half of the 1940s. The failures of the revised Geneva Conventions to make the scourge of war less terrible, the inability of the League of Nations to broker peace effectively and manage the fallout of a breakdown in relations, as well as the continued perpetration of crimes against humanity by state actors challenged the foundation on which the first Formal Humanitarian System had been built.

The signing of the fourth Geneva Convention in 1950 along with the creation of the United Nations and its humanitarian agencies and programmes (High Commissioner for Refugees (UNHCR), Food and Agriculture Organisation (FAO), World Food Program (WFP), etc.) paved the way for the Formal Humanitarian System 2.0. During this period, secular and especially faith-based INGOs experienced unprecedented growth; in the United States alone nearly 200 NGOs were created in the latter half of the 1940s (Barnett 2013). The proliferation and development of humanitarian INGOs accelerated further during the decolonisation period where "the skills, material and money wielded by Northern organisations were called upon to supplement those of the newly established Southern governments … after the rapid withdrawal of the colonial power" (Davey et al. 2013, p. 11).

6 *Strategic foresight for transformation*

During this age of what Barnett (2013) coins as 'neo-humanitarianism', the Formal Humanitarian System 2.0 grew in terms of the number of actors involved, the scope of what was being attempted and the funding which was being put into humanitarian activities (Reimann 2006). This period, culminating in the Biafra War (Nigeria 1967–1970), showed how the agility and impact of INGOs could push the system forward as yet another generation of INGOs came into being. Once again, seeing the failure of many of the existing actors and structures to meet the spiralling need in Biafra, a new, more strident and interventionist generation of INGOs was born. These INGOs stand out from those that came earlier in the period by adapting their operating methods and principles to be more confrontational. Showing how the use of testimonials, advocacy and campaigns could achieve impact was in stark contrast to the discretion and silence of the International Red Cross and Red Crescent Movement (Maietta 2015, p. 54). With the signing of the second protocol of the Geneva Conventions in 1977, the Formal Humanitarian System 2.0 reached maturity.

The Formal Humanitarian System 2.0 would not survive the turmoil of the end of the Cold War. The 1990s ushered in the beginning of the age of what Barnett (2013) calls 'liberal humanitarianism' and what we will call the Formal Humanitarian System 3.0, which continues to the present day. The reflection of formal humanitarian actors on their failures in the aftermath of the Rwandan genocide (1994) initiated the design and implementation of a new set of humanitarian standards, for example the Humanitarian Accountability Partnership (HAP) and the Sphere Standards. It was intended that these measures would enhance the quality of humanitarian action, making humanitarian actors more effective in their mission.

The creation of bureaucratic processes and norms designed by institutional donors to control the way that money is spent and ensure greater oversight of funds (e.g. in the setting up of the Project Cycle Management quality system by USAID in 1971 and the European Commission in 1992) solidified the dependency between INGOs and state actors. In the Formal Humanitarian System 1.0 and 2.0, INGOs were game changers. However, during the third iteration of the system, they would gradually lose their agility and independence. An increasing need to feed their growth-oriented economic models began to overwhelm their original purpose.

The process of bureaucratisation completely transformed the ways of working for both formal and non-formal humanitarian actors who were receiving ODA funding, even indirectly. As part of this process, approaches and resources for 'strategy development' began to be

Strategic foresight for transformation   7

adopted from the business sector, without much consideration for how they needed to be adapted for a non-profit mission. First, UN agencies and then INGOs began designing and implementing strategies with the support of management consultancy firms like Deloitte, BCG and Accenture, a process which is still common today. This relationship is predicated on the understanding that formal humanitarian actors receiving the support believe that business strategies would make them more effective, while business sector actors hope their partnership with INGOs could "possibly lead to gains in their reputations" (CSR Europe 2004, p. 4). This shift in organisational culture where formal humanitarian actors began to behave more like businesses (particularly in terms of how they manage risk) fuelled the creation of gargantuan organisations whose economic models required them to be increasingly concerned with their financial growth and market share. Many of the formal humanitarian actors who engaged in these processes would lose their original purpose: to put people affected by crises at the centre of their mission. The result of this trend was epitomised when, in the first decade of the 21st century, most of the biggest INGOs had in place top-down strategies aimed at growing the brand of their organisations, without meaningful consideration or contribution of people affected by crises.

Since the beginning of the Formal Humanitarian System 3.0, the ways of working and laws guiding humanitarian action have not significantly evolved. Humanitarian actors' value chains, meaning the sequence of strategic activities of an organisation (Kaplinsky and Morris 2001), are mostly unchanged since the nineties. Worse, the economic models of many have cemented, creating disturbing (and paradoxical) dependencies between INGOs and the state actors that are their primary donors. Moreover, the dominance of formal humanitarian actors over the proportion of ODA spent on humanitarian endeavours has created significant barriers to entry for non-formal actors to key decision-making spaces and impedes the ability of new actors from communities affected by crises to set standards and norms. This bottleneck protects the colonial structures that define the roots of formal humanitarian actors and has been imbibed into each iteration of the system since its foundation (Davey et al. 2013, p. 6). The dependence of INGOs on the state actors that fund them directly and indirectly make it more challenging for them to address the deep-rooted causes of modern poverty and vulnerability, which are fundamentally political.

Often humanitarian action still saves lives in the short term. However, the Formal Humanitarian System 3.0 as it currently operates has become expensive, ineffective and can be disruptive to local resilience (Spiegel 2017). A new iteration is not only needed but is imperative in a world

8 *Strategic foresight for transformation*

that is regionalised, affected by complex crises, and where addressing inequality and injustice are necessary for success.

High-level decision-making (e.g. the setting of standards and guidelines or the prioritisation of resources) is still heavily dominated by formal humanitarian actors. Despite some progress towards the commitments made in the Grand Bargain (signed in 2016), for a participation revolution and to channel funds more directly to local organisations (IASC n.d.), these objectives are still far from being realised. Signatories to the Grand Bargain themselves reported that while there had been gains in localising aid, "progress remains at the normative level – there is as yet no system-wide shift in practice" (Metcalfe-Hough et al. 2020, p. 54). Given the lack of progress by formal actors to make the space more inclusive, it is necessary that the change in the dynamics of power will be driven by non-formal actors who create parallel systems, making formal actors obsolete, or who force a change of practice on formal actors.

The Formal Humanitarian System 3.0 has become a very conservative structure and is incredibly resistant to any change and transformation that challenges its underlying power structures. In biology and medicine, the condition that causes the stiffening of a part or parts of an organism is called 'sclerosis'. The only way to fight against the sclerosis of the Formal Humanitarian System 3.0 is to incept change and transformation from the outside, namely from non-formal actors in the ecosystem. Non-formal actors – mainly communities and people affected by crises – are the new potential game changers. Actors in the Formal Humanitarian System 3.0 need to begin to see their roles differently. The humanitarian ecosystem is on an evolutionary journey towards a new age of humanitarianism, where formal actors must embrace humility, understand that complexity can only be faced collaboratively, and that their ultimate goal is not growth (or even their own existence) but to leverage their investments and expertise into transformation for the benefit of others.

What is strategic foresight?

Strategic foresight is a process that enables actors to use collective intelligence to build their understanding of possible futures and identify pathways to achieve their vision: "it is about understanding the whole landscape of a particular situation and the options that a decision maker has in it" (Kuosa 2011, p. vii). We break down strategic foresight into three discreet phases: foresight, strategic development and planning. This book will focus on the first two phases of foresight and strategic development.

Foresight

Foresight is not a prediction. It is a process of looking forward in time and using collective intelligence and imagination to consider a range of possible futures (definition derived from Lustig 2017). The exact origin of foresight is disputed, as roots of futures thinking can be found the world over dating back centuries. However, there is a general consensus that in its modern form it developed in Europe and America in the late 1940s and 1950s (Hines 2020). Though there are many institutions from a variety of countries that each brought different approaches to the development of the field, many give credit of the institutionalisation of foresight and futures studies to the formation of the RAND Corporation, which grew out of a partnership between the United States Air Force and Douglas Aircraft Company signed in 1946 (Dreyer and Stang 2013, p. 9). Since then, foresight has been used for decades by military organisations to achieve a strategic advantage, by governments to try to ensure long-term efficacy and by business sector actors to maintain their competitive edge. The foresight phase of strategic foresight as we define it includes two stages: structural analysis and scenario building. There are a few key tenets of foresight which have guided our work that we feel are important to highlight.

The first is that the future does not evolve in a linear fashion (Godet 2006, p. 13). There are many dimensions of complexity in the systems in which we live and work, and it is not reasonable to simplify the full array of uncertainty generated into a single, unique version of the future. There are no facts about the future, and foresight requires managing the discomfort that comes with having to deal with incomplete information. Although foresight will not tell you what the future will be, through the process of exploration it builds an understanding of the multiple ways a system could evolve and "gives us increased power to shape our own future even when times are unsettled" (Lustig 2017, p. 12).

The second, related concept is that the degree of uncertainty grows as the length of your outlook extends. As is represented by the futures cone in Figure 1.1, the scope of possible futures widens as time passes. With fewer fixed parameters, a longer time frame often offers more opportunities for change and transformation.

Finally, foresight provides simple tools for complex problems (Godet 2006, p. 14). The purpose of foresight is to provide you with a way to unpack complexity, not to add to it. As a result, useful foresight tools must be easy to engage with.

Foresight is a foundation on which better decisions can be made by developing an understanding of the system in which you are operating

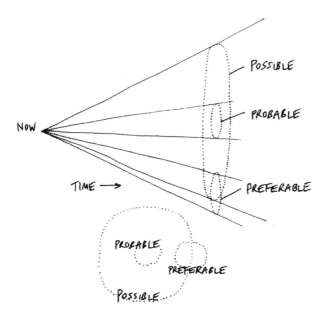

Figure 1.1 Possible, probable and preferable futures as subsets of possibility space (Candy 2010, p. 35)

and the myriad of ways that it may evolve, as well as what the role of your organisation is within it. Foresight can help make actors more impactful when it is paired with strategic development.

Strategic development

Strategic development is the second phase in strategic foresight. It is a process which articulates possible futures with a strategy. Through the process of strategic development actors evaluate their strategic options, consider choices and decide which strategy to implement. A strategy defines an overall objective and its underpinning hierarchy of objectives. Before we can discuss what the term 'strategy' means for humanitarian actors, we must first understand how the concept evolved.

The concept of strategy is rooted in military culture and it is even older than the word 'strategy' itself. The concept has evolved across centuries of history and its interpretation has changed through transculturation. Sun Tzu (2014), Machiavelli (1961) and Clausewitz (2007)

Strategic foresight for transformation 11

are widely recognised as the leading thinkers in strategy and warfare. The concept of strategy we embrace in this book, and in our work, is more in line with the roots of Sun Tzu's teachings, which, over time, have been enriched by the approaches of the Arabic schools of strategy.[3] Both schools of thought believed that the goal of war was to dissuade the enemy without even engaging in combat. Sun Tzu advanced an approach using misdirection, espionage and agility, while the Arabic schools added the values of embracing patience and wisdom. Ultimately, they are about engaging higher-level systems, thinking to understand your opponent and adapting your strategy to discourage him.

We find Sun Tzu's work and the Arabic schools of strategy more applicable to humanitarian action, as they are founded more on systems thinking and persuasion, considering all dimensions of engagement rather than focusing narrowly on the tactical dimensions of combat and prevention (Handel 2005, p. 24 and Khawam 2010, pp. 9–10). For our use, we transpose the thinking of these eminent strategists from winning wars to achieving equity and justice.

The strategic development process operationalises collective intelligence. It shapes an organisational culture enabling decision-making and agility, containing risk, and finally enhancing actors to a higher level of performance. The utility of strategic development, recognised by governments and business actors for decades, has still not been adapted and systematically implemented by the majority of humanitarian actors.

Actors, and particularly formal humanitarian actors, have the tendency to be focused on their identity and performance. Strategic development offers actors the opportunity to think differently about how they work. The strategic development process opens the possibility to converge with other actors uniting around a common vision. It has the potential to enable them to align their actions to increase their agility and impact. Developing a strategy is a process through which teams build a collective understanding of the journey that an organisation is undertaking towards a shared vision. A strategy does not determine the future (Mackay et al. 2020) but is a journey towards a possible one. When strategic development is associated with solid leadership, it enables decision makers to build high-performing teams.

Why humanitarians need strategic foresight

Many humanitarian actors are focused on delivering lifesaving aid, meeting the immediate needs of the communities they serve. While such interventions are certainly necessary, they do very little to build local

12 *Strategic foresight for transformation*

resilience and can have deleterious effects on communities in the long term.[4] The majority of organisations and funds channelled through formal humanitarian actors are directed at responding to crises rather than preventing them or alleviating the structural causes of vulnerability. Humanitarian actors are largely reactive in nature (McGoldrick 2011, p. 968).

Strategic foresight has huge potential for all actors in the humanitarian ecosystem seeking to increase their long-term impact and create a more effective and equitable system. Here are just some of the particular ways that strategic foresight can support better decision-making in the humanitarian ecosystem.

Strategic foresight can help humanitarian actors to think beyond the real-time challenges that they face and to consider how they can better contribute to the achievement of long-term goals, such as the SDGs. There are few, if any, challenges faced by humanitarian actors and the communities they serve which can be overcome in a matter of months or a year. Moreover, there are many protracted crises which have lasted multiple decades. Not addressing the root causes of a crisis, but solely focusing on the immediate needs that are created by it, considerably reduces the impact of humanitarian action. The creation of parallel systems which are predominantly funded by external sources can create dependency and disempower communities. Without thinking long term, humanitarians cannot support communities to address the structural dimensions of a crisis. Foresight studies and strategic development can lay the groundwork to challenge the short-termism which has become a stumbling block to genuine impact and transformation.

Strategic foresight can help humanitarian actors to address complexity. Some of the underlying dynamics which drive complex crises are exacerbated by the world's inability to resolve the protracted social discord created by inequality (in all aspects – income, gender, race, etc.), the continued scourge of conflict, our failure to manage the demands of economic and social progress in balance with the environment, and the increasing strain of climate change. Many of the structural problems which have underpinned longer humanitarian crises are likely to be intensified by the COVID-19 pandemic. For example, in 2020 there was an increase in the number of people living in extreme poverty for the first time in over 20 years (UNOCHA 2021, p. 9). Humanitarian actors need to grapple with these structural challenges if they are going to be successful in alleviating suffering in the long term. The fact that humanitarian actors see their funding rising incommensurately with the needs that they seek to address adds even more pressure to be strategic with the resources we have.

Strategic foresight for transformation 13

Not thinking with a long-term or systemic perspective means that humanitarian actors are more likely to do harm and waste money in complex crises. If the actor is not local to the context in which they are working, they must consider if and how they can bring value and continue to question themselves as time passes so they understand when they should leave. Operating in the same way year on year without thorough reflection can use up precious resources at best and yield damaging results at worst. All organisations (local or international) either need an exit strategy, a medium-term strategy (three–five years) or a long-term strategy (five–ten years) to be able to really consider how to have an impact on communities. Strategic foresight is critical for all of these processes.

Strategic foresight can help humanitarian actors to be more agile. By understanding the complexity of the systems in which they intervene and the ways in which they can evolve, humanitarian actors can learn to better manage uncertainty. Strategic foresight provides humanitarian actors with the tools to develop strategies for multiple futures, providing them with the ability to be prepared to make rapid changes in a volatile context. Having multiple strategies that are fit for different futures already designed is a significant advantage for operational actors that are trying to maintain their impact while having to respond to everyday challenges in humanitarian action.

Strategic foresight can help humanitarian actors to evolve. Strategic foresight can encourage actors to question their value chain and transform it – i.e. to find where they have the greatest added value in intervening in complex crises and how they can complement other actors in the space. Humanitarian actors (particularly formal humanitarian actors) have not changed their view of what strategic activities on the value chain they should invest in since the beginning of the Formal Humanitarian System 3.0, predominantly focusing on fundraising, programming and operations. This has resulted in many organisations maintaining a structure which has not kept pace with the changes in the world around them. Formal humanitarian actors continually overestimate their own importance as they do not take the time to truly understand and appreciate the capacity of the other actors they engage with. This means that many humanitarian organisations often do not complement the strengths and support systems of local communities and people affected by crises but rather overrun them. This is an incredibly inefficient use of resources, which could be improved by transforming their value chain. The commitments to the participation revolution, to ensure that funding more directly reaches local organisations and to making equitable partnerships, could all be more easily realised if humanitarian leaders systematically

14   *Strategic foresight for transformation*

used strategic foresight to visualise possible paths of transformation and had the managerial courage to pursue change.

To properly review their value chain, formal humanitarian actors need to question their mental models and the 'white saviour' complex which infects many aspects of humanitarian action. Collaborative intelligence and inclusive decision-making could be used to challenge the Western bias that dominates structures in the formal humanitarian system, to integrate more and different perspectives, and to challenge the plethora of assumptions that underpin both large and small decisions. Strategic foresight can help individuals and organisations to break out of their worldview and consider the systems they intervene in from different angles. Approaching humanitarian action from a different vantage point is key to changing the underlying structures which perpetuate the imbalances that deny affected communities a voice in decisions about their own lives.

Non-formal humanitarian actors can use strategic foresight to challenge the dominance of their formal humanitarian counterparts in key decision-making fora. In addition, strategic foresight can help local actors to challenge their existing structures, consolidate their value chain and enhance their economic model to become more independent and influential. Strategic foresight tools can support non-formal humanitarian leaders to channel their knowledge, culture and experience into change and transformation.

To achieve sustainable change, the goal of humanitarian action, humanitarians need to break from their path dependence – basing what they will do next on what they have done in the past rather than a critical evaluation of what would be most effective in the future. Path-dependence reinforces a broken system, as "the system, to a large extent, causes its own behaviour" (Meadows and Wright 2008, p. 2). Strategic foresight is a critical tool to support humanitarian decision makers in reflecting on their role within the humanitarian ecosystem.

This book focuses on how to respond to the strategic and existential questions that humanitarian actors face. It does not comprehensively cover how to implement a strategy on a tactical or operational level, i.e. it does not include the planning phase of strategic foresight. This is because most humanitarians are good tacticians, skilled at taking a strategy and transforming it into a plan. Humanitarian organisations are routinely comprised of technical experts, logisticians and managers who have varying levels of experience in implementing programming in a myriad of contexts. Where organisations seem to struggle is in figuring out which strategic questions they should be trying to address, how to break down complexity without falling into siloed thinking and how to prepare to be effective in multiple futures.

Strategic foresight for transformation 15

Toolkit approach

The development of the approach we put forward in this book is built on the outputs of an operational research programme titled the Inter-Agency Research and Analysis Network (IARAN) in which a team of analysts and strategists were embedded in an international think tank and two networked INGOs. Lasting over six years, this programme explored the use of different methods and strategic foresight tools for humanitarian actors. The approach we propose here has been tested and refined through over 150 projects carried out with a plethora of different organisations of a variety of sizes and mandates working across the globe, principally in sub-Saharan Africa, the Middle East and Asia. Over the course of the test and pilot phases of the IARAN project, the different approaches and methods that we explored coalesced into a set of flexible, accessible tools to deliver quality strategic foresight support with limited resources and on tight timelines. Though the research which underpins this book spans more than six years of operational work, the context in 2020 and 2021 when this text was being drafted made the value in a flexible approach all the clearer as the COVID-19 pandemic changed working patterns and perspectives.

In writing this book our overarching goal was to synthesise our learning into a manual for humanitarian practitioners interested in integrating strategic foresight into the culture and the practices of their organisations and their decision-making processes. To this end, we have identified the following aims:

- To demonstrate how foresight and strategic development can enhance long-term impact and transformational change
- To provide humanitarian actors with a suite of foresight tools that they can use to analyse the complexity of the contexts in which they operate and project themselves into the future, in collaboration with other stakeholders
- To equip readers with the approach and the method to design agile and robust strategies

To achieve these aims, we have adopted the structure of a toolkit to ensure that what you need to know to use the approaches which we recommend is communicated as clearly and as practically as possible. The toolkit contains 13 files, each of which explores a particular tool; we outline its uses, the expected outputs and give you a step-by-step guide of how to do it. These tools can be combined to support you through the phases of foresight and strategic development from the selection of a strategic question, through the creation of exploratory scenarios and finally onto developing an agile strategy for your organisation or context (see Figure 1.2).

16 *Strategic foresight for transformation*

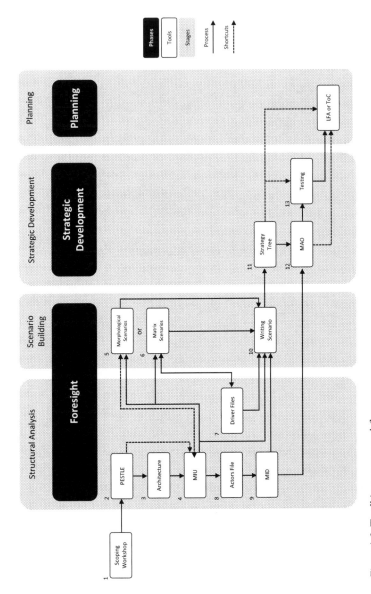

Figure 1.2 Toolkit contents and flow

Strategic foresight for transformation 17

The toolkit itself is preceded by a narrative section which, building on this introduction, discusses the ways in which strategic foresight can be used in the humanitarian space and weaves together a process to create a set of detailed, contextualised scenarios, and an agile and robust strategy. If you are already familiar with strategic foresight, you can turn directly to the toolkit in Chapter 4 for practical guides on how to implement our tools.

This book is laid out according to the following outline.

Chapter 2, "Embracing uncertainty with foresight", deepens the introduction into foresight methodologies and outlines how to combine the tools explored in the toolkit to formulate a set of exploratory scenarios, using two different scenario approaches. This chapter introduces ways in which you can support the 'uptake' of your scenarios by decision makers by proposing several communications methods/workshops which you can explore. Finally, Chapter 2 closes by highlighting two complementary approaches to scenario development and providing sources for each for further reading.

Chapter 3, "Developing a strategy for effective change", discusses the current ways of planning in the humanitarian ecosystem, their origins and limits. This chapter will explain how the approach to strategic foresight presented in this book can enhance strategy design and decision-making to concretise your vision in effective and agile strategic plans for change and transformation. It covers both how to build a robust, futures-oriented strategy and how to optimise a strategy that you already have.

Chapter 4, "A toolkit for humanitarian action", includes guides on how to use and implement the 13 individual tools. These guides give a step-by-step process of how to implement each tool in the foresight and strategic development phases, and provide details of how these tools can be used collaboratively in a virtual setting.

Notes

1 For details of how international humanitarian assistance is measured, please see A Thomas and A Urquhart (2021) *Global Humanitarian Assistance Report 2020*, Bristol, Development Initiatives, pp. 85–86.

2 Eleanor Davey *et al.* describes them exhaustively in *A History of the Humanitarian System: Western Origins and Foundations* (2013, p. 13).

3 The Arbabic schools of strategy are excellently summarized in *Le Livre des ruses: La strategie politique des Arabes* (Khawam 2010).

4 For specific examples, consider the investments in the Democratic Republic of Congo (Smith 2018, p. 1), the response to Rohingya (Khaled 2021) or the lack of investments in Somaliland (Moscovici 2021).

18 *Strategic foresight for transformation*

References

Barnett, M (2013) *Empire of Humanity: A History of Humanitarianism* (Reprint ed.), New York, Cornell University Press.

Bhagat, A et al. (2021) What does it mean to decolonize the future?, *Diaspora Futures Collective*, accessed on 13 April 2021, https://medium.com/diaspora-futures-coll ective/what-does-it-mean-to-decolonize-the-future-98baf6c294a7

Brown, D, Donini, A and Knox Clarke, P (2014) Engagement of crisis-affected people in humanitarian action, Background Paper of ALNAP's 29th Annual Meeting, 11–12 March 2014, Addis Ababa. London, ALNAP/ODI.

Candy, Stuart (2010) The futures of everyday life: politics and the design of experiential scenarios (PhD dissertation). University of Hawaii at Manoa. DOI: 10.13140/RG.2.1.1840.0248

Clausewitz, Carl (2007) *Carl von Clausewitz: On War*, translated by Michael Howard and Peter Paret. Oxford, Oxford University Press.

CSR Europe (2004) *Engaging with NGOs: Challenging but Rewarding? Workshop Series Report*, Paris, accessed on 22 March 2021, https://www.orse.org/fichier/2406

Davey, E et al. (2013) *A History of the Humanitarian System: Western Origins and Foundations*, London, Humanitarian Policy Group: Overseas Development Initiative.

Dreyer, I and Stang, G (2013) Foresight in governments: practices and trends around the world, in *Yearbook of European Security YES* [online], accessed on 11 February 2021, https://www.iss.europa.eu/sites/default/files/2.1_Foresight_in_governm ents.pdf

Godet, M (2006) *Creating Futures: Scenario Planning as a Strategic Management Tool*, London, Economica.

Handel, Michael (2005) *Masters of War: Classical Strategic Thought*, London, Taylor & Francis.

Hines, A (2020) When did it start? Origin of the foresight field, *World Futures Review*, 12(1), 4–11. https://doi.org/10.1177/1946756719889053

Inter-Agency Research and Analysis Network (IARAN) (2016) *Future of Aid: INGOs in 2030*, London, IARAN, accessed on 11 February 2021, https://www .iaran.org/future-of-aid

Inter-Agency Standing Committee (IASC) (n.d.) About the Grand Bargain, United Nations Office for the Coordination of Humanitarian Affairs (UNOCHA), accessed 11 February 2021, https://interagencystandingcommittee.org/about-the -grand-bargain#:~:text=The%20Grand%20Bargain%2C%20launched%20during ,efficiency%20of%20the%20humanitarian%20action

International Committee of the Red Cross (ICRC) (n.d.) *Convention for the Amelioration of the Condition of the Wounded in Armies in the Field*, Geneva, 22 August 1864, accessed on 11 March 2021, https://ihl-databases.icrc.org/applic/ihl/ihl.nsf/State s.xsp?xp_viewStates=XPages_NORMStatesParties&xp_treatySelected=120

Kaplinsky, R and Morris, M (2001) *A Handbook for Value Chain Research*, Brighton, UK, Institute of Development Studies, University of Sussex.

Khaled, A F M (2021) Do no harm in refugee humanitarian aid: the case of the Rohingya humanitarian response, *International Journal of Humanitarian Action* 6(7), https://doi.org/10.1186/s41018-021-00093-9

Khawam R R (2010) *Le Livre des ruses: La stratégie politique des Arabes*, Paris, Libretto Editions Phebus.

Kuosa, Tuomo (2011) *Practicing Strategic Foresight in Government: Cases of Finland, Singapore and European Union*, Singapore, S. Rajaratnam School of International Studies.

Lustig, Patricia (2017) *Strategic Foresight: Learning from the Future*, Axminster, Triarchy Press.

Machiavelli, Niccolò (1961) *Il Principe*, edited by Luigi Firpo, Torino, Enaudi.

MacKay, B, Arevuo, M, Meadows, M and Mackay, D (2020) *Strategy: Theory, Practice, Implementation*, Oxford, UK, Oxford University Press.

Maietta, M (2015) Origine et évolution des ONG dans le système humanitaire international, *Revue internationale et stratégique*, 2(2), 53–59. https://doi.org/10.3917/ris.098.0053

McGoldrick, Claudia (2011) The future of humanitarian action: an ICRC perspective, *International Review of the Red Cross*, 93(884), 965–991. DOI:10.1017/S1816383112000306

Meadows, D and Wright, D (2008) *Thinking in Systems: A Primer*, London, Chelsea Green Publishing.

Metcalfe-Hough, V et al. (2020) *The Grand Bargain Annual Independent Report 2020*, London, Humanitarian Policy Group: Overseas Development Institute.

Moscovici, B (2021) A miracle on the horn of Africa, *Der Spiegel*, accessed on 14 April 2021, https://www-spiegel-de.cdn.ampproject.org/c/s/www.spiegel.de/international/world/boom-in-somaliland-a-miracle-on-the-horn-of-africa-a-c7fb91cc-4b0a-4561-977d-dd985cf48256-amp

Oxfam International (n.d.) Our history, Oxfam, accessed on 15 March 2021, https://www.oxfam.org/en/our-history

Ratha D et al. (2020) *Migration and Development Brief 32: COVID-19 Crisis through a Migration Lens*, Washington, DC, KNOMAD-World Bank.

Reimann, K (2006) A view from the top: international politics, norms and the worldwide growth of NGOs, *International Studies Quarterly*, 50(1), 45–67, accessed on 14 April 21, http://www.jstor.org/stable/3693551

Smith, A N (2018) Foreign aid and development in the democratic republic of the Congo: an analysis of international barriers to development, *Perceptions*, 4(2), 19. https://doi.org/10.15367/pj.v4i2.110

Spiegel, P (2017) The humanitarian system is not just broke, but broken: recommendations for future humanitarian action, *The Lancet: Health and Human Services Series*, accessed on 14 April 21, https://www.thelancet.com/journals/lancet/article/PIIS0140-6736(17)31278-3/fulltext, DOI: https://doi.org/10.1016/S0140-6736(17)31278-3

Thomas, A and Urquhart A (2020) *Global Humanitarian Assistance Report 2020*, Bristol, Development Initiatives.

Tzu, Sun (2014) *The Art of War*, translated by John Minford, London, Penguin.

United Nations Office for the Coordination of Humanitarian Affairs (UNOCHA) (2021) *Global Humanitarian Overview 2021*, Geneva, UNOCHA.

2 Embracing uncertainty with foresight

Foresight in the humanitarian ecosystem

Strategic foresight has been used in many sectors to augment an organisation's competitive advantage, to enable organisations to adapt to a changing environment and to help organisations become increasingly effective. However, many of the tools and approaches that are most commonly used in foresight take a significant investment of time and money, two resources which are often limited for humanitarian actors. The majority of humanitarian actors have not routinely included strategic foresight as part of their planning processes, and in many instances the development of a strategy is predominantly based on what has been done in the past. In order to encourage more humanitarian actors to explore strategic foresight we have piloted some adaptations to the tools and processes that were developed for the business sector and governments to find a more flexible approach, one that can be implemented on a shorter time-scale and better adapted to the pace of humanitarian decision-making. Depending on the level of consultation and collaboration which you want to engage in, the toolkit we propose in this book has been developed to deliver a robust scenario analysis from conception to final edit in 6 weeks – though this is a challenging endeavour!

To create and validate a process well suited to humanitarian action it was necessary to test tools and approaches to ensure that they could be carried out in a myriad of different circumstances. The tools also had to be easy to engage with to enable humanitarians to include as many actors as possible while simultaneously relying on easily accessible resources and mostly free software. Having the buy-in of stakeholders in your organisation, partners and the communities with whom you are working is critical to ensuring your foresight analysis is used. As a result, the tools that we have included in this toolkit all have a participatory component which you can scale up or scale down depending on your time and resources.

DOI: 10.4324/9781003094753-2

Embracing uncertainty with foresight   21

Tools from the schools of early warning, strategic foresight and the use of quantitative modelling were all explored in the development of this toolkit. Through this process of exploration, the tools that brought the most value to the planning and decision-making processes of humanitarian actors were honed and adapted. Though each approach has provided insights which have been integrated into the toolkit, the majority of the tools that we will explore in this book stem from strategic foresight.

Within the practice of foresight there are many different approaches. However, most have the same three broad elements: an analytical stage (which we call structural analysis), scenario building and use of the information for decision-making. In this chapter, we will focus on the first two stages.

Structural analysis is the foundation of foresight. It is a combination of tools that helps you to gather information, categorise the information that you have collected, analyse the complexity in your system, consider the way in which your system will evolve and synthesise the outputs so that they are digestible and easy to engage with. It helps us to break away from linear thinking and begin to operate in a more systems-based way, focusing on the connections between the critical drivers of our system and building our understanding of how those interactions shape the context where we are, and will be, working in. David Stroh (2015) synthesises why thinking outside silos and in a systems way is critical for social change: "it enables you to achieve better results with fewer resources, in more lasting ways" (p. 1). In short, it is essential to achieve the ambitions of humanitarian and development actors, and doing it with a futures lens brings even more value.

Though the process of structural analysis can help to build your understanding of the structures and drivers of change that underpin your system, making them useful in and of themselves, the development of scenarios takes your analysis one step further. Scenarios are images of possible futures. They are narratives created to explore how the dynamics of a system could change over a given time period. Scenarios are a critical tool in strategic foresight. They are a way of efficiently presenting a lot of complex information in a way that decision makers can easily engage with.

Scenarios are a useful tool for decision makers, as they are a way to immerse them in the futures that they are contemplating. Part of the difficulty in thinking strategically is that the future is unknown and uncertainty can paralyse decision makers or convince them that there is little point in long-term planning, as their context may change dramatically. However, scenarios present decision makers with images of the futures they may

22 *Embracing uncertainty with foresight*

face, representing them as reality, which can help them think through some of the changes that they need to prepare for and demonstrate the consequences of their actions (or inaction) on their environment.

The process of building scenarios is a learning journey that does not end once a report is written. The best scenarios are living documents which are monitored and updated as time passes. The skills you gain, the common vision that you develop and the resources that you create through this process add up to be more than the sum of its parts.

Identifying a strategic question

Getting started: the Scoping Workshop

Before you begin a foresight study it is necessary to ensure that you have clearly identified the question you wish to answer and considered how you will approach it. A key tool that helps you to identify what your strategic questions might be is called the Scoping Workshop (for more details on this tool, see pp. 82–93). This process supports you to think through what the critical changes are that face your organisation or the context in which you are intervening, and asks you to consider your level of preparedness to meet each change. In this exercise, changes can be both challenges that you have to overcome and opportunities which you could take advantage of, were you sufficiently strategic in your investments/positioning. This kind of exercise shows you where your strengths lie, what you are not prepared for and where you need to focus your attention in order to change direction.

The Scoping Workshop can be an excellent entry point into foresight work, as it is quick to implement and can yield very interesting results which prompt reflection from the participants about core questions facing many humanitarian organisations such as:

- Where are your strengths/weaknesses?
- Are you positioned to be effective as your context changes around you?
- What challenges do you need to overcome?
- What do you need to do to take advantage of opportunities of transformation?

While you may feel that you are already clear on the topic which you would like to investigate, thereby eliminating the need for a Scoping Workshop, you still need to set the parameters of your research. Throughout your strategic foresight journey you will be taking a systems

Embracing uncertainty with foresight 23

approach to work. Though there are many definitions of what a system is, this is a succinct way of thinking about the concept: a system is "a set of elements or parts that is coherently organised and interconnected in a pattern or structure" (Meadows and Wright 2008). Before you can begin your investigation into any system you must first define its boundaries. You can do this by setting the viewpoint of your study – deciding if you are going to investigate your topic from the perspective of your organisation (organisational) or your context (geographic or contextual), and you must decide on your time horizon – the length of your outlook (see prerequisites in Scoping Workshop, pp. 82–93). Once you have fixed these two parameters you have defined what we call your 'system of study', the foundation of any strategic foresight work.

With a clear system of study you must now consider how your mental model might affect your analysis.

Mental models

As you are defining your system of study, it is essential to be aware of your mental model. Mental models are defined as "cognitive representations or constructs of situations that may be real, imagined, or hypothetical" (Al-Diban and Ifenthaler 2011 and Gentner and Stevens 1983, cited in Glick et al. 2012, p. 488). Everyone has a mental model shaped by each individuals' unique experiences of culture, race, religion, community, education, work and values. You can never rid yourself of your mental model; it is something that changes over time, and is shaped by the way your life and thinking progresses. Mental models have social and cultural purposes, but can also represent an obstacle when it comes to imagining alternative futures. Being aware of one's mental models is often a prerequisite to challenge them and to become open to seeing and accepting information that might not fit within those moulds.

Biases, blind spots, preconceived notions and the ways in which you have been conditioned to learn (assuming you know things about a system, people or context before gathering facts or updating your information) can wreak havoc with your ability to constructively engage an analytical project. It is too often the case that those in leadership positions in the formal humanitarian system (often not from the community about whom decisions are being made) bring their biases and preconceived notions to the table. Without meaningful engagement with local partners and national staff, these misconceptions can severely, adversely affect critical decisions which are made over how to use limited resources. The best way to ensure that you are challenging your mental model, covering blind spots in your knowledge and learning as you progress through an

24 *Embracing uncertainty with foresight*

analytical project is to ensure that you are representing as wide a range as possible of people and perspectives in your work. The majority of participants in your study should stem from the community within the system that you are exploring. The tools that we are proposing here have been adapted to be easy to use for people not familiar with strategic foresight work to enable you to use them flexibly with different stakeholders. When you are not able to include an actor in the foresight phase, you should explore how you can integrate their perspective using other data sources such as existing surveys, adding in questions to ongoing monitoring and evaluation processes, and conducting interviews.

Other steps which you must take to counter your mental model include being clear about your assumptions, externalising your thinking, being transparent about any inferences you're making and inviting criticism. All of these steps can be accomplished by going through a process of structural analysis.

Foresight: using structural analysis to develop scenarios

The foresight phase is made up of the structural analysis and scenario-building stages. In this chapter we will present the sequence and approach to exploit these tools to conduct a structural analysis of your system and give you two different approaches to creating scenarios. The sequence of tools for the foresight phase are as follows: the PESTLE, Architecture, Importance/Uncertainty Matrix, Morphological Scenarios or Matrix Scenarios, Driver Files, Actors File, Influence/Dependency Matrix, and Writing Scenarios (tools 2 to 10 in the toolkit, see Figure 2.1). You should use only one method of scenario generation (Morphological or Matrix) and as such, while there are nine tools presented here, you will only use eight of them in any one project.

Structural analysis stage

Structural analysis is a process of deconstruction and externalisation. It is a combination of tools that helps you to gather information, categorise the information that you have collected, analyse the complexity in your system, consider the way in which your system will evolve and synthesise the outputs so that they are digestible and easy to engage with. Through the process of structural analysis we create what we call the foresight base. This is a set of analytical outputs which are the foundation of your study and represent all the research you have done and information you have gathered. Out of the whole process of building scenarios, the phase of structural analysis takes the longest time to complete. It is critical that

Embracing uncertainty with foresight 25

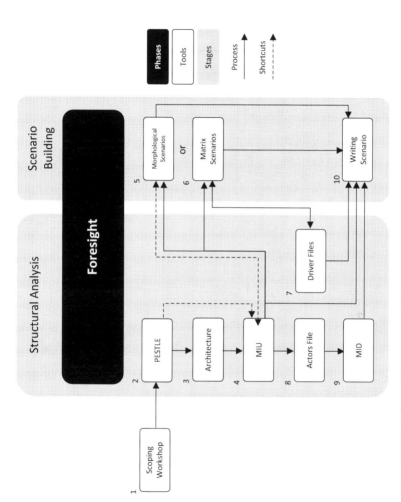

Figure 2.1 Foresight toolkit contents and flow

26 *Embracing uncertainty with foresight*

you create a solid understanding of your system and the phenomenon you are analysing.

PESTLE

The first phase of structural analysis is brainstorming. You have likely already engaged with many of the tools that are useful in this phase, as they are frequently used to do context analysis and other forms of assessments. There is a rich library of literature on ways to stimulate and organise your thoughts, and finding the tools which best align with your way of thinking or organisational culture is a process in which it is worthwhile to invest some time. We have exploited many of these tools as part of foresight work, and usually a combination (if you have the time and interested participants) yields the most interesting results, as each tool can encourage you to think differently and to look at your system from a different perspective. However, in this book we are proposing the tool which we use most often and which can often suffice to be the only brainstorming tool you use – a framework for identifying the *political, economic, social, technological, legal* and *environmental* dimensions of any system, a PESTLE (see pp. 94–99 for more details).

The goal of the brainstorming phase is not to fulfil any specific tool or template but rather it is to think as divergently and expansively about your system as you can. You may find it more intuitive to create your own approach to answering the critical question that you are trying to unpack here, namely: What are the component parts (both actors and factors) of your system? What are the underlying trends that have been (and continue) to cause your system to change? What are the potential events or 'triggers' which could cause a sudden shift in the way your system evolves? Can you decompose the culture and structures which underpin the behaviours and values of the system you are analysing? What are the changes that occur around your system which impact how it develops? Who are the actors operating within your system, and outside of it, which can influence how the system is shaped? In short, what are the elements of your system that you need to understand in order to confidently estimate the different ways they may evolve in the future and understand how their interactions could create new realities.

While you are constructing your PESTLE, it is necessary to define the components that you have identified. In order to take your analysis to the next stage you need to ensure that each component is clearly delineated and that there is a common understanding of what is included under that term. It is essential that you are able to build a shared language between your stakeholders, because as you involve new or different

Embracing uncertainty with foresight 27

people through the process a lexicon of your system of study is a vital document to enable them to participate effectively.

Once you have completed your brainstorming process it is necessary to ensure that it is summarised into an easily digestible output – a PESTLE table (see Table 4.2 in Chapter 4 for an example). This step is essential as you should always invite people who are knowledgeable about your system to critique your work, asking them to flag anything that is missing or challenge any of the ways in which you have defined the components that you set out, and providing them with a format that is easy to use is most likely to encourage them to engage.

Architecture

The next step of the structural analysis process is to create a map of the system that you are exploring; in our toolkit we call this the Architecture (see pp. 100–106). As with brainstorming tools, there are a plethora of different approaches that you can use to do this. System maps range from highly complex representations of hundreds of components and the pathways between them to basic mind maps which represent a system in broad groupings. There is value in any kind of graphical representation which translates the list of components you have gathered into a map which gives you an organisational paradigm of your system. The Architecture which we propose in our toolkit does not ask you to map the connections of the components of your system (that analysis comes later). It focuses on segregating these components of your system into different levels, categorising them according to their spatial or thematic relevance to the crux of your scope of work. This approach allows you to create a way to visualise your system in an accessible manner.

The creation of your system map is a valuable step and key output in your analytical process. The output you create here can be a guiding document for a multitude of planning processes for your organisation, even without taking your analysis any further. By going through this process as a team you create a shared vision of the system in which you are working and this is a key step towards effective teamwork.

Reducing complexity

Once you have identified the components of your system, defined each of them and arranged them in an Architecture, you can begin the process of reducing the scope of your system to the actors and factors that are the most influential and impactful. Without engaging in this exercise, you may find yourself struggling to manage the vast quantity of data that you

28 *Embracing uncertainty with foresight*

have collected. Without a process to reduce the number of components you need to consider, it can be difficult to choose where to focus your attention.

To reduce the complexity of your system we recommend using an Importance/Uncertainty Matrix (MIU; see pp. 107–116), an incredibly valuable tool. By assessing each of the components in your system according to two metrics – their importance in the system and the uncertainty of their evolution – it provides a new lens through which you can increase your understanding of your system of study. The output of your MIU can be interpreted in multiple ways and is useful throughout the scenario-building stage and strategy development phase. The MIU provides you not just with a way to reduce the complexity of your system to your critical drivers but also to identify the actors in your system which merit further analysis and to identify the levers of change in your system. The MIU is a visual demonstration of how dynamic or static your system of study is.

The metrics of importance and uncertainty are concepts which are easy to understand, and the way in which you fulfil the matrix is intuitive. The implementation of this tool is highly flexible and easy to adapt to the circumstances of your project. In addition, it allows you to assess your actors and factors in the same tool, taking only the most important forward in your research. As such, it is often the approach that we recommend.

However, there are other ways you can reduce the complexity of your system, such as through a Matrix-Based Multiplication Applied to a Classification (MICMAC). The MICMAC tool is focused on assessing the details of the interaction between the factors of your system by assessing the influence of each factor on all the others (the MICMAC does not support you to reduce the number of actors that you are considering). A MICMAC asks participants to assign a numerical value to the level of influence of one factor on another and enter the results in a spreadsheet. The creation of the MICMAC is an intense process, and it can be challenging to find participants with the time and inclination to complete it. However, the results of the MICMAC can yield very interesting insights, some of which can seem counterintuitive, and so the somewhat laborious process is often worthwhile. The output of the process is a graphical representation of the influence/dependency of each factor on all the other factors of your system. It highlights which factors are determinant in your system, which ones can be influenced and which have influence. From this graph you can select the most influential factors in your system on which to focus your research and analysis. Though we do not explore this tool in the toolkit, we wanted to introduce it as an alternative option and provide you with the resources where you can find more detail.[1]

Embracing uncertainty with foresight 29

When it comes to selecting the number of actors and factors that you will take forward in your study there is no magic number, as it depends on the structure of your system of study (e.g. how dynamic it is) and your time and resources. While there isn't a strict number of actors or factors you should be aiming to include, we can give some general guidance. When using the MIU to reduce the number of actors you are considering, we would recommend that you do not take more than 25 actors on to the next stage of your project. When considering how to select the critical factors, the potential number varies more widely. We have run global projects such as *The Future of Aid: INGOs in 2030* (IARAN 2016) where 23 critical factors were selected and more commonly, smaller country/regional focused projects where we highlighted between 3 and 10 critical factors. If you are taking your analysis forward to write scenarios, the number of factors you identify is determined by the type of scenarios that you will be writing (see Steps 1 and 2 of Matrix Scenarios, pp. 126–136, and Morphological Scenarios, pp. 117–125, for more details).

Ultimately, the process of reducing the complexity of your system is vital and there are benefits to both tools we present here. The benefits of the MIU are that it allows you to treat your actors and factors simultaneously, it takes less time to complete and it is an easier process in which to engage your stakeholders. One of the benefits of the MICMAC is that it is a very detailed analytical process which requires you to really delve into the dynamics of your system to assess how the relationship of influence works.

The process of reducing the complexity of your system lessens the burden of research, but more importantly it simplifies your system to the essential components which can bring clarity to your thinking and analysis.

Note: A MICMAC measures the influence/dependency of factors, whereas an MIU measures importance/uncertainty of all factors and actors. While influence and dependency are perceived as very distinct characteristics of a component, facilitators and attendees might find the difference between importance and influence to be confusing. You should try to be very clear with which tool you are using and clarify these concepts before using either one.

Deepening your research into the drivers of change and most influential actors

After you have identified the critical drivers to be included in your scenarios (using the approaches outlined in the Morphological and Matrix Scenario approaches) and reduced the number of actors you are

30 *Embracing uncertainty with foresight*

considering in your study you must conduct further research on each of these components. It is at the point where the critical factors for your scenarios are selected that we begin to think of them as our critical drivers.

To research the critical drivers in your system, we recommend using the framework of a Driver File (see pp. 137–140). Driver Files are structured to help you to research the history, current context, trends and uncertainties of each of the drivers you are investigating. The format presented encourages you to explore the aspects of your system which you have identified as being important so that you are more confident in projecting how they may evolve in the future.

In addition to the Driver Files, you should complete your Actors File (see pp. 141–145) to investigate the ways in which the most important actors in your system (identified in your MIU) will operate. If you chose to complete a MICMAC instead of an MIU you would need to include all the actors in your Architecture in your Actors File. The Actors File asks you to identify the agendas and analyse the role of each of the most important actors in your system. It is a vital step towards better understanding how your system of study could change over the course of your outlook and it yields very useful insights into how to best interact with the actors in your system today.

To take your analysis of the role of actors further, it is at this stage that you should perform an Influence/Dependency Matrix workshop (MID; pp. 146–162) on the actors in your Actors File. The MID enables you to focus on the game of actors, meaning to consider how each of the actors in your system interacts with those around them. It is a detailed workshop which requires a relatively significant investment of time as you consider the relationship of each actor with all of the others one by one. In its process, it is similar to the MICMAC. Though it is time-consuming, the detailed analysis the MID provides can shed new light on how to interpret the actions of the actors in your system of study and help you to identify potential allies, partners and targets for your work. It is a robust way of bringing added nuance to your analysis of one of the most complex aspects of your system of study.

Your research into the most important actors and factors can be used to inform your work in many different ways. Their value is not limited to the construction of scenarios; the outputs from your Actors File and MID are also essential in the strategic development phase. In addition, by creating a library of resources about the critical components of your system, you can draw on this information for a plethora of decision-making needs. Your Driver Files and Actors File can become a useful repository for information which you can, and should, continue to update as your context evolves.

Embracing uncertainty with foresight 31

The research into the critical drivers of change and most important actors in your system is the culmination of your structural analysis. It is the point where you have come from the widest analysis of your system (created through brainstorming and represented in your system map) to a detailed analysis into the most important elements that you are working with. These become the focus of your scenarios moving forward.

Scenario building

The process of scenario building begins from the outputs of the structural analysis stage – your foresight base. In writing scenarios, we first begin by looking at the critical drivers in your system of study, the ones which you identified through your MIU/MICMAC and have written up as Driver Files. The reason we focus our attention on these drivers is that the value of creating multiple scenarios is to explore how the critical components in your system of study may evolve in different directions. When writing scenarios using the Matrix and Morphological approach you begin by focusing only on the drivers you have identified, and after your scenario framework has been developed you will integrate your analysis from your Actors File and MID workshop.

You can create scenarios to explore contexts at many levels – programmatic areas (subnational), countries, regions or even global projects. There are several different types of scenarios which can be used depending on your analytical and decision-making needs. Some of the most commonly used include predictive, normative, hypothetical and exploratory scenarios.

Predictive scenarios are scenarios which include a dimension of likelihood as they postulate different evolutions for a particular phenomenon or context. Predictive scenarios are usually based on (or at least include a component of) quantitative analysis. As such, they can provide a very interesting picture of potential futures where robust data is available to be exploited but can be more limited in their ability to explore complex and unquantifiable phenomenon comprehensively without significant resources and investments.

Normative scenarios are used to design pathways to a desired future. They do not explore the full spectrum of what may occur but rather hone in on how to make a particular future a reality. As a result, they can be particularly useful in designing advocacy strategies as they can show multiple pathways to achieving a particular goal while exploring the trade-offs in each one.

Hypothetical scenarios ask the question what if. They have a catalysing event (e.g. what if there is a severe earthquake) in mind and then work

32 *Embracing uncertainty with foresight*

forwards from that starting point rather than your present reality. These are useful for examining the possible ramifications of different events and can be especially useful for contingency planning.

Exploratory scenarios, as is suggested by the name, explore a broad range of futures. This approach casts a wide a net as possible to understand the complexity and uncertainty that is encapsulated in any system. Exploratory scenarios seek to represent the scale of possible change in your system. As a result, exploratory scenarios are useful in many different aspects of decision-making and planning.

Each of the different types of scenarios produces a different kind of image of the future and can be useful for different decisions. Though all kinds of scenarios have value in answering different organisational and decision-making needs, we have found exploratory scenarios to be the most useful in the majority of situations. You can use several different methods to create exploratory scenarios. In this toolkit we illustrate two different methods: Matrix and Morphological Scenarios. We have selected these two approaches to generate exploratory scenarios as they are the tools we have used the most often and find to be the best adapted to the majority of humanitarian decision-making needs.

Matrix Scenarios

Matrix Scenarios (see pp. 126–136) are a very commonly used approach to scenario generation. By framing your scenarios across two axes which are defined by the critical drivers you have selected you are able to create four distinct images of the future which are easy to represent and understand. The process of coming to these scenarios is simple yet the framework offers you the opportunity to make the scenarios as detailed and robust as you are able to by fleshing out the narrative in each quadrant with the details you can draw from your structural analysis research. For first time futurists, this form of scenario generation can be an excellent entry into the field.

CASE STUDY OF MATRIX SCENARIOS: 2025 – AGRI-FOOD
SYSTEMS IN A PLUS COVID-19 WORLD (CIMMYT 2021)

The 2019/2020 COVID-19 pandemic prompted many organisations to think about how they need to work differently and some, such as the International Maize and Wheat Improvement Center (CIMMYT), embraced the challenge to think about how they could leverage this period of disruption to increase their effectiveness in the near term and

Embracing uncertainty with foresight 33

Figure 2.2 Matrix Scenarios, 2025: Agri-food systems in a plus COVID-19 world (CIMMYT 2021)

in the future. To do this, a virtual, collaborative foresight project was launched, structured using a series of workshops, multilingual surveys and participatory seminars. Over the course of the project which lasted several months, insights from over 300 staff members and experts were gathered and integrated into the analysis. Using the methodology outlined in the toolkit presented in this book, a set of Matrix Scenarios was constructed (Figure 2.2).

The matrix for this set of scenarios provided a frame for how the world could evolve between 2020 and 2025. The two groups of drivers that were created around the efficacy of governance and the economic/social consequences of the pandemic and the policy responses to it shape the reality of many industries, but this project went further thinking through what each of the four distinct scenarios means for the agricultural sector and food insecurity more generally. Ultimately these scenarios were used for a comprehensive engagement strategy, working with partners and investors to think through what the consequences of the global disruptions are for them and the work that they do.

34   *Embracing uncertainty with foresight*

Morphological Scenarios

Morphological Scenarios (see pp. 117–125) are also explored in the toolkit. Morphological scenarios give you an approach to creating scenarios that are framed by more than two dimensions and as such are a useful complementary tool to ensure that if you are analysing a system which you feel is best expressed by exploring the evolution of between five and ten drivers you are able to do so robustly. Morphological scenarios explore the different potential evolutions of each driver, synthesising each option in a hypothesis before weaving together hypotheses from each driver to create a cogent and stimulating image of the future. This process is repeated as many times as you need to create a set of scenarios that explore the range of uncertainty that you are looking to represent. While Morphological Scenarios can be more time-consuming to construct and are not as intuitive or easy to represent as Matrix Scenarios, they are able to explore more dimensions of your system in a rigorous and transparent way. Morphological Scenarios have been our go-to approach for studies focusing on country-level or regional dynamics for several years.

CASE STUDY OF MORPHOLOGICAL SCENARIOS:
EAST AFRICA AND THE HORN IN 2022

This foresight project was initiated by multiple country offices of an international non-governmental organisation (INGO) operating in East Africa and the Horn that were eager to create a shared vision of the future of the region to improve their effectiveness and plan a regional response. This study explored how the politically dynamic region, which is also regularly affected by environmental stresses, would change over the coming 5 years. For the construction of the scenarios the study used most of the tools outlined in the toolkit, though a MICMAC opposed to an MIU was used to identify the critical drivers.

Building on the analysis of the heavy trends including demography, urbanisation and climate change, this study identified the critical drivers of the scenarios, those that would be the most influential over the course of the outlook. The critical drivers that were selected included:

- Changing development landscape
- Commodity price fluctuations
- Competition over infrastructure projects
- Geopolitical spheres of influence
- Kenyan elections
- Regional rivalries

Embracing uncertainty with foresight   35

Multiple hypotheses for each of these drivers were then created and weaved into three distinct scenarios: Tanzanian Stability–Regional Fragility, Sunrise over the Indian Ocean and The Warmth of Consensus. To support the organisation in its strategic development, this foresight study also identified some potential triggers to be monitored: the death of a long-time leader in Uganda, Rwanda, Eritrea or Sudan; or the occurrence of a pandemic. The robustness of this analysis was built from the input of staff and experts. It helped the decision makers in the organisation to consider the multiple paths for long-term prosperity and highlighted the challenges which need to be overcome.

With both Matrix and Morphological Scenarios, you must complete the exercise by integrating your analysis of the actors in your system of study. To do this you should consider each scenario in turn and assess how the role of the actors you have researched could affect or be affected by the future that you are describing. This stage of scenario writing is pivotal as it brings an additional level of detail and enables you to embed into your final product your understanding of how the actors in your system operate.

As discussed in Chapter 1, the principal aim of using foresight and ultimately, of writing scenarios, is to provide decision makers with the space to open their minds and move beyond the everyday pressures of their work to think creatively about what strategic interventions they should invest in or what they should stop doing to increase their effectiveness, prepare for upcoming challenges and leverage opportunities to change the world in which they are working. However, in order to do that, scenarios have to be written coherently and presented in a fashion which stimulates decision makers and provokes discussion of key issues (see Writing Scenarios, pp. 163–169). Reading scenarios and working with the output of foresight analysis should be an immersive experience. It is key that you structure all outputs of your work in a way that makes them easy to engage with. It is also necessary that you support decision makers in translating analysis into learning and decision-making.

Designing scenarios using a base of structural foresight can be a time-consuming process and often requires the efforts of a dedicated analyst to lead the project and carry out the research, and/or a project manager to support a team to co-create a foresight report. While we would always recommend the approach outlined earlier and explored further in the toolkit, we understand that in the humanitarian space there are often times when decisions need to be made quickly and resources for analytical work are hard to come by. As a result, in the following we present a light-touch approach you can exploit if you find yourself so constrained.

36 *Embracing uncertainty with foresight*

Foresight on a tight timeframe

As we have mentioned throughout, any of the tools in the structural analysis section of the toolkit can provide you with a useful way to analyse your system and think through what your operating environment looks like and how it may change. We have already outlined a thorough and detailed approach to the structural analysis and building scenarios stages, but we also wanted to present a couple of suggested steps for a scenario process if you find yourself very short on time. It has been our experience that, though it is not ideal, many humanitarian actors either require analytical input on a much faster timeline than you may be able to deliver using the aforementioned process (e.g. to inform proposals or as a preliminary exercise to launch a partnership) or that they simply do not have the human resources to dedicate to as involved a process. If you are exploring a short time-horizon (less than one or two years) and you do not have the time or resources to conduct a full structural analysis or write a comprehensive set of scenarios, then we would recommend the following steps to you.

Three tools are recommended for foresight on a tight timeframe: PESTLE (pp. 94–99), MIU (pp. 107–116) and Matrix Scenarios (pp. 126–136).

A) Conduct a PESTLE: The PESTLE tool allows you to do a quick but thorough scan of your system to identify the components of it that you should be aware of. Even just going through this exercise can help you to identify some of the actors and factors that you want to explore further.

B) Use your PESTLE to complete an MIU: While an Architecture is a very helpful output, you can skip this step and move straight to conducting an MIU, which will give you a lot of information about your system and help you to identify the areas that you need to consider in your work. Just knowing what the most impactful factors and who the most influential actors are is critical information for any decisions that you are making.

C) You can also run a Matrix Scenario workshop straight from your MIU and create a set of short scenarios in approximately two hours. As you will not have had time to invest in researching your Driver Files, Actors File or running an MID workshop, the makeup of the participants in the group you work with is even more critical. Without a broad range of knowledge, you are unlikely to come up with analysis that is interesting or reliable. However, if you are able to create a group of well-informed stakeholders, then the scenario matrix workshop can provide you with some very interesting insights in a short time. We recommend the Matrix Scenario approach rather than the Morphological Scenario approach here as it is more intuitive for participants who can sometimes struggle with the creation of lots of hypotheses, it provides a frame on which you can continually add detail as your time allows and it provides a ready-made communication tool for you to use with other actors.

D) As you write up your scenarios (which can be done in bullet points) you should be sure that each future you are designing considers how the most influential actors in your MIU (those of both high and low uncertainty) might behave in each scenario you present.

A process such as this could be completed in approximately 6 to 10 hours of work. We would not recommend this process for longer-term outlooks where the range of uncertainty grows, as it is difficult to contemplate the full potential spectrum of change and really dig into where the opportunities for transformation lie. However, we understand that there are many occasions in humanitarian action when time and resources are short, and even in these moments, structured, systems thinking with a futures lens can be of value. You will find this approach less useful for long-term strategising, but it can be very useful for things such as contingency planning in a rapidly changing context or to respond to an urgent change in organisational direction.

Whether you create scenarios using the full approach that is recommended earlier in the chapter or the more light-touch version outlined here, it is vital that you consider how the output of your foresight work will be used.

The next section of this chapter will begin to discuss different ways to engage decision makers with your work before the approaches to strategic development are discussed in Chapter 3.

Using scenarios

The creation of scenarios only has value if they are used for broadening people's thinking and informing strategic decisions. In order to ensure that there is uptake of your foresight analysis you will often find that you need to support the stakeholders who you are engaging. In this section, we will outline a few ways that you can do that. Scenarios in particular and futures-focused systems thinking in general can be useful for humanitarians in several different ways.

38 *Embracing uncertainty with foresight*

For decisions relating to the future of organisations, foresight can be used to rally staff and partners around a shared understanding of the opportunities and challenges you face. It can be used to develop a new organisational vision, to consider different structures which would enable you to operate more effectively in the future, and to engage partners and donors more constructively and creatively.

While the uses of strategic foresight for making decisions in humanitarian operations are similarly varied, we have seen foresight employed most often in the design of country strategies. This can be long-term planning to enable humanitarian actors to contribute to significant transformations in their context or for contingency planning to prepare for disruptive events. Integrating foresight at the level of country office planning usually fits well with the existing decision-making system and economic model of most formal and non-formal humanitarian implementers.

Using foresight in this way can help to ensure that humanitarian interventions are contextually driven rather than shaped by the priorities of any donor or organisation. However, there are other ways to use strategic foresight that are becoming more common, for example in creating regional strategies to approach transnational challenges and complex crises. A regional approach can help to increase how effectively resources are used and, more importantly, increase the potential impact of interventions by creating a multipronged approach to tackling underlying causes of vulnerability which are often not bound by national borders. Other opportunities to use foresight for decision-making include in contingency planning for security and for the design of exit strategies for organisations looking to shrink their programmatic footprint and transfer power to actors better placed to perform effectively.

Finally, scenarios and futures thinking can be enormously valuable to inform, design and enact advocacy strategies or campaigns. By being able to show multiple pathways to achieving a specific goal, while outlining all the trade-offs that each would entail, organisations can demonstrate how to make their desired future a reality. In addition, the power analysis which is encapsulated in your Actors File and MID output can be hugely useful in improving your understanding of how to engage allies and targets in your advocacy work. Strategic foresight can be a powerful communications tool to challenge the thinking of decision makers who are not ready or able to contemplate systemic change on the scale that is necessary to secure a safer and more just world. By providing the space and tools to create a shared vision of the potential futures that exist, collaborative foresight work can be critical in creating alliances of different actors who share a common goal.

Embracing uncertainty with foresight 39

While foresight is a powerful and flexible tool which can be put to many uses, in general the main way that scenarios are used are for strategic development at organisational and operational levels (see Chapter 3 for more). The toolkit which has been developed in this book will support you to move from the generation of your scenarios to a robust, futures-focused strategy. However, there are other exercises which you can use to either complement your process of strategic development or simply to help decision makers internalise the analysis that you have created so that it can be used in other ways.

Uptake of foresight analysis

One of the best ways to ensure uptake of your analysis and encourage decision makers to use the scenarios that you have developed in their decision-making is to run light (or a series of light) workshops to present your findings. The goal of these workshops is to immerse decision makers in the futures that you have created, asking them to consider what each of these futures would mean for the organisation and the actors with/for whom they work.

It is possible that some of your decision makers will describe one or a few of the futures that you present as unlikely or unimaginable (especially if they have not been part of the scenario-building stage). It is in these cases that workshops such as the ones we suggest in the following section can be most useful in helping them to open their minds and contemplate how the futures you present could affect them and their work. While the suggestions we have outlined here are very light-touch in their approach, they follow the same ethos as the methods used in experiential futures. Experiential futures "involves designing and staging interventions that exploit the continuum of human experience, the full array of sensory and semiotic vectors, in order to enable a different and deeper engagement in thought and discussion about one or more futures" (Candy 2010, p. 3). In other words, it creates an experience which uses many different approaches (acting and improvisation, product design and the use of symbols for example) to transport the decision maker from their present-day reality into the future scenarios that you have created. By feeling a greater connection to that future, the decision maker becomes better able to think through its consequences, challenges and opportunities, and to learn from them to make strategic decisions in the present day.

Immersing decision makers in the new realities you have designed

The first two suggestions for how to better engage your decision makers and encourage them to fully play out the scenarios is by challenging them

40 *Embracing uncertainty with foresight*

to produce documents or hold meetings which stem from that reality. Divide the decision makers you are working with into groups so that there are between three and six people who each work on one of the scenarios from the suite of futures that you have produced. The results of their exercises are then presented back to the wider group. If you do not have enough participants, you can divide into fewer groups and ask each group to work on more than one scenario.

In our experience, asking decision makers to produce a detailed situation report for their organisation for each scenario forces them to think through what the consequences of that scenario would be for the communities they work for. The process of capturing that thinking into a format with which they are familiar (such as a situation report) grounds it in their reality. This mix of the unknown and the familiar can help decision makers become more comfortable with the uncertainty they face, and translating the scenario (which may feel is a bit far-fetched) into concrete hypotheses about what the impacts of that future could be on their work helps them to see the value in thinking through several different eventualities. If situation reports are not commonly used in your organisation or line of work, the alternative is to ask the decision makers with whom you are working to write a short news article or prepare a short news briefing reporting on the humanitarian situation in the future that they are working on. By asking people to write a situation report, news article or news script they internalise the dynamics of the scenarios they have been presented with and create another communications resource for you to use when sharing the scenarios with other actors.

If you want a more dynamic way to immerse decision makers in the futures that you have created you can also ask them to simulate a meeting, for example a humanitarian coordination meeting. In this workshop each participant would be assigned a role which would ensure that different actors are represented (you select the actors to consider from your MID) and each participant would be asked to represent the organisation that they have been assigned, acting as though they are in the scenario which you have created. This can help decision makers to think through not only what some of the consequences of the scenario would be for the communities they work for but also what some of the challenges and opportunities are for the actors in their space. You can draw on your actor analysis to inform the positioning of the actors you are seeking to represent. Depending on the number of participants you have, this is an exercise which can be done in groups (one group for each scenario) or you can ask each participant to play the same stakeholder in multiple simulated meetings (you can make these just 15 or 20 minutes long) so that they see how the context changes for them as an actor across your multiple futures.

Embracing uncertainty with foresight   41

Considering what the futures you have created mean for an organisation or community

If you would prefer to move immediately to focus more directly on what the futures you have created mean for your organisation, there are a couple of simple exercises that can help you to do that. If you are conducting an organisational study, the first option is to ask your group of decision makers to conduct a SWOT analysis (drawing on the organisational factors and actors listed in the specific system of their architecture). This analyses the strengths, weaknesses, opportunities and threats (SWOT) to your organisation in each of the futures that you have designed. This process asks participants to think through how their organisation will operate in each future and contemplate where they have the capacity to be effective and where the gaps lie. The other outcome of this style of exercise is that it helps to highlight what the no-regret actions are. These are the strategic decisions which would make the organisation more effective in multiple (or even every) scenario and as a result offer a path to increase effectiveness with minimal risk.

If you are working on a contextual study in which you do not want to inject your organisation at this stage, you can consider what the challenges and opportunities are to some of the different actors that you work with or for. This is a simplified version of a SWOT in which you do not consider capacities or gaps, as you may not have access to that information, but rather think about opportunities and challenges. When engaging in this type of exercise you should always endeavour to include the actors you are hypothesising about in the process or be very clear in your communication of the results that they were not included in the process to avoid misunderstandings. By putting decision makers in the shoes of other actors it can increase not only the rate at which they internalise the findings of your study by making them reflect on the differences between each scenario but also to consider how they could be better partners or allies to the other actors in their space as they try to view the different evolutions from their perspective.

These examples of how to encourage the uptake of scenario analyses and support decision makers to internalise the findings can be a very useful exercise to go through after having developed a set of scenarios as they each perform the function of transporting the decision maker from the present day into the images of the future that you have created. You may find, even if you are going to engage in a full strategic development process (see Chapter 3), that some of these preliminary exercises can be useful as an icebreaker, especially if you are involving decision makers

42 Embracing uncertainty with foresight

in the strategy development process who were not part of the scenario-building stage.

Alternative types of scenario building and their uses

While we feel that that the tools we are presenting in this book (and explore in detail in the toolkit) provide you with a firm foundation to conduct foresight projects for humanitarian interventions and transformations, we also want to offer a very brief introduction into two different approaches we feel have a lot of value for you to consider along with some resources you can use to explore them further.

Causal layered analysis

Causal layered analysis (CLA) is a research method to generate "transformative spaces for the creation of alternative futures" (Inayatuallah 2004, p. 8) conceptualised and popularised by Sohail Inayatullah. CLA is an excellent tool to use to unpack and digest the structures and dynamics which have underpinned the historical changes and present context of your system of study and will continue to shape the futures you explore. The focus on dissecting the different layers of facts, myths, behaviours and beliefs which exist in every system provides you with the space to deepen your understanding of how your system of study functions and integrates these different levels of analysis into a coherent and stimulating

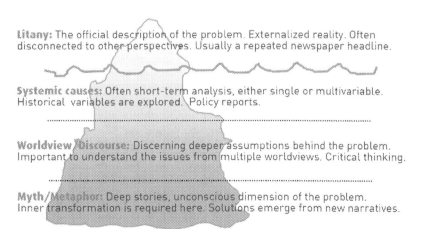

Figure 2.3 The CLA iceberg image with layers (Inayatuallah 2017, p. 5)

Embracing uncertainty with foresight 43

vision of a transformed future reality. CLA pursues systemic change by unpacking the drivers at the very core of each context.

CLA creates four separate levels of analysis: the litany, systemic causes, worldview/discourse, and myths and metaphors. These are summarised in Figure 2.3.

You can use the CLA as a method as part of the process of structural analysis and scenario building that we have summarised in this book or as a standalone approach to generating alternative futures. The approach of CLA encourages you to view your system of study from many different vantage points and as such can yield deeper insights. For more detail on how to use CLA, please see resources such as *Causal Layered Analysis* (Inayatuallah 2017) or *The Causal Layered Analysis (CLA) Reader: Theory and Case Studies of an Integrative and Transformative Methodology* (Inayatuallah 2004).

Alternative futures

Alternative futures is another approach to scenario generation which can be an interesting visioning tool. Through many years of research analysing as many images of the future as they could, from corporate visioning, government scenarios, opinion polls, students and science fiction to name but a few sources, James Dator at the Manoa School of Futures identified four generic piles into which the vast majority of scenarios fit (Dator 2009, p. 6). These four generic piles each encapsulate "common theoretical, methodological and data bases which distinguish them from the bases of the other three futures" (Dator 2009, p. 7). These four generic futures are titled continued growth, collapse, discipline and transformation.

The alternative futures approach asks facilitators to draft images of what their system of study would look like using the four rationales for continued growth, collapse, discipline and transformation. Subsequently, facilitators share the four possible futures with participants, asking them to have a structured discussion about what that particular future could mean. For a step-by-step guide, please see "Alternative Futures at the Manoa School" (Dator 2009).

Each of the potential futures that are developed under this method has elements that can be both positive and negative; there should not naturally be a best- or worst-case scenario. While many people may be tempted to routinely ensure that the continued growth scenario is always a positive extrapolation of the present day, doing so would ignore the very real stress that continued growth can put on the earth's resources or its consequences for inequality. Similarly, people may view collapse as a fully negative scenario, but episodes of collapse can create opportunities

44 *Embracing uncertainty with foresight*

for new ideas and structures to be born and as a result are often not negative from everyone's perspective.

Dator's alternative futures provides a very interesting and different approach to scenario generation than we have presented in this book. It can be a useful approach to take with a larger group of people, as you can divide the exercise between the four groups and there is little preparatory work for participants to do before engaging directly with the futures that you have created. The four generic futures provide you with the framework to create very distinct images of the future, which you can make as detailed and disruptive as you can by fully embracing the rationale presented in each one, considering how those dynamics would change your system of study and taking them to their conclusion over the time horizon you have set.

There are many different ways to develop scenarios other than the tools we have outlined in this book. However, unlike both CLA and Dator's alternative futures, many are a variation on the tools that we have presented rather than an entirely different approach. That is why we have chosen to highlight these two approaches to you as we feel they complement the toolkit that we have developed and each can add value in their own way depending on how you are going to use your analytical output and the conditions in which you are conducting your project.

Conclusion

Regardless of the methodology you choose, the benefits of integrating a futures-focused approach to your analysis are manyfold.

Foresight tools can help to break out of siloed thinking to create more effective, integrated programming approaches. Considering humanitarian action in a comprehensive way can help to identify opportunities to leverage existing programmes to complement other ongoing or new initiatives to increase their effectiveness. Making progress against the structural conditions which make chronic vulnerability a reality for many communities across the globe requires systems thinking about the challenges they face. Many of these structural issues are condensed into the Sustainable Development Goals (SDGs) which all humanitarian actors are committed to working on, but towards which progress thus far has been too slow to have a realistic chance of being met. Identifying the levers of change is vital to changing this trajectory and making real progress.

Better understanding complexity and system dynamics not only helps to integrate programmes and approaches, but it can also lay the foundation for genuine partnerships to implement multisectoral work. A collaborative foresight project is one of the ways through which you can

Embracing uncertainty with foresight   45

establish a team's collective mental model which can increase their efficacy and overall impact. This is one of the best side effects of engaging in a strategic foresight project and a key reason why the end result is often so much more than the final report.

Integrating foresight into your research and decision-making processes can help to induce a cultural change in your organisation and eventually challenge short-termism in the wider humanitarian sector. By habitually thinking beyond the present to consider the impact of your work and the role of your organisation in 5, 10 or even 20 years, you can focus your time and resources on the most impactful and transformational initiatives. You can begin to think about where your organisation can be most effective and focus on developing your organisational capacity in those areas, divesting yourself of the areas of work at which other actors in the system are better placed to implement and considering how to ensure that the power of affected communities is reflected in humanitarian decision-making processes.

Each of these benefits provides a reason to begin to explore how foresight can be better used in your organisation. While it can feel daunting, and there may be times when you require additional support, you do not need to be an expert to get started. As you begin this endeavour there are a few things to keep in mind. Firstly, consistency is critical; once you choose an approach that you would like to follow you would do well to continue along that track. As you become more experienced, you will better understand how you can integrate tools from different schools of futures studies into your work, but without having practised each it can be difficult to see the potential pitfalls in doing so.

Secondly, the communication of findings is key if you want your analysis to be used. You need to consider the ways in which you will try to encapsulate your analysis as you are going through the process. By gathering input from the decision makers that you hope will use the output of your foresight work throughout the process or at the very least updating them on outputs of the analysis as you are progressing, you will increase the buy-in of your audience. Upon conclusion of your foresight study, having multiple different products of varying lengths and structures (e.g. a full report, a short summary, a selection of infographics and presentations) is critical to engaging with your audience. Scenarios which are developed but not well communicated are rarely used.

Finally, scenarios which have no 'uptake' are not worth writing. As a result, before you begin a foresight report you should identify the ways in which you can support decision makers to use it. This can be done through some of the workshops outlined in this chapter which can help decision makers to immerse themselves in the futures that you have

46   *Embracing uncertainty with foresight*

created, or it can progress to the next step to engage in a strategic development process.

The strategic development tools which are outlined in the following chapter provide the best opportunity to get the most out of your foresight. The approaches to strategic development outlined in this book offer you the chance to improve your organisational agility and to increase your impact.

Note

1 For more details on how to embark on a MICMAC, please see the brief on the software at http://en.laprospective.fr/methods-of-prospective/softwares/59-MICMAC.html.

References

Candy, Stuart (2010) *The Futures of Everyday Life: Politics and the Design of Experiential Scenarios* (PhD dissertation). University of Hawaii at Manoa. DOI: 10.13140/RG.2.1.1840.0248

Curedale, Robert (2013) *50 Brainstorming Techniques for Team and Individual Ideation*, Los Angeles, California, United States, Design Community College Incorporated.

Dator, Jim (2009) Alternative futures at the Manoa School, *Journal of Futures Studies*, November 2009, 14(2): 1–18.

Glick, Margaret B *et al.* (2012) Effects of scenario planning on participant mental models, *European Journal of Training and Development*, 36: 488–507.

Heuer, Richard (2014) *Structured Analytic Techniques for Intelligence Analysis*, Washington D.C., CQ Press.

IARAN (2016) *Future of Aid: INGOs in 2030*, London, IARAN, accessed on 11 February 2021, https://www.iaran.org/future-of-aid

Inayatullah, Sohail (2004) *The Causal Layered Analysis (CLA) Reader Theory and Case Studies of an Integrative and Transformative Methodology*, Taipei, Tamkang University Press.

Inayatullah, Sohail (2017) Causal layered analysis, in *The Prospective and Strategic Foresight Toolkit*, Paris, Futuribles.

International Maize and Wheat Improvement Center (CIMMYT) (2021) 2025: Agri-food systems in a plus COVID-19 world: Global Perspective, Unpublished.

La Prospectif (2010) *MICMAC: Structural Analysis*, accessed on 4 January 2021, http://en.laprospective.fr/methods-of-prospective/softwares/59-MICMAC.html

Meadows, D and Wright, D (2008) *Thinking in Systems: A Primer*, London, Chelsea Green Publishing.

Stroh, David Peter (2015) *Systems Thinking for Social Change: A Practical Guide to Solving Complex Problems, Avoiding Unintended Consequences, and Achieving Lasting Results*, Hartford, VT, Chelsea Green Publishing.

3 Developing a strategy for effective change

Strategy and planning in the humanitarian ecosystem

The culture of reactivity is evident in the humanitarian ecosystem in many (if not all) aspects of humanitarian work (McGoldrick 2011, p. 968). This creates a trap of recurring "action in the short-term reality" (Godet 1994, p. 2). While this type of intervention saves lives it does not necessarily contribute to long-term resilience or development. As a result, the short-termism trap means that most actors intervene, expending resources, without addressing the root causes of the vulnerability that created the crisis.

The only way to break out of this short-termism trap is to reconfigure our thinking by extending our perspective so that we are working on a timeframe where change and transformation are achievable and the root causes of humanitarian crises can be addressed by the people and the communities concerned or by supporting them embracing the principle of subsidiarity when they cannot. A culture of long-term and anticipatory thinking could enable true effectiveness. Humanitarian actors should not see themselves as locked into their role of 'responders to emergencies' but also as 'change agents', fulfilling their full purpose to alleviate the suffering of people and communities affected by crisis over the long term.

The Formal Humanitarian System 3.0 has taken some steps to create a culture of anticipation, such as through the introduction of disaster preparedness norms and standards and an increasing number of initiatives focused on anticipatory action (Tanner et al. 2019). The driving force behind these shifts has predominantly been their potential financial advantages. While the strength of the evidence varies depending on the context, it is widely agreed that "in the absence of preparedness actions, it costs more and takes longer to respond to humanitarian needs when a disaster strikes and when humanitarian needs peak" (OECD 2017).

DOI: 10.4324/9781003094753-3

48 *Developing a strategy for effective change*

However, despite the growing interest in disaster preparedness, the proportion of official development assistance (ODA) going to disaster preparedness is still negligible (UN 2017). In 2018, in the majority of countries that were allocated disaster risk reduction (DRR) funding, it constituted only 1% of the ODA they received (Thomas and Urquhart 2020, p. 13). The dependence of formal humanitarian actors on ODA funds and the dominance on the upward flow of accountability (towards donors, deprioritising communities) prevents actors from moving beyond the short-termism trap.

To move past the short-termism trap, the way that strategy development and planning are done in the humanitarian system needs to change, for formal humanitarian actors in particular. As they were encouraged to do when adopting strategic processes from the business sector, the top-down way that strategies are designed by formal humanitarian actors must be reversed. Formal humanitarian actors must abandon the false equivalency that organisational growth equals impact by no longer focusing on branding, growth and competition, and must begin prioritising genuine contributions from people affected by crises. This could be achieved by introducing bottom–up ways to design strategies, developing more collaborative approaches, reinstating their original purpose (which is not their own organisational growth but the well-being of people affected by crises), opening the governance of formal humanitarian actors to communities concerned by their mission and creating a culture of anticipation that prizes sustainable development.

Strategic foresight offers us the tools with which we can pursue this kind of change. To incept the shift towards more futures-focused, systemic thinking we propose an approach which would integrate new tools into the existing decision-making processes of most humanitarian actors, embedding them within Project Cycle Management (PCM) systems.

The Project Cycle Management heritage: challenges, risks and opportunities

At the start of the 1990s, as part of an effort to revise how they approached their work, humanitarian actors looked to business actors for approaches and resources they could employ for their financial consolidation and quality control. During this era, they discovered PCM as a quality assurance system and adopted many related business tools. Under the umbrella of PCM systems, two distinct approaches have been adopted by the majority of humanitarian actors: the Logical Framework Approach (LFA) and theory of change (ToC). Some organisations use both approaches.

Developing a strategy for effective change 49

LFA is a four-by-four temporal matrix that defines a project as a set of linked hypotheses: if inputs then outputs, if outputs then purpose, if purpose then goal. The rows describe the initiatives that need to be implemented: activities, outputs, purposes, goal. The columns describe the information to be collected by event: narrative, indicators, sources, assumptions.

Originally conceived and developed by the military and thereafter by business actors, the LFA was implemented in the humanitarian eco-system for the first time in 1971 by the US Agency for International Development (USAID), a state actor (USAID 1971). Its adoption followed the successful implementation of a project by Fry Consulting Inc. to design an evaluation and appraisal reporting system (Rosenberg 1970). In 1993 the European Commission (EC) adopted the LFA and made its use mandatory for those applying to access its PCM system. Since the 1990s, the use of LFAs has been widely required by most institutional and multilateral donors including all major OECD countries. It is now part of the set of norms and standards that regulate the flow of money through ODA.

One of the main advantages of the LFA is that it offers a synthetic project outlook, guiding implementers and evaluators through a systematic and logical analysis of the linked hypotheses underpinning a project. It provides all the information needed for planning, monitoring and evaluation, and it improves the quality of the project if regularly and well used (EuropeAid 2004). The limits of the LFA are that this tool requires high-quality information and regular review, which takes time and calls for a collaborative approach. Time and collaborative approaches are often economised in the trap of short-termism, and in that context the LFA can quickly become a rigid administrative tool that generates poor outputs (following the principle of 'garbage in, garbage out').

The ToC was conceived of by business actors in the fifties as an approach to management by planning (Drucker 1954) and emerged as a method of programme theory and evaluation for social and political change in the nineties. While the LFA approach focuses on the achievement of the objective by combining outputs, the ToC focuses on a more detailed hierarchy among objectives and considers intermediary objectives as outcomes to achieve an ultimate, long-term goal. The innovation in the ToC approach, compared to the LFA, lies in the agility of its logic to differentiate desired and actual outcomes and by requiring stakeholders to plan according to the desired outcome. The potential downsides of the ToC approach are that it requires more time and information than the LFA and the desired outcomes that are identified may not take

50 *Developing a strategy for effective change*

into consideration the full complexities of the reality in which they are implemented.

In terms of strategic thinking, both the LFA and ToC, have an Achilles heel. In the complex and interconnected global context in which these approaches are used, they both attempt to address long-term goals, but both lack the comprehensiveness to manage the uncertainty of multiple possible futures. As a result, defining a long-term goal using these approaches can be risky and, even worse, irrational, especially if it is done without the very people and communities that are concerned by the goal you define and the future you pursue. While there are pros and cons to both the LFA and ToC approaches, for better or worse, they both dominate the current practices in PCM systems applied by humanitarian actors. As they are so well engrained in the decision-making structures of the humanitarian ecosystem, the LFA and the ToC are ideal entry points to incept a culture of anticipation and integrate a collaborative way of working to design bottom-up, grassroot strategies.

Enhancing Project Cycle Management systems with strategic development

Our strategic development process is not meant to design strategies for emergency responses. The process that we recommend is not well suited for decisions that need to be taken to determine a path of action for the next 48 hours, nor are they suited to serve the objectives of hurried proposal writing. While we understand that all interventions require resources, the intention of our methodology is to focus your attention on how to be impactful in a complex context rather than how to tailor your work to the priorities of donors.

Every context in which you intervene is made up primarily of people. At the individual, household and community level there are a diverse set of skills and resources which people and organisations marshal to support themselves and one another during times of crises. Respecting people affected by crises and leveraging their considerable capacities requires you to invest time and effort in better understanding that complexity. Whenever you are writing a proposal or developing a strategy in a hurry, you risk betraying the very purpose of humanitarianism and serve only the financial growth of your organisation.

The strategic development process that we want to explain in this chapter builds on traditional PCM systems used by humanitarian actors to design strategies and to plan their interventions. Our strategic development process integrates strategic foresight techniques into the LFA and

Developing a strategy for effective change 51

ToC approaches, enhancing traditional PCM systems to build a culture of anticipation and embed a collaborative way of working.

The PCM includes between five and six phases, depending on the various PCM versions and related guidelines available today. The PCM guidelines from the European Commission describe five iterative phases: identification, formulation, implementation, evaluation, programming then back to identification. This system describes a virtuous cycle within which projects adapt and improve in terms of quality (EuropeAid 2004). The integration of the foresight and strategic development phases begins by integrating tools from the structural analysis and scenario-building stages (see Chapters 2 and 4) in the identification phase of a PCM system, enhancing the LFA or ToC approach from the beginning of the project cycle.

The ToC describe six distinctive stages in the PCM phase of identification according to the Center for the Theory of Change: identifying long-term goals, backwards mapping and connecting the preconditions necessary to achieve that goal, identifying your basic assumptions about the context, identifying the interventions to create your desired change, developing indicators to measure your outcomes, and writing a narrative to explain the logic of your initiative (CFTOC 2021).

The LFA approach to the phase of identification, consists of two stages: the analysis stage and the planning stage. The PCM guidelines from the European Commission, which take an LFA approach, suggest that you perform the analysis stage of the identification phase with four tools: Stakeholder Analysis, Problem Analysis, Objective Analysis and Strategy Analysis (EuropeAid 2004, p. 60).

Instead of following either the ToC or LFA approaches to the phase of identification, we recommend that you engage in a more detailed process of structural analysis of the system of study that you are targeting. Moreover, we suggest that you dive into an exploratory journey on the possible futures of that system of study and, for each possible future, you design a strategy that can be implemented effectively in the game of the actors you have analysed. The ability to rapidly shift your strategy to adapt to a changing context is a benefit of strategic development which is critical for most operational humanitarian actors. Though this takes more time (it replaces four tools in the LFA analysis stage and the first two stages of the ToC with 12 strategic foresight tools) your outputs and therefore your strategy will be more robust.

It is for this reason that we put forward a process that helps humanitarian actors to think long term about their work and to be more collaborative in their approaches.

52 *Developing a strategy for effective change*

Strategy and plan for humanitarian actors

During our experience using strategic foresight to enhance humanitarian action, we realised that the distinction between 'strategy', 'plan', 'tactics' and 'operations' is often blurred, so we have defined them next.

What are operations? The operational dimension is activities-output focused; it is the implementation of the activities according to a sequential workplan to produce outputs (or results).

What are tactics? The tactical dimension is outputs-goal focused; it is the sequential combination of the outputs (or results) produced by the activities to achieve a goal (or a specific objective or lower-level objectives).

What is a plan? A plan achieves one or multiple specific objectives, it is often presented under the combined form of a logical framework and a chronological workplan. A plan is very concrete and execution oriented, with a focus on the operational and tactical dimension.

The strategic planning phase encapsulates the processes to design the tactical and operational elements and their sequential logic (see Figure 3.1 for a visual representation) and a 'plan' is its final output.

What is a strategy? The strategic dimension is focused on higher-level and lower-level objectives; it is the sequential combination of the goals (or specific objectives or lower-level objectives) to contribute to a mission (or general objective or higher-level objective).

A strategy is a journey towards a possible future. A strategy is the final output of a strategic development phase.

It is very important for our strategic development process to understand that objectives have a hierarchy: the higher they are, the more likely it is that they relate to a high level of strategic thinking. A mission, or an end of state, is the highest objective in a strategy; specific objectives are the highest objectives in a plan but the lowest in a strategy. Activities are the lowest objectives in a plan (see Figure 3.1).

Our learnings from piloting the strategic development phase with humanitarian actors flagged another misperception among humanitarian actors when it comes to defining and applying the terms 'programme' and 'project' and to identifying their subset of objectives. Adding more confusion, there is no consistency in the uses of these terms among the different PCM systems. According to the PCM guidelines from the EC, a project has one specific objective or goal to achieve, whereas a programme is a combination of many projects contributing to an overall objective or general objective (EuropeAid 2004). It is the EC's interpretation that we adopt in this book (see Figure 3.1).

Figure 3.1 is intended to clarify how these different dimensions and terms intersect, while also allowing you to visualise what can be achieved

Developing a strategy for effective change 53

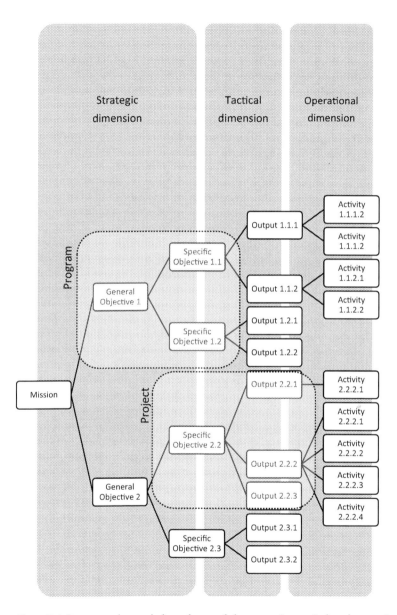

Figure 3.1 Strategy, plan and the subsets of the strategic, tactical and operational dimensions

54 *Developing a strategy for effective change*

with our strategic development process. The final output of following the toolkit that we have provided in this book will be a strategy and not a plan. Once you have defined your strategy, you can create plans to implement it using either the LFA approach by moving to the planning stage of the identification phase (EuropeAid 2004, p. 60) or the ToC approach by moving on to the stage of identifying the interventions to create your desired change (CFTOC 2021) according to your PCM system.

What to do if you don't have a strategy

Now that we have clarified key concepts and set our expectations, we are ready to start our strategic development process.

The foresight base and scenarios

We assume at this point that you have defined your system of study and that you have already explored the complexity of that system and its possible futures with a set of scenarios that you have created with your stakeholders (discussed in Chapter 2).

If this is not the case you have two options. In the first option, you need to source a set of quality scenarios and the analytical outputs that make up the foresight base, such as the Actors File and Driver Files – then you can begin your foresight process by performing an Influence/ Dependency Matrix workshop (MID), tool 9 in the toolkit (see pp. 146– 162). This allows you to skip the first eight tools of structural analysis and scenario building, dramatically reducing the amount of time you need to invest. For option two, if you can't find any exploratory scenarios on your system of study, we strongly recommend that you follow the nine tools as recommended and discussed in Chapter 2. Once you have sourced or built a set of scenarios and you have amassed your foresight base, you can start the strategic development process.

It is necessary to have a set of scenarios, as one of the advantages of our strategic development process is that you are going to design a set of strategies and not one single strategy for your system of study. For each scenario that you have, you will create a strategy specifically designed to ensure that you are fit for that future. By strategising for multiple different potential futures, you enhance your agility. Though in the end you will select one strategy to implement, in the eventuality that the dynamics of your context shift, you will have alternative strategies ready to replace it with to ensure your continued impact.

The sequence for strategic development is described by three tools: the Strategy Tree, the Actor/Objective Matrix (MAO) and Testing (tools 11, 12 and 13, respectively, in the toolkit).

Strategic development

Through the process of structural analysis and scenario building we deconstruct your system of study and consider the different ways it could evolve. Through the process of strategic development, we build a path for change and transformation in each future. Strategic development, like foresight, requires contributions from the people concerned in your system of study to create a basis for collective intelligence, which is the cornerstone for successful change and transformation.

Strategy Tree

The first strategic development tool is a combination of a causal analysis followed by an objective analysis. A rich collection of tools for causal analysis and objective analysis already exists, for example, in the planning stage in EC PCM. Rather than reinvent them, we have used the problem and objectives analysis tools in the analysis stage of the LFA (EuropeAid 2004) as the foundation from which to conceive a tool that exploits your foresight base for a richer and more detailed analysis. This tool, designed by the IARAN and tested and piloted in different contexts (local, regional and global) and with different humanitarian actors (formal and non-formal), is called the Strategy Tree.

The Strategy Tree enables you to build on your foresight base to design a systemic strategy for each scenario. By 'systemic strategy' we mean a performant strategy that is adapted to the complexity of your scenario. The Strategy Tree builds on the possibilities of change offered in each potential future and not on the present, contrary to the LFA or ToC approaches. This is the foundation of the disruption that we have introduced into the current ways of designing strategies used by humanitarian actors. By building strategies with only an understanding (and often not a complete understanding) of your present context, humanitarian actors might be effective in the short term, but they risk doing harm and struggling to make sustainable change. The only way to achieve sustainable change is to anchor your present response in an understanding of your possible futures. Only by envisioning the possible futures, can we engineer a response that has the potential to be performant over the long term, sustainable and, most of all, transformative. Integrating futures thinking into the traditional methods of PCM is imperative if humanitarian actors are to break out of the trap of short-termism explained earlier in this chapter.

The strategic development process we put forward starts from the future, immersing your participants (a group of stakeholders) in the possible futures of your system of study. Gathering people concerned by

56 *Developing a strategy for effective change*

your system of study is very valuable in your strategic development process. Many times, especially in the work of formal humanitarian actors, projects and programmes in the humanitarian ecosystem are designed by people who are foreign to their system of study and following standards that are poorly adapted to the complex environments in which they are implemented. The integration of perspectives from within the communities that they are seeking to serve is therefore vital if they are to develop a robust strategy to implement.

To conduct a Strategy Tree exercise, participants first analyse the relationship of cause–effect among problems and opportunities emerging from a specific scenario, then they transform those relationships of cause–effect between problems and opportunities into a relationship of means–end objectives (Strategy Tree, pp. 170–180). Finally, from the relationship of means–end between objectives they identify a draft strategy.

The diagram of causality is the first output of the Strategy Tree. One diagram is created for each scenario, elaborated by a subgroup of your participants. The diagram of causality offers a synthetic map of connections between problems and opportunities emerging from the specific scenario. In most of the existing approaches to PCM, the focus is on the problems of a system. In the LFA, for example, opportunities are completely ignored in the 'Problem Tree' tool (EuropeAid 2004). While problems are usually the focus of humanitarian actors, to ignore opportunities means that you disregard the factors that already exist within your context, which could be the foundation of greater resilience. By focusing only on the problems, the LFA approach overlooks these critical elements of every system. With the Strategy Tree tool, you set the base for a holistic response, not only looking at the system in all its dimensions, but also considering how it changes over time. By including the future and the positive factors at the beginning of your strategic development phase, you create a multidimensional playing field on which you can design agile strategies.

The diagram of objectives is the second output of the Strategy Tree. It describes the relationship of means–end among a hierarchy of objectives. Moreover, the diagram of objectives allows for the identification of the strategic options (Strategy Tree, pp. 170–180), which are systemic groups of objectives where you can distinguish one higher objective at the top and a chain of connected lower objectives below with their own logic of means–end. These can overlap in a system. In a diagram of objectives, once you have identified the strategic options, you will realise that the differentiation of higher- and lower-level objectives is quite intricate. Objectives can be a lower objective in a specific strategic option and a higher objective in another one; this is why it is important that you write all your strategic options on a separate document (see the example in the

Developing a strategy for effective change 57

following case study). Some objectives might be repeated across different strategic options, but this is not an issue, particularly at this point. Your strategic options make up your draft strategy, the third and final output of the Strategy Tree tool.

Case study on the Strategy Tree: A study on South Sudan with an outlook to 2018

As a case study to demonstrate how these tools are used, we will use a strategic development pilot project that was started in June 2016 by a formal humanitarian actor operating in South Sudan to design their biannual country strategy. This strategic development process was built on an initial foresight study for North-Central South Sudan which created four scenarios with an outlook to 2018 that were finalised in April 2016. Because the context was very volatile, before starting the strategic development process, we revised the foresight base and updated the study to reflect the changes in the situation. As part of this process the team realised one of the four scenarios that was developed was obsolete, and, as such, only three were taken forward to the strategic planning exercise.

Three scenarios, focused on the humanitarian ecosystem in South Sudan, were deemed to still be relevant and valid and are summarised next.

Scenario 1: 'A Temporary Peace'. In this scenario donors grow tired of funding a war without end, and humanitarian aid dries up, forcing hard decisions on many currently displaced people to begin moving to refugee camps outside the country. The conflict lasts into the foreseeable future at a high level of violence and volatility, with constrained road access and the possibility that Juba could be cut off from overland trade routes and markets in Uganda.

Scenario 2: 'Fragmented Power, Economic Collapse'. In this scenario fighting in Juba forces another evacuation of the international community. Angered by the return to war, the Troika pressure the United Nations (UN) to impose economic sanctions shortly thereafter but, critically, do not impose an arms embargo, allowing weapons to proliferate across the country. An unsecured border gives free rein to Sudanese militia groups, who took advantage of their mobility and began to severely threaten the Sudan Armed Forces (SAF) in South Kordofan during the 2018 dry season campaign.

Scenario 3: 'Dictatorship and Dinka Dominance'. In this scenario, with peace on the table, South Sudan qualified for and received an International Monetary Fund (IMF) bailout, which helped stabilise

58 *Developing a strategy for effective change*

the economy. Hardliners within the government continued a brutal crackdown against rebellions around the country, making full use of helicopter gunships, heavy weapons and attacks on civilians. Human rights and protection actors decried the violence through 2017 to no avail. By June 2018, the government looks increasingly authoritarian and has passed non-governmental organisation (NGO) and media bills that have greatly constrained any criticism.

To carry out the strategic development process we organised three subgroups (one for each scenario). Following the instructions in the Strategy Tree tool (pp. 170–180) each subgroup identified a draft strategy for their scenario, with a combination of general objectives (GOs) underpinned by various specific objectives (SOs).

For the scenario 'A Temporary Peace', the draft strategy 'Reaching the Unreachable':

GO1: Malnutrition among the vulnerable population decreased
    SO1. Households' livelihoods and food production is improved
    SO2. Malnutrition is treated
    SO3. Local market systems and access are strengthened
    SO4. Health care services access
    SO5. Access to clean water
    SO6. Access to basic sanitation and hygiene
GO2: Reduce the harmful effects of displacements
    SO1. Gender and protection are mainstreamed
    SO2. Health care services access
    SO3. Access to water and sanitation
    SO4. Access to food and to shelter
    SO5. Displaced people access to land and cattle
GO3: Humanitarian access is guaranteed to vulnerable population
    SO1. Negotiation capacity to access is enhanced to both sides
    SO2. Local NGOs and staff are empowered to deliver aid
    SO3. Gender and protection are mainstreamed
    SO4. Population resilience is built up where possible
GO4: Psychological traumas are contained and managed
    SO1. Gender and protection are mainstreamed
    SO2. Psychological counselling access
    SO3. Children are protected
    SO4. Anti-violence campaigning
GO5: Youth is empowered and protected
    SO1. Gender and protection are mainstreamed
    SO2. Youth livelihoods are improved

Developing a strategy for effective change 59

SO3. Youth capacities are built up
SO4. Financial services, literacy and access

For the scenario 'Fragmented Power, Economic Collapse', the draft strategy 'Feeding the Markets':

GO1: Improve the food security for the most vulnerable population during the lean season
 SO1. Internally displaced persons (IDPs)/refugees access to food and livelihood opportunities
 SO2. Financial services access
 SO3. Veterinarian services access
 SO4. Agricultural production increased
 SO5. Food security surveillance and information access
GO2: Malnutrition among the vulnerable population is decreased
 SO1. Dietary intake improved
 SO2. Acute malnutrition is treated
 SO3. Health care services access
 SO4. Agricultural production increased
 SO5. Food security surveillance and information access
 SO6. Access to clean water and sanitation
 SO7. Access to basic sanitation and hygiene
GO3: Vulnerable population improves their financial resilience
 SO1. Livestock restocked
 SO2. Small farmers capacity empowered
 SO3. Financial services, literacy and access
 SO4. Access to livelihood opportunities
GO4: Increase small-scale farmers' production
 SO1. Livestock improvement
 SO2. Farmers are empowered
 SO3. Basic infrastructures access
 SO4. Crop diversification and protection
 SO5. Nutrition behaviours improved
 SO6. Hosted IDPs access to land and cattle
 SO7. Financial services access
GO5: Movement of population is contained
 SO1. Gender and protection are mainstreamed
 SO2. Hosted IDPs access to land and cattle
 SO3. Basic infrastructures access
 SO4. Host and IDP women are empowered
 SO5. Conflicts are mediated and resolved
 SO6. Regional migration coordination is advocated

60 *Developing a strategy for effective change*

GO6: Strengthening the local markets in the most vulnerable areas
  SO1. Food security surveillance and information access
  SO2. Local network of traders is strengthened and improved
  SO3. Basic infrastructures access
  SO4. Short trade circuits are improved
  SO5. Financial services, literacy and access

For the scenario 'Dictatorship and Dinka Dominance', the draft strategy 'Communities are Key':

GO1: Malnutrition and morbidity are addressed among the most vulnerable population in case of emergency
  SO1. Clean water access
  SO2. Cash access
  SO3. Malnutrition treated
  SO4. Vaccination campaigning
  SO5. Agricultural resilience strengthening
GO2: Communities' resilience is strengthened against market disruptions
  SO1. Basic infrastructure access
  SO2. Agricultural resilience strengthening
  SO3. Livestock improvement
  SO4. Food security surveillance and information access
  SO5. Income generating activities (IGAs) access
GO3: Increase small-scale farmers' production
  SO1. Livestock improvement
  SO2. Farmers are empowered
  SO3. Basic infrastructure access
  SO4. Crop diversification and protection
  SO5. Nutrition behaviours improved
  SO6. Hosted IDPs access to land and cattle
  SO7. Financial services access
GO4: Community tensions are contained and vulnerable groups are protected
  SO1. Gender and protection are mainstreamed
  SO2. Hosted IDPs access to land and cattle
  SO3. Basic infrastructure access
  SO4. Host and IDPs women are empowered
  SO5. Conflicts are mediated and resolved
  SO6. Regional migration coordination is advocated
GO5: South Sudanese immigration and exploitation in neighbouring countries decreased
  SO1. Small-scale farmers' production is secured

SO2. Hosted IDPs/refugees access to land and cattle
SO3. Regional migration coordination is advocated
SO4. IDPs/refugees/host community tensions are contained
SO5. Livelihood options are available
SO6. Financial services, literacy and access
SO7. Refugees/IDPs/hosts access to basic services

At this point the Strategy Tree output was finalised into three draft strategies. You will notice that there are many similarities and some repetition between the specific objectives and even between a few of the general objectives. As explained earlier, some repetition is completely normal at this point. When the final strategy is refined, only repetitions between lower objectives (SOs) are tolerated. If there are repetitions among specific objectives in the refined strategy, it means that those projects will contribute to achieving more than one general objective or programme, making it a highly strategic investment.

Game of actors and the design of stratagems

The game of actors analysis is an important tool in your structural analysis stage, as it enables you to understand the role and the power of different actors in your system of study and to enrich the scenarios you build. In the strategic development phase, the game of actors analysis allows you to test your draft scenario strategies to assess how they would be received by other actors in your system and allows you to refine your draft strategies.

The Actor/Objective Matrix (MAO)

The MID output is part of the foresight base you will exploit in the strategic development phase. The cross-analysis of your draft strategy with the game of actors of your system of study is possible using a tool called the MAO. You begin to fill your MAO tool by selecting the most influential actors identified in the MID chart according to the role they play in the game (MAO, pp. 181–194).

With the MAO tool you continue to engage in an objective analysis, corresponding to the last tool of the LFA analytical stage (EuropeAid 2004). However, while the EC PCM guide remains very light and short in its analytical process for this tool, we dive into a more detailed cross-analysis with the stakeholders of your system of study. The combination of the MID and the MAO is a smart approach that provides more enlightening insights than the classical actor mapping tools like 'Power Mapping'. The use of actor analysis across the foresight and strategic development

62 *Developing a strategy for effective change*

phases makes the results of your study even more compelling and puts your system's actors at the centre of your strategic development process. By not engaging in a detailed actors analysis, the traditional PCM tools have a methodological bias that likely contributes to the lack of consideration of the actors in their outputs. As a result, they are not as well adapted to inspire considerations and discussions of partnership and alliances.

While your draft strategy is designed from the possible future (the specific scenario) that you have been engaging with, the MID chart you developed during the structural analysis stage is a map of the current game of actors in your system of study. Through the MAO tool, you will assess each of your draft strategies by considering how the actors in your MID could support or challenge the objectives you have outlined, intersecting the present and future dimensions of your analysis.

The reason the insights you gain from the MAO are useful is that whatever strategies you have designed to be effective over the course of your outlook (in the possible futures you identified) you are going to implement them in the present. Therefore, understanding how the most important actors in your system will engage with your strategic options is critical. Transparency of your strategy is intrinsic to the values of the humanitarian ecosystem. However, that doesn't mean that when confronted with specific actors, particularly those that are highly political, you cannot adapt tactics and use some misdirection to achieve higher objectives.

The use of misdirection is a cornerstone of the Sun Tzu approach to strategy and it is central in the definition of a stratagem. A stratagem is a subset of a strategy that is created by reorganising the lower objectives in the tactical dimension to pursue a conflictual higher objective in a more unconventional way. The idea is to embed more controversial or sensitive lower objectives under a more consensual higher objective, which can give you the space to achieve the change you are working to pursue while avoiding direct conflict. The output of the MAO can help you to identify different configurations of consensual and conflictual objectives that might enable you to build a stratagem and be more effective (MAO, pp. 181–194). While in most cases the insights of the MAO will help you to refine your strategy in this way, occasionally you may find that you do not have conflictual objectives which you are pursuing. In this case you would maintain the original draft of your strategy.

Case study on MAO: A study on South Sudan with an outlook to 2018

We will continue to use the strategic development pilot project implemented in June 2016 for a formal humanitarian actor operating in

Developing a strategy for effective change   63

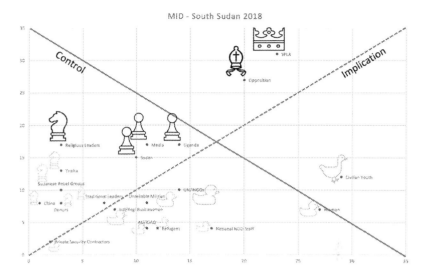

Figure 3.2 MID chart of the study North-Central South Sudan 2018, with MAO-selected actors in black

South Sudan as a case study. The foresight base for the study North-Central South Sudan 2018 included a game of actors analysis represented in a MID chart. Figure 3.2 depicts that MID chart, and the actors in bold correspond to the most influential ones selected to perform the MAO.

Each draft scenario strategy was tested with the game of actors illustrated in the MID chart. For the draft strategy 'Reaching the Unreachable' from the scenario 'A Temporary Peace', the MAO revealed two conflictual objectives (in grey) and two consensual objectives (in black) (Table 3.1).

For the draft strategy 'Feeding the Markets' from the scenario 'Fragmented Power, Economic Collapse', the MAO revealed only one consensual objective (in black) (Table 3.2).

For the draft strategy 'Communities are Key' from the scenario 'Dictatorship and Dinka Dominance', the MAO revealed only one conflictual objective (in grey) and one consensual objective (in black) (Table 3.3).

While the MAO for the draft strategy 'Feeding the Markets' revealed a very simple configuration with just one consensual objective (Table 3.2), the MAO for the draft strategy 'Reaching the Unreachable' and 'Communities are Key' (Table 3.1 and Table 3.3, respectively) revealed

Table 3.1 MAO for the draft strategy 'Reaching the Unreachable'

	Decreased malnutrition and hunger among vulnerable populations	Reduce the harmful effects of displacement	Humanitarian access is guaranteed to vulnerable populations	Psychological trauma is contained and managed	Youth are empowered and protected	Implication absolute
SPLA	2	1	−2	0	−3	8
Opposition	2	1	−2	0	−3	8
Media	2	3	1	0	2	8
Uganda	2	3	1	0	1	7
Religious leaders	2	2	2	3	3	12
Sudan	1	1	1	0	1	4
Implication Absolute	11	11	9	3	13	
Number of agreements	11	11	5	3	7	
Number of disagreements	0	0	4	0	6	

Table 3.2 MAO for the draft strategy 'Feeding the Markets'

	Improve the food security for the most vulnerable population during the lean season	Malnutrition among the vulnerable population is decreased	Vulnerable population improves their financial resilience	Increase small-scale farmers' production	Movement of population is contained	Strengthening the local markets in the most vulnerable areas	Implication absolute
SPLA	0	0	0	0	0	0	0
Opposition	1	0	0	1	2	2	6
Media	1	0	0	1	2	3	7
Uganda	0	0	0	0	2	1	3
Religious leaders	2	1	1	2	1	2	9
Sudan	0	0	1	1	0	2	4
Implication absolute	4	1	2	5	7	10	
Number of agreements	4	1	2	5	7	10	
Number of disagreements	0	0	0	0	0	0	

Table 3.3 MAO for the draft strategy 'Communities are Key'

	Malnutrition and morbidity are addressed among the most vulnerable population in case of emergency	Communities' resilience is strengthened against market disruptions	Increase small-scale farmers' production	Community tensions are contained and vulnerable groups are protected	South Sudanese immigration and exploitation in neighbouring countries decreased	Implication absolute
SPLA	2	1	1	−3	0	7
Opposition	1	1	1	−2	1	6
Media	1	1	1	2	2	7
Uganda	1	0	0	0	2	3
Religious leaders	2	2	1	3	1	9
Sudan	0	0	0	0	0	0
Implication absolute	7	5	4	10	6	
Number of agreements	7	5	4	5	6	
Number of disagreements	0	0	0	5	0	

Developing a strategy for effective change 67

some conflictual objectives, which suggests that it is worth reconfiguring those draft strategies and potentially designing more effective stratagems (MAO, pp. 181–194).

For example, in the draft strategy 'Communities are Key' a Trojan Horse stratagem was designed. According to the MAO, the higher objective 'Communities tensions are contained and vulnerable groups are protected' (GO4) is conflictual. The actors 'SPLA' and 'Opposition', respectively 'queen' and 'bishop' in our MID chart North-Central South Sudan 2018, were strongly against it. If the implementer wanted to contribute to GO4, he needed to find a more subtle way of pursuing that goal.

To design this stratagem and at the same time refine the overall strategy 'Communities are Key', we first needed to find a consensual higher objective within the draft strategy 'Communities are Key', then verify that our queen and our bishop were openly in support of it. The MAO revealed that the higher objective 'Malnutrition and morbidity are addressed among the most vulnerable population in case of emergency' (GO1) was not only the most consensual one, but the actors 'SPLA' and 'Opposition', respectively queen and bishop in our MID chart North-Central South Sudan 2018, were openly supporting it in the scenario 'Dictatorship and Dinka Dominance'.

Once we had identified our ideal consensual objective, we could start to design our Trojan Horse stratagem (MAO, pp. 181–194). GO1 was going to play the Trojan Horse to misdirect our queen and our bishop, while we engineered a way to embed the lower objectives of GO4 under GO1. As a reminder, the original structure of the strategic option GO4 was the following:

GO4: Communities tensions are contained and vulnerable groups are protected
    SO1. Gender and protection are mainstreamed
    SO2. Hosted IDPs access to land and cattle
    SO3. Basic infrastructure access
    SO4. Host and IDP women are empowered
    SO5. Conflicts are mediated and resolved
    SO6. Regional migration coordination is advocated

While the original structure of the strategic option GO1, our Trojan Horse was the following:

GO1: Malnutrition and morbidity are addressed among the most vulnerable population in case of emergency
    SO1. Clean water access

68   *Developing a strategy for effective change*

SO2. Cash access
SO3. Malnutrition treated
SO4. Vaccination campaigning
SO5. Agricultural resilience strengthening

The final output was a new engineered GO1 with seven lower objectives instead of five, and the following transformations noted in underlined text:

GO1: Malnutrition and morbidity are addressed among the most vulnerable population in case of emergency.

SO1. Clean water and sanitation access among the most vulnerable population
SO2. Cash, financial training and services access to vulnerable households
SO3. Hosted IDPs access to land and cattle
SO4. Malnutrition treated
SO5. Vaccination campaigning
SO6. Agricultural resilience strengthening
SO7. Regional migration coordination is advocated

Because the most controversial lower objectives in GO4 were 'Gender and protection are mainstreamed', 'Host and IDP women are empowered' and 'Conflict are mediated and resolved', respectively SO1, SO4 and SO5, it was important to mainstream them in most of the lower objectives of GO1, embedding and nuancing them. Note that the word 'women' has disappeared, while 'household' appeared and vulnerable population has been expanded. SO2 and SO6 in GO4 have been simply added to GO1 because they were less controversial and became, respectively, SO3 and SO7 in GO1. Finally, SO3 and SO4 in GO4 have just disappeared; the remaining lower objectives GO1 already covered basic infrastructure access (health and micro-economy), while SO1 in GO1 has been reinforced with 'sanitation'.

After eliminating some duplications among lower objectives and reinforcing the overall consistency among higher objectives, the 'Communities are Key' refined strategy for the scenario 'Dictatorship and Dinka Dominance' towards 2018 was presented as follows:

GO1: Malnutrition and morbidity are addressed among the most vulnerable population in case of emergency

SO1. Water and sanitation access among the most vulnerable population
SO2. Cash, financial training and capital investments found access to vulnerable households

Developing a strategy for effective change   69

SO3. Malnutrition treated
SO4. Vaccination campaigning
SO5. Agricultural resilience strengthening
GO2: Communities resilience is strengthened against market disruptions markets
    SO1. Basic infrastructure access
    SO2. Livestock improvement
    SO3. Food security surveillance and information access
    SO4. IGAs access
GO3: Increase small-scale farmers' production
    SO1. Livestock improvement
    SO2. Farmers are empowered
    SO3. Basic infrastructure access
    SO4. Crop diversification and protection
    SO5. Nutrition behaviours improved
GO4: South Sudanese immigration and exploitation in neighbouring countries decreased
    SO1. Small-scale farmers' production is secured
    SO2. Hosted IDPs/refugees access to land and cattle and basic services
    SO3. Regional migration coordination is advocated
    SO4. IDPs/refugees/host community tensions are contained
    SO5. Livelihood options are available

There is a repetition of SO 'Livestock improvement' in GO2 and in GO3 of this refined scenario strategy. It means that the project 'Livestock improvement' will contribute respectively to the programme 'Communities resilience is strengthened against market disruptions and the programme 'Increase small-scale farmers' production' making it a highly valuable investment.

Making a decision

Once you have refined a strategy for each scenario that you have built, you can start the process of deciding which strategy you will pursue.

Note: If you are a facilitator, it is important that you do not participate in the decision-making process.

It is vital to leave space for the people and communities from within the system of study, not only to contribute to the strategic development process but, most importantly, to make the decision about which strategy

70 Developing a strategy for effective change

to implement. Our experience with collaborative foresight and strategic development processes showed that participants develop expectations about their role in the ultimate process of decision-making. If you are a facilitator, you should be very mindful of this and make sure that the decision-making process is designed and owned by the whole group and not dominated by a single person (regardless of seniority). How the group makes the decision will be informed by many different avenues of analysis.

While until this point we have not discussed the likelihood of the scenarios that have been created to ensure that participants in the strategic development process consider all the potential eventualities, one of the metrics you could now use to identify which strategy you would like to pursue is which future you think you will be working in. This approach requires you to take a bet on what you think the most likely future will be and follow the strategy that was designed for it. Alternatively, you may feel that you are not prepared to bet on one single scenario as your context is very dynamic; in this case you would work to find the most robust strategy, one that is the most effective across multiple futures to ensure that you have maximum agility as your context changes.

Another potential metric which you can consider when deciding which strategy to pursue would be how well aligned the strategy you have created is to the mission and mandate of your organisation, i.e. How relevant is the strategy for your structure? In the Testing tool, we propose steps which can help you to conduct this analysis efficiently and give you the information you need to decide how to proceed.

Testing

Testing is a succession of two tests that provide further information on the finalised strategies (Testing, pp. 195–203). More specifically, it enables you and the collaborative group to identify the robustness of the final strategies towards all the possible futures you have identified and the relevancy of those strategies within the strategic frame of an upper structure (alliance, network, confederation or global entity, etc.). Regardless of the strategy you choose, the other draft strategies that were created should not be discarded, as you may find them useful as you move through the course of your outlook.

Before you begin the Testing tool you must remember that the outcome of these tests is designed to provide you with more information on which to base your decision-making process; they are not designed to replace you as a decision maker.

Developing a strategy for effective change 71

Case study on Testing: South Sudan with an outlook to 2018

Let's go back to our case study of South Sudan with an outlook to 2018. After the MAO has helped us to refine all the draft scenario strategies, and because the collaborative group felt the situation was too dynamic to bet on one scenario, we decided to perform the Testing tool to provide complementary information for their decision-making process. To do this we needed to gather more information about their upper organisational structure and their global strategy. From their global strategy we extracted three strategic 'pillars': 'Mitigate the consequence of hunger', 'Address the cause of hunger' and 'Change the way hunger is view and addressed'. Tables 3.4 and 3.5 depict the outcome of the robustness test and the relevancy test performed on the three final scenario strategies: 'Reaching the Unreachable', 'Feeding the Markets' and 'Communities are Key'.

The robustness test demonstrated that the strategy 'Feeding the Markets' was the most adaptable across all three scenarios which were being considered. The outcome of the relevancy test was that the strategy 'Communities are Key' was the most relevant strategy according to the global objectives of the upper structure.

After considering the Testing outputs, the final decision taken by the collaborative group was to implement the refined strategy 'Communities are Key', designed from the scenario 'Dictatorship and Dinka Dominance'. The refined strategy 'Communities are Key' wasn't the most robust but the most relevant strategy according to the Testing tool, and it was the

Table 3.4 The robustness test and the most robust strategy (in grey)

	Temporary Peace (Civil War)	Fragmented Power, Economic Collapse	Dictatorship and Dinka Dominance
Strategy 1 Reaching the Unreachable			
Strategy 2 Feeding the Markets			
Strategy 3 Communities are Key			

72 Developing a strategy for effective change

Table 3.5 The relevancy test and the most relevant strategy (in grey)

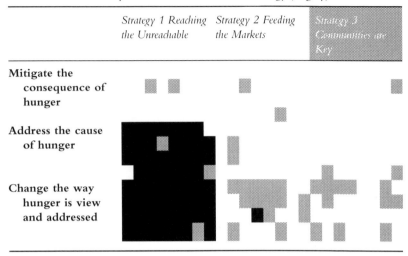

strategy that the collaborative group considered the most pertinent to implement at the time of the workshop. Knowing that it was not as robust as the other strategic options, the group also reflected on the fact that they would need to closely monitor how their context evolved and be prepared to make amendments (integrating elements from the other draft strategies or switching completely) to ensure their continued effectiveness. The fact that a specific strategy was chosen by the collaborative group meant that they had more ownership over its implementation, already paving the way for success.

In July 2016, one month after the workshop, the Battle of Juba and the exile of Machar were clear signals that strategy that had been selected would not be as effective as the other strategies designed during the workshop. The collaborative group subsequently changed their mind, and 'Feeding the Markets' was implemented as the country strategy for the following two years.

Planning

Once the decision is made on which refined strategy to implement, you can archive the alternatives strategies with their respective scenarios and start to plan. Most humanitarian actors use two approaches for planning: the LFA and the ToC.

If you use the LFA, once your chosen strategy is outlined, you can follow the "planning stage" of the identification phase (EuropeAid 2004,

Developing a strategy for effective change 73

p. 60), transferring the hierarchy of high and low objectives from your refined strategy into a logical framework and finalising the planning stage with the identification of the outputs to achieve the lower objectives of the strategy and the activities necessary to produce those outputs. Each lower objective, or SO in our case study, would correspond to a project, and each higher objective, or GO in our case study, would correspond to a programme.

The integration of our strategic development method is best placed at stage two of the ToC, when you start backwards mapping from the long-term goals. The long-term goals in the ToC are your higher objectives in your refined scenario strategy, the GOs in our case study. Therefore, you should consider how the lower objectives are connected as 'actual outcomes', and start to backwards map their complementary 'outcomes' and their respective preconditions. The ToC allows you at this stage to add 'desired outcomes' or to consider some 'actual outcomes' as desirable. This is where the integration of your strategy based on foresight becomes more vulnerable to corruption compared to the relatively simple process of integrating it with an LFA. By having the opportunity to reframe your objectives, you run the risk of breaking the logic of your original strategy (designed from the foresight base) and reverting back to present thinking and original assumptions. However, if you are mindful of this risk, you can mitigate it by ensuring that you are abiding by the logic of your original strategy when you identify desired outcomes and ensuring that the process is collaborative.

What to do if you already have a strategy (optimisation)

How our structural analysis, scenario-building techniques and strategic development processes can be integrated with traditional methods of PCM has been extensively explained. However, we also want to discuss what to do if you have already designed a strategy that you are implementing and how you can use foresight and strategic development to enhance it.

Now that you are familiar with the foresight phase explained in Chapter 2 and the strategic development ones explored in this chapter, we are going to suggest another process which can help you run a diagnostic on your strategy and optimise it to be fit for the future.

In order to optimise your existing strategy and make it fit for the future, we suggest a sequence of three stages that will enable you to identify the critical objectives that you want to optimise or alert you to the

74 Developing a strategy for effective change

fact that you need to design a new strategy: creating your foresight base, testing and optimisation.

Create your foresight base

It is important that before you engage in an optimisation process to fit your existing strategy for the future that you create a foresight base and a set of scenarios for the system covered by your strategy. The definition of your strategy should provide you with the key parameters of a well-structured system of study: the viewpoint (organisational or contextual) and the time horizon (Scoping, pp. 82–93). Your defined system of study gives you the place to start the foresight phase described in Chapter 2. Alternatively, you can endeavour to find applicable exploratory scenarios produced by an external source. However, you should ensure that you have the outputs from their structural analysis in order to be able to use them effectively.

Test and optimise

Now that you have your foresight base and your scenarios, you can proceed by testing your strategy with the game of actors using the MAO (pp. 181–194). If your strategy is structured with one higher objective at the top (like in a programme for example) proceed to test the lower objectives of your strategy. The MAO will reveal if it is worth it to reconfigure your strategy by designing and implementing a potential stratagem to be more effective (see Figure 3.3). If the output of the MAO suggests that a restructure of your strategy could make you more effective, then you should begin to refine your strategy accordingly (MAO, pp. 181–194). Once you have performed the MAO and your strategy has been refined, you can proceed to test your strategy in terms of its robustness across all the possible futures you identified, using a robustness test (Testing, pp. 195–203).

If your robustness test concludes that your refined strategy is not fit for the futures which you are facing, you should acknowledge that a new strategy is needed. In that case, starting from your foresight base, follow all the processes of strategic development described in this chapter. If it is still effective, you can continue to implement it and monitor its effectiveness.

Developing a strategy for effective change 75

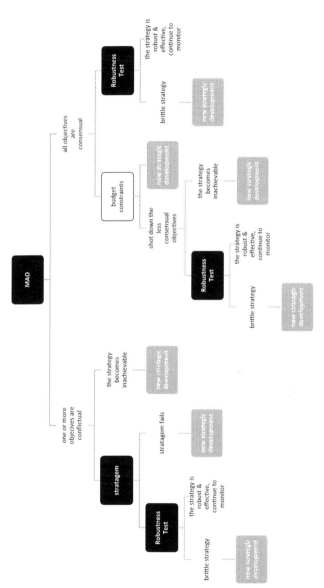

Figure 3.3 Optimisation chart flow

Conclusion

Strategic development provides you with three tools (Strategy Tree, MAO and Testing) with which you can increase your impact and agility. The way in which the process has been designed to fit with both the LFA and ToC PCM systems means that it can be easily integrated into the existing decision-making processes of most humanitarian actors, reducing the friction that can be created by trying to think in a different way. Many staff in humanitarian organisations have limited time to invest in learning new tools or rethinking their ways of working. By creating tools that are easy to implement and fit within their existing decision-making processes, we hope that strategic development can provide an avenue through which everyone can explore how to create strategies in a more futures-focused way. There are many benefits to strategic development, three of which we wanted to highlight in closing this chapter.

Our experience with formal and non-formal actors has evidenced substantial differences between strategic development processes conducted with people affected by crises and without. There have always been reasons to not include people affected by crises: security reasons in conflict contexts, time, a lack of resources (e.g. for translation), etc., but those reasons don't change the fact that the quality of the output and the relevance of the strategy is weaker when people affected by crises weren't around the table. The strategic development approaches we have presented are all collaborative in nature and rest on a strong understanding of the system in which you are intervening. As a result, they offer humanitarian actors the opportunity to be more inclusive in their strategy development processes and, as a result, to have a greater impact.

In addition to increased participation, one of the greatest benefits of strategic development is that through the process of designing multiple strategies, humanitarian actors can increase their agility. This helps them to ensure that they can still be effective as their context changes. Many humanitarian actors operate in areas where rapid changes due to both environmental factors and manmade causes are relatively common. It is therefore prudent to invest in a strategic foresight system which enables you to not only consider what these different futures might be but also how you can be effective in them so that you can prepare ahead of time rather than having to scramble to adapt.

Finally, by placing an emphasis on the way in which your system of study might evolve in the future and preparing for those eventualities, you are challenging the short-termism that defines the ways that many humanitarian actors operate. Thinking more long term and being

Developing a strategy for effective change   77

prepared to be an effective actor in your system even as the context shifts (which could mean both increasing or decreasing the scale of your programming) is a huge benefit of strategic development, especially in an era where change within the humanitarian ecosystem itself is occurring.

The way we have tested and piloted our strategic development process has shown that a transition from traditional PCM methodologies to an enhanced version is possible. By incepting a culture of anticipation and collaborative ways of working, not only do humanitarian actors acquire immediate strategic agility, but its Western-centric biases are continually challenged, paving the way for transformation. Grass-rooted strategies have the power to seed change and transformation for the organisations that are implementing them, challenging their purpose. A transformation from the bottom, that with time and strong leadership can inspire revolution. In the end, it's always a question of leadership.

References

Centre for Theory of Change CFTOC (2021) How does theory of change work? *New York*, 30 March 2021, https://www.theoryofchange.org/what-is-theory-of -change/how-does-theory-of-change-work/

Clausewitz, Carl (2007) *Carl von Clausewitz: On War*, translated by Michael Howard and Peter Paret, Oxford, Oxford University Press.

Drucker, P. (1954) *The Practice of Management*, New York, Harper.

EuropeAid (2004) *Project Cycle Management Guidelines: Aid Delivery Methods* Vol.1, Bruxelles, accessed on 19 March 2021, https://europa.eu/capacity4dev/iesf/docu ments/aid-delivery-methods-project-cycle-management-guidelines-europeaid -2004

Godet, M (1994) *From Anticipation to Action: A Handbook of Strategic Prospective*, Paris, UNESCO Publishing.

Handel, Michael (2005) *Masters of War: Classical Strategic Thought*, London, Taylor and Francis.

Khawam, R R (2010) *Le Livre des ruses: La strategie politique des Arabes*, Paris, Libretto Editions Phebus

Levi, J (2016) *L'art de la guerre: Sun Tzu*, translated by: Jean Levi, Paris, Fayard.

Machiavelli, Niccolò (1961) *Il principe*, edited by: di Luigi Firpo, Torino, Enaudi.

McGoldrick, Claudia (2011) The future of humanitarian action: an ICRC perspective, *International Review of the Red Cross*, December 2011, 93(884), 965– 981, DOI:10.1017/S1816383112000306

Organisation for Economic Co-operation and Development OECD (2017) Finance preparedness: world humanitarian summit, *Putting Policy into Practice: The Commitments into Action Series*, OECD, accessed on 15 March 2021, https ://www.oecd.org/development/humanitarian-donors/docs/financingprepared ness.pdf

78   *Developing a strategy for effective change*

Oxford Advanced Learner's Dictionary (2021) *Definition of Strategy Noun,* accessed on 9 April 2021, https://www.oxfordlearnersdictionaries.com/definition/english/strategy?q=strategy

Rosenberg, J L (1970) *Final Report Contract No. csd-2510 Project Evaluation and the Project Appraisal Reporting System,* Washington DC, FRY Consultants Inc., accessed on 19 March 2021, https://pdf.usaid.gov/pdf_docs/PNADW881.pdf

Tanner *et al.* (2019) Scoping and design for taking forecast-based early action to scale: three case studies, Overseas Development Institute, accessed on 4 April 2021, https://odi.org/en/publications/scoping-and-design-for-taking-forecast-based-early-action-to-scale-three-case-studies/

Thomas, A and Urquhart (2020) *Global Humanitarian Assistance Report 2020,* Development Initiatives, accessed on 14 April 2021, https://devinit.org/resources/global-humanitarian-assistance-report-2020/

Tzu, Sun (2014) *The Art of War,* translated by: John Minford, London, Penguin.

UN (2017) Too important to fail: addressing the humanitarian financing gap, in *High-Level Panel on Humanitarian Financing Report to the Secretary-General,* New York, accessed on 15 March 2021, https://interagencystandingcommittee.org/system/files/hlp_report_too_important_to_failgcoaddressing_the_humanitarian_financing_gap.pdf

United States Agency for International Development (USAID) (1971) Practical concepts incorporated, in *Guidelines for Teaching Logical Framework Concepts,* Washington DC, accessed on 19 March 2021, https://web.archive.org/web/20110409170601/http://pdf.usaid.gov/pdf_docs/PNABI452.pdf

4 A toolkit for humanitarian action

The second half of this book is dedicated to exploring the tools of foresight and strategic development that were introduced in Chapters 2 and 3. The toolkit is designed to be a manual for people working in the humanitarian ecosystem who want to be more strategic. As such it is structured as a series of clear, step-by-step guides, taking you from selecting a critical question to designing a systemic strategy for more sustained impact.

Each of the tools follows the same structure. They open with an introduction to the tool itself, which states the purpose and what the expected output will be. It then outlines what, if any, prerequisites there are for using the tool. The bulk of each guide is made up of the 'How to do it' section which details, in a clear and methodical way, how you can implement each tool. Understanding the resource and time constraints under which most humanitarian actors operate, there is a selection of tools (particularly in the structural analysis and scenario-building stages) which can be completed as a solitary exercise. However, all of the tools which we propose in this book can be conducted as participatory workshops, and we strongly recommend you to include stakeholders in your work. Regardless of how you approach each tool, you should always allow time to challenge and validate your outputs with a group of external experts. After a brief 'Frequently asked questions' section, each guide concludes with a set of facilitation notes to assist you in implementing the tool as a collaborative exercise. While we include general guidance as to how you could host a workshop, we have invested more attention in giving comprehensive facilitation notes for how you could host a virtual workshop.

Though the research which underpins this book spans more than 7 years of operational work, the context in 2020 and 2021 when this

DOI: 10.4324/9781003094753-4

80 *A toolkit for humanitarian action*

text was being drafted made the value in a flexible approach all the clearer as the COVID-19 pandemic changed working patterns and perspectives. During the pandemic, demand for support to organisations considering how they could better understand the context in which they found themselves and manage the extreme uncertainty they faced increased, but many strategic foresight projects had to be adapted to be delivered entirely virtually. While it is more than likely that in-person meetings and workshops return in the coming years, we believe that the benefits of conducting these processes at least partially online, such as the opportunity to include more people at different stages of the process, greater flexibility in allowing people to participate on their own time, and reducing the carbon and financial costs of moving people to one central location will all support continuing to conduct at least some parts of strategic foresight workshops and processes virtually.

The guides in this toolkit have been arranged in an order designed to make it as easy as possible to progress through all the tools of a strategic foresight project.

1. Scoping Workshop...pp 82–93
2. PESTLE..pp 94–99
3. Architecture ....pp 100–106
4. Importance/Uncertainty Matrix ....pp 107–116
5. Morphological Scenarios ....pp 117–125
6. Matrix Scenarios..pp 126–136
7. Driver Files ....pp 137–140
8. Actors File...pp 141–145
9. Influence/Dependency Matrix ....pp 146–162
10. Writing Scenarios..pp 163–169
11. Strategy Tree...pp 170–180
12. Actor/Objective Matrix ....pp 181–194
13. Testing..pp 195–203

However, there are occasions when we present tools that can be used in multiple ways and times, and when we present two different options for tools you could employ to progress through your work. In order to try to bring some clarity to the process we have created Figure 4.1 to graphically represent how you can flow through a project.

A toolkit for humanitarian action 81

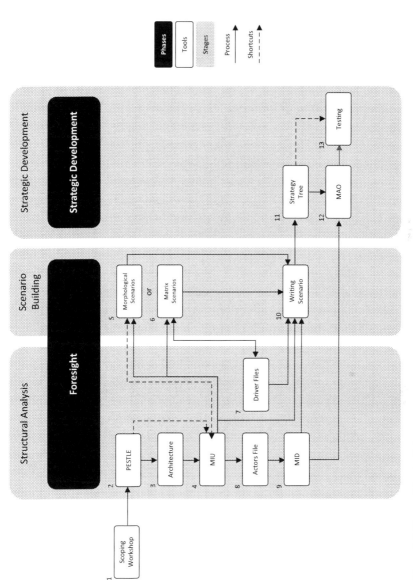

Figure 4.1 Flow of the toolkit

82 *A toolkit for humanitarian action*

SCOPING WORKSHOP

It is critical to take the time to clearly define the topic that you want to investigate before starting any foresight work. A good definition of your topic sets the parameters of your research and takes you halfway on your strategic foresight journey.

The Scoping Workshop is structured to prompt a discussion on the critical changes that your organisation or the context in which you are working in will face over the coming years or decades. Through the process, you will build consensus among participants, create a shared vision of the critical changes that may occur, consider which of the changes you identify you are prepared to meet and, finally, highlight what changes you need to explore further to master.

You may already have a clear idea of the topic you want to explore, such as creating a global outlook for your organisation or investigating how environmental stress will evolve around Lake Chad. If this is the case, you do not need to conduct a Scoping Workshop, but you do need to set the parameters of your research by following steps (a) and (b) of the 'Prerequisites' in this guide and begin to examine your assumptions (Step 7: Listing assumptions).

If you are unclear about what topic you want to investigate, or you feel your topic is too broad, the Scoping Workshop is an iterative process that will help you to refine it (follow all the steps of this guide).

The output of the Scoping Workshop will allow you to identify one or multiple topics to explore.

Prerequisites

Regardless of whether you feel you have a clear topic or not, it is important, to set the parameters of your research by answering two questions:

a) **Are you exploring critical changes for an organisation (e.g. what are the challenges your organisation/team would face in the future) or for a context (geographical and/or thematic; e.g. the future of Sudan, how digitalisation in Cote d'Ivoire will unfold, or the future impacts of extreme weather on global agriculture)?**

The answer to this question gives you the viewpoint of your study (whether it is organisational or contextual). The reason you need to set the viewpoint as a parameter of your research is that the perspective you take will affect the way in which you approach some of the tools in this toolkit.

From an organisational viewpoint, the structure and dynamics of your organisation are part of the system that you are exploring. From a contextual viewpoint, your organisation will be considered as an actor among the others actors of the system you are exploring and the focus will be on the evolution of the context.

It is not easy to shift between an organisational or contextual study once you have begun, so it is worth spending some time considering which viewpoint best suits your needs.

b) What is the time horizon you are looking at?

The answer to this question defines the length of the outlook of your study, e.g. 2 years, 5 years, 10, years, etc. By identifying your topic and answering these two questions, the parameters of your research are set and your system of study is defined.

A well-structured system of study looks something like these examples:

Organisational: 'An organisation that is fit for purpose in 2040'; 'A new economic model for your organisation in 2035'; 'The future of your organisation in South America in 2040'.

Contextual: 'The future of Eritrea in 2035'; 'The future of work in 2050'; 'A sustainable food system in East Africa in 2040'.

If you would like to focus on a specific geographic, you should include that within your system of study; if you do not enumerate a geographic area it is assumed that you are investigating your topic at the global level.

If you are content with the system of study that you have identified by using these two dimensions, you can skip to Step 7 of this guide to begin to identify your assumptions. However, if once you have set these parameters, you feel that your system of study is still too broad or insufficiently clear to give you the analysis that you need, then you can use a Scoping Workshop to refine it further.

Scoping Workshop

If you want to refine your system of study using a Scoping Workshop, you need to select the workshop participants according to the viewpoint of your system of study:

For an organisational study: you will engage with the senior leadership team of the organisation. They will constitute three-fifths of the panel and they should identify the other one-fifth of participants

84　*A toolkit for humanitarian action*

from among the mid management and junior staff, and the remaining one-fifth from their key partners or/and external experts.

For a contextual study: you will engage with a choice of internal and/or external experts, with a high level of understanding of the geography and/or thematics and an interest in building a collaborative vision.

The quality and diversity of the participants is critical not only for the validity of the scoping output, but also for getting buy-in and building consensus around the overall strategic foresight process.

How to do it

Step 1 Preparation

First, attendees need to do some light preparatory work before attending the workshop. You should circulate an introduction to the exercise (being clear what the expected outputs are) and two questions they should answer prior to the exercise workshop:

a)　**What have been the most impactful changes for the organisation or for the context?** (use your time horizon as the limit; e.g. if the time horizon for your project is 10 years in the future, then you should ask people to consider the past 10 years)

b)　**What do you anticipate being the most impactful changes for the organisation or for the context in the future?** (use the time horizon of your study as the limit)

Gather the responses and summarise the information in a handout which you can circulate at the beginning of the workshop.

Step 2 Introduction and selection of critical changes

Anticipate key changes for the organisation or for the context: after a short introduction on the workshop, a presentation of the agenda and an introduction of the participants, you will share the summarised outputs of the questions gathered in Step 1.

Then you ask the attendees to list (in 10 minutes) a predetermined number of main changes (we often set the number at three) they anticipate being the most impactful for the organisation or the context in the time horizon set. They can select from the responses collected at Step 1 or list new ones.

Each attendee will create their own list and, in turn, present it to the group – writing their contributions on a shared list or sticking the

A toolkit for humanitarian action 85

Post-it notes that they have written on a wall that can be seen by the whole group. Following a roundtable discussion about the changes that have been presented, all the ideas that were expressed should be placed on the board and should be optimised (you should try to synthesise long phrases, eliminate any duplications and group changes which you feel speak to the same topic). Your final list of changes should be written on clean Post-it notes and placed randomly on a white board/wall/screen.

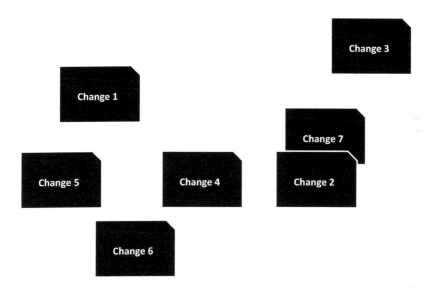

Figure 4.2 Optimised list of changes for a Scoping Workshop

Step 3 Rank the level of impact each change will have on your system of study

To rank the level of impact of the changes that are represented in Figure 4.2, you will organise a ranking exercise with the attendees. First, you have to create an empty frame on a white board/wall/screen following the template in Figure 4.3. Note that the line delineating the boundary between high impact and moderate impact is not centred but rather is only one-third of the way above the x axis, leaving more space for high impact.

Once you have drawn your frame (you can prepare this beforehand) you should explain to the attendees how the ranking exercise will work.

86 *A toolkit for humanitarian action*

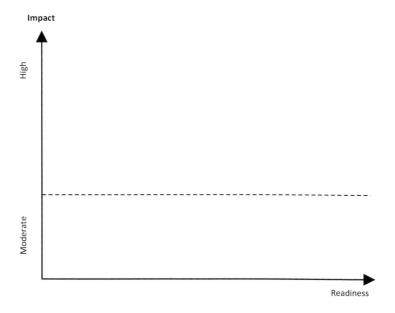

Figure 4.3 Impact–Readiness chart

Each participant will be given an equal number of points (as determined in the following) which they can allot to the changes they feel are the most impactful.

Then you distribute the points to each of the attendees and ask them to individually attribute the spread of points to the changes on the board according to their interpretation of their impact on the system of study. The changes that they consider to be the most impactful is where they should allot most of their points. They can place all their points on one change or spread them out across several changes that they feel are important.

To calculate the total number of points that each attendee will have to distribute, use this formula: (Number of changes expressed by each participant × Number of participants) / 2. For example, with ten participants, each of whom lists three main changes: (3 × 10) / 2 = 15 individual points.

Whether the workshop is virtual or in person, allow to the attendees enough time to distribute their points. As a facilitator you will then need to add up all the points that each change has received and

A toolkit for humanitarian action 87

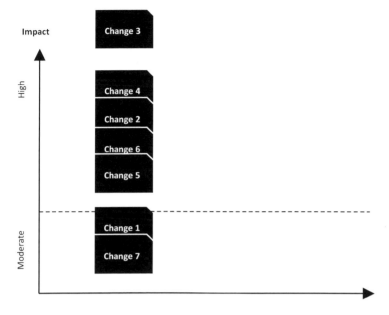

Figure 4.4 X–Impact chart with changes ranked by impact

rank the changes in a vertical line according to which received the most points from the participants. Changes receiving zero points are eliminated.

The final result should look similar to the example in Figure 4.4, where Change 3 has collected the maximum of points and Change 7 the minimum (but still above zero):

***Step 4 Discuss the readiness of the organisation
or the context to meet these changes***

Finally, the attendees identify – collectively – the degree of readiness of the organisation or the context has to manage each change.

Before engaging in the discussion, you need to introduce and explain the concept of readiness using the frame in Figure 4.4 and a few examples. Readiness is a metric used to assess the current state of your organisation or the context's preparedness and ability to respond to the considered change. This can either be the degree of readiness to overcome a challenge or to take advantage of an opportunity.

88 *A toolkit for humanitarian action*

Organisation example: the generational change in workforce culture and the ability of your organisation to handle that change strategically

If there is no mention of that change in the current strategy and nothing has been done to adapt your human resource policy to the changes in the behaviours of the workforce to come, then your organisational readiness against that change is very low.

Contextual example: the acceleration of south–north migrations in Europe resulting from increasing temperatures in the southern Mediterranean

If climate change is at the core of strategic discussions among the European countries and most of them have started to consider in their policies to integrate the potential exponential number of migrants into their economies and societies by 2030, then the contextual readiness against that change is high.

When engaging in the discussion (which should last approximately one hour), start with the change ranked highest in impact. Once a consensus on the level of readiness is reached, move the changes accordingly on the readiness axis of the matrix, maintaining their relative position of impact. Do this with each change in turn. As you progress, you can also discuss the readiness of the following changes by comparing them with the ones already set.

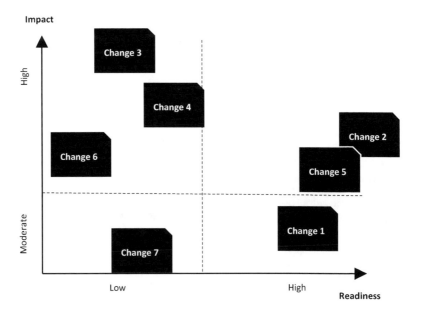

Figure 4.5 Readiness–Impact chart with ranked changes by impact and readiness

Benchmark: crossing the middle vertical line indicates a higher level of readiness meaning that the participants can demonstrate performed actions or an existing strategy/programme/documents which exhibit their readiness to meet this change.

The final result should look similar to Figure 4.5.

Step 5 Interpretation

Once all the changes are placed on the Impact/Readiness matrix, you can explain the interpretation to the participants. The interpretation should not be made clear to the participants before the workshop is completed or it could create bias in their responses.

The matrix is divided by the middle line of the readiness axis and the line dividing high and moderate impact resulting in four distinct areas: A, B, C, D, as in Figure 4.6.

Critical changes in the top, left area A: all the changes placed in this area are critical future challenges/opportunities for which the organisation or the context is unprepared; they lack the capacity to act or respond to the considered change.

Important changes that are well mastered in the top, right area B: all the changes positioned here are important and well mastered by the organisation or the context.

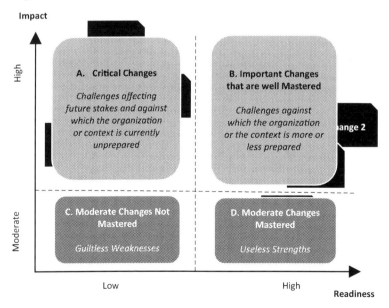

Figure 4.6 Readiness–Impact chart with ranked changes by impact and readiness plus interpretation

90   *A toolkit for humanitarian action*

Moderate changes not mastered in the bottom, right area C: all the changes set in this area have a moderate impact and while the organisation or the context is unprepared and without capacity to act or respond to them, it is not critical.

Moderate changes that are mastered in the bottom, right area D: all the changes positioned here are moderately impactful and well mastered by the context or the organisation; however, that capacity and preparedness is relatively useless.

Step 6 Refining your system of study

Choosing an area to explore further (in essence to become your system of study) should come from those listed among the critical changes in the top, left area A and be decided by considering how each are ranked in terms of importance.

If the critical changes quadrant is empty, then you can focus on some important changes that are well mastered in the top, right area B, particularly the ones with high impact, near the middle readiness line. These changes present opportunities to improve the existing strategic foresight of the organisation or the context to increase its preparedness and effectiveness in meeting that change.

The chosen change can help you to refine your system of study. While you began the scoping exercise with a topic in mind, framed by the parameters you set of the viewpoint and time horizon, the Scoping Workshop enables you to set the focus and to explore it further.

For example, if you began your Scoping Workshop looking at the rights of lesbian, gay, bisexual, transgender, and intersex (LGBTI) people in Uganda with an outlook to 2030, then you may end your Scoping Workshop having identified access to healthcare as being the most important critical change to address. Therefore, you would refine your system of study to become *the rights of LGBTI citizens in Uganda to access quality healthcare: an outlook to 2030.*

Now that you have refined and finalised your system of study, it is important understand what preconceived notions you have of your system of study and what assumptions you are making about the system you will be exploring.

Step 7 Listing assumptions

Everyone has their own mental model, their particular thought process which is informed by their experiences and biases. Without challenging your mental model and outlining your assumptions, you are open to integrating bias into the foundation of your system of study which can severely limit your thinking and the end result.

As such, you should begin your work by writing down what assumptions you are making to frame your investigation. Once you have a list of assumptions you should research each one and gather evidence that supports or refutes them. Those that you find evidence for, and you think are reasonable, should be formally included in your study. Be careful when selecting your assumptions, as you will not consider any future which challenges them. Assumptions are a part of most foresight exercises, as they are often necessary to focus a study. However, they should all be validated with a diverse panel of experts who bring a different perspective to your exercise and can challenge your mental model.

Once finalised, your list of assumptions should be added to the opening of every output you produce during the course of your study, along with the system of study.

Next are examples of a set of hypotheses used to frame a study on the Future of Aid in 2030.

The following changes are likely to take place too slowly to be relevant before 2030:

- A reform of global governance structures, which would enable global governance institutions to significantly expand their role vis-à-vis other actors
- Stabilisation of chronically fragile countries (Yemen, Syria, South Sudan, etc.)

Frequently asked questions

If I focus on a critical change for which I have already a strategy, should I engage in a foresight study?
If you focus on a critical change for which you have already a strategy, it is important to first check if you have a foresight base that underpins those documents. If not, you should engage in a foresight process starting from Chapter 2 using the PESTLE (PESTLE, pp. 94–99) or source external scenarios and their underpinning analysis. If you have already a foresight base, then we suggest that you engage in a strategy optimisation process (see Chapter 3, pp. 73–74).

Facilitation notes

The Scoping Workshop is a collaborative exercise that can be performed physically or virtually, and should take between 3 and 4 hours.

92 *A toolkit for humanitarian action*

In the Scoping Workshop, you should pay particular attention to the optimisation of the list of changes (ensuring that you don't have any duplicates and the grouping of changes summarising similar dynamics is coherent). Grouping of changes is a delicate process: the facilitator should identify duplications and suggest grouping fluidly, ensuring that a consensus emerges on the edits that you are making. That process can be significantly time-consuming if the facilitator is uncertain about the process.

Tip: For a physical workshop, ensure you leave a 30-minute break between Step 3 and Step 4 (which will allow you to also do the arithmetic and prepare the ranked chart for Step 4).

Virtual facilitation notes (2.5–4 hours, with no breaks)

You can run a scoping workshop virtually, following the same steps as those outlined earlier, using a virtual whiteboard. Here is some guidance on how to adapt the steps to an online setting.

Preparation

  i. Follow the instructions in Step 1 to introduce your participants to the workshop and ask for their initial reflections on past and future changes. Create the summary sheet and circulate it to all participants prior to the workshop.
 ii. Before the workshop, prepare your virtual whiteboard with the impact/readiness chart (as seen in Figure 4.3) and in a blank open space next to the chart place a selection of empty Post-it notes (for clarity these should be all the same colour).

Tip: To reduce confusion for the participants, hide the area of your whiteboard with the empty chart for the start of your exercise and reveal it only in Step v when you are placing the Post-it notes upon it.

Workshop

 iii. Open the workshop with an introduction to the exercise and ensure that all participants are confident in being able to manipulate the software. (15 minutes)
 iv. Begin with Step 2, asking all participants to fulfil or create Post-it notes denoting the changes that they feel are most significant. As in the earlier instructions, you should lead the process of optimising

A toolkit for humanitarian action 93

their input, synthesising their input, removing duplicate notes and grouping. (30–60 minutes)

v. You now need to rank the changes that you have identified. Most virtual whiteboard software have an inbuilt feature which allows for voting, and so you can structure the voting session as described earlier. If it does not have a voting feature, you should create symbols or coloured dots that denote the points which the participants have been allocated and ask them to place their points on the Post-it notes in the same fashion as described in Step 3. (5–20 minutes)

vi. You will then need to calculate the final results (if you are able to use a voting function on the software this should be instantaneous). Once you have the final results you should place the Post-it notes on your impact/readiness frame in order of descending impact (see Figure 4.4). (5–20 minutes)

vii. Once the ranking is complete you need to introduce the concept of readiness and facilitate a discussion to place each change on the chart. The details of how to do this are discussed in Step 4. You should move the Post-it notes on the whiteboard as the discussion is unfolding, keeping their relative level of impact the same. (50–70 minutes)

viii. After assessing the readiness for each change, you should proceed to Step 5 and explain the interpretation of your chart. You can do this by placing shapes, labelled as in Figure 4.6, on top of your chart. (10 minutes)

ix. Finally, you should move on to Step 6 (discussion of how you want to refine your system of study) and Step 7 (identification of initial assumptions) with the group before closing the session. (20–40 minutes)

Resources: a summary sheet of the past and future changes, a pre-prepared virtual whiteboard.

94 *A toolkit for humanitarian action*

PESTLE

Francis Aguilar is most commonly credited with creating the original framework for the PESTLE tool in his 1967 work *Scanning the Business Environment*. While the tool has evolved under many different acronyms since its first conception, its purpose has always been to support decision makers in better understanding the big picture in which their work takes place.

At the outset of your strategic foresight process, you need to begin developing your understanding of the dynamics that you are looking to explore. Building from the parameters and assumptions you have set, you need to identify the important components (the actors and factors) which make up your system of study.

A PESTLE (sometimes referred to as a PESTEL or STEEPLE) provides you with the prompt to consider all the different components you want to think through – the political, economic, social, technological, legal and environmental dimensions of your system of study. The goal of this exercise is to think as broadly as possible about what should be included to ensure that you do not overlook any critical actors or factors.

The output of your PESTLE exercise is a comprehensive list of the actors and factors that are relevant for your system of study and their definitions. Even without taking your analysis further, a PESTLE can be a very productive exercise for any team hoping to be more strategic in its thinking.

Prerequisites

Before you begin your PESTLE, you must have identified a clear system of study – the viewpoint of your study, the topic (including geographic considerations if you have them) and the time horizon.

How to do it

Step 1 Introduction

It is necessary to, first, be clear about what the 'component' parts of your system are. These are made up of actors and factors.

By *actors* we mean a person, a group, a movement, an organisation, an enterprise or an institution with a role in your system of study.

By *factors* we mean the dynamics, phenomena and events both natural and manmade which exist in your system of study. These can be as diverse as poverty, climate change, disruptive technologies, national legislation, local levels of unemployment, social exclusion, terror attacks, peace talks and social media campaigns.

Step 2 Create the PESTLE table

Once this is clear, you can begin to identify the actors and factors that are relevant for your system of study. You can do this in list form or it can be helpful to create a table by assigning each of the PESTLE dimensions their own column and fulfilling the table with the components you want to include (see Table 4.1 for an example).

Table 4.1 Example of a PESTLE table

PESTLE dimension	Factor/actor	Abbreviation	Full name	Definition

Sometimes it is useful to have a set of questions which you can use to provoke thinking about each of these dimensions. Some examples include:

Who are the actors who hold power in your system?
What has changed in your context over the last ten years?
What are the global changes which affect your context?

Note: Grouping – When you are creating your list of factors and actors you need to decide the granularity you want to include in your study. Some factors and actors can be grouped together to create one entry which can simplify the complexity that you are seeking to represent. This can be a very useful exercise, but before engaging in any grouping you must ensure that your approach is coherent.

For factors, this means considering whether the factors you are grouping behave in the same way in your system. For example, you should not group factors which look at different phenomena in your study and could evolve in divergent ways, such as 'GDP' and 'health system strengthening'. However, in a study looking at a national level conflict, factors such as 'malnutrition' and 'levels of childhood vaccinations', which represent different facets of the same dynamic, could be grouped together to form one coherent factor of 'childhood health outcomes'. You should not 'overgroup' factors you think are most relevant to your study in case you

96 *A toolkit for humanitarian action*

lose some of the interplay between different dimensions of the question you are trying to explore.

For actors, you need to consider if the motivations, capacities and agenda of the actors you are grouping are similar enough to form a sensible group. For example, states such as those in the European Union can often be grouped together or a government can be represented as one entry opposed to listing its individual departments. Other times, often for political reasons, you need to subdivide actors such as the leadership of a factious armed group and its foot soldiers or organisations within a loose alliance that have very different levels of power.

Step 3 Filling a PESTLE

As you are building your list of factors and actors (or once your list is complete), you should write or source a definition of each one (see Table 4.2 for an example). You will be sorting, categorising and analysing these components for the duration of your study, thus you need to be as clear as possible about what they are. For example, if you include a factor such as poverty you need to make clear what measurement of poverty you are using. Is its relative poverty or absolute poverty? Are you using the national poverty line or the international poverty line?

All your factors and actors must be distinct and well formed to allow you to engage with them effectively. If you have overlap between multiple factors or actors it can cloud your analysis. For example, if you include a dimension of inequality in your definition of poverty but also have inequality as a separate factor, you will have redundancies throughout your study and it can make your system harder to understand.

Table 4.2 Example of a filled in PESTLE table

PESTLE	Factor/ actor	Abbreviation	Full name	Definition
Economic	Factor	Rem.	Remittances	Remittances are understood as cross-border, private, voluntary monetary and non-monetary (social or in-kind) transfers made by migrants and diaspora, individually or collectively, to people or to communities not necessarily in their home country (European Parliament, 2014).

PESTLE	Factor/actor	Abbreviation	Full name	Definition
Political	Actor	OECD	OECD Members	States that are members of the OECD group, which are predominantly high- and middle-income states (OECD Members, n.d.).
Social	Factor	Food dem.	Changes in food demands	Shifting tastes, changing diets and changes in ways of eating. This can be both long term (such as the consumption of less meat) and sudden (such as people eating less food outside of the home due to social distancing). In some cases, it reflects an improvement in the public's understanding of the inputs, processes and outputs of the local and global food system.
Social	Actor	Civ ser.	Civil service	All administrative departments of the national government, including the departments of treasury, health, education, etc. that implement the policies of the political leadership. This excludes elected bodies and the military.

Step 4 Reviewing

Once you have a completed PESTLE, you may want to share it with colleagues or external experts to see if they have any actors or factors to add and ensure that any groupings you have made are coherent.

Frequently asked questions

How many actors and factors should I include in my PESTLE?

The number of factors and actors that you include in your study depends on the complexity of your system and the time you have to dedicate to the process. It is difficult to set guidance on how many components are needed to make your analysis sufficiently detailed to be robust without considering the particularities of your system of study. However, in general it is recommended to have a minimum of 25 factors and 15 actors in your PESTLE and a maximum 60 components in total (combined actors and factors).

98　*A toolkit for humanitarian action*

Facilitation notes

You can draft your PESTLE yourself using literature reviews, surveys and/or interviews to source the information you need, or you can host a workshop or survey (physical or virtual) to gather the input you need. The approach you choose will likely be determined by your time constraints and the level of interest of the colleagues you are engaging. Regardless of how you create your PESTLE it is best if it can be reviewed by colleagues or experts to see if they can identify anything that is missing and check its coherence (Step 4).

In physical workshops, you can use breakout groups to brainstorm for each dimension of your PESTLE before you allow all groups to present their findings and ask the other participants to add anything that is missing. In workshops, pay particular attention to the optimisation of the list of factors and actors, ensuring that you don't have any duplicates in your PESTLE and the grouping of factors/actors which makes sense.

Virtual survey (at least 1 week for survey completion)

There are several ways that you could approach this, but we present a detailed guide to one option here. If you are working virtually, we would advise that you run an online survey to collect the list of factors and actors that you will then work to rationalise, group and define alone before validating your findings.

Preparation

i. Prepare a survey which asks participants to list the factors/actors that they think are relevant for your system of study. Divide your questions according to the PESTLE categories and ensure that you have adequately explained the exercise and clearly described the system of study when you circulate the survey. You can also include some broader questions that stimulate people's thinking in a different way such as, What are the most significant changes you foresee in this system over the course of your outlook? or Who are the most important actors in this space? (Allow at least one week for responses)

Survey

ii. Collect the input and create a comprehensive list of factors and actors. At this point you should group the factors/actors where necessary, but, for the sake of transparency, be sure to document how

A toolkit for humanitarian action   99

you have done this, e.g. Stability of livelihood + Income + Assets = Household resilience.

Follow-up

iii. Work out definitions for each of the component parts (see Table 4.2 for an example).
iv. Distribute the table with the components and definitions you have created to all participants and ask for their validation of the final product.

Resources: a prepared survey

100 *A toolkit for humanitarian action*

ARCHITECTURE

The Architecture is a kind of graphical representation of a complex system. In it we do not identify the interactions between the component parts but rather list them in a structured way which illustrates the complexity of your system of study.

The Architecture is a framework through which you can organise all of the different components (factors and actors) of your system of study that you need to unpack in order to understand its complexity. An Architecture is the foundation of your study; building it is a vital step that should not be skipped or rushed. Even without taking your analysis any further, an Architecture provides you with a map of the factors and actors that are critical for your study and as a result is a useful standalone document.

It is important to note that the way you organise the factors and actors you identify in the Architecture depends on the viewpoint of the study that you are conducting. If the viewpoint of your system of study is contextual (i.e. an outlook of a country context in five years' time or the future of education in 2040), then you will organise your Architecture slightly different from an organisational viewpoint (e.g. how could an alliance of non-governmental organisation (NGOs) working on hunger be effective in 2030). As a result, you must be very clear on your system of study before starting this exercise (please refer to the Scoping Workshop).

Prerequisites

Before you begin your Architecture, you must have identified a clear system of study and conducted a PESTLE exercise.

How to do it

Step 1 Preparation

Once you have identified and defined all the factors and actors that are relevant to your system of study using your PESTLE, you need to create a template for your Architecture (Figure 4.7).

For clarity and ease of interpretation, underneath your Architecture template you should include your completed PESTLE table which names and defines the factors and actors that will be added, as well as the abbreviation with which each component will be labelled on your Architecture.

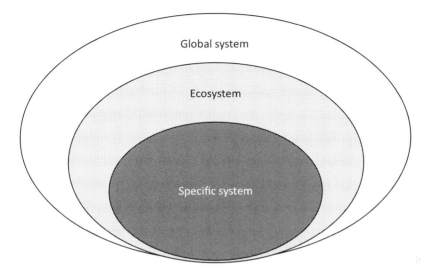

Figure 4.7 An Architecture template

Step 2 Set the logic of the Architecture

Once you have the template of your Architecture, with your PESTLE table embedded, you need to consider the logic of how you will fill it. While the same frame can be used for each type of foresight study that we are exploring in this book – organisational or contextual – there is a slightly different logic for how to place the components you have identified on the template depending on the viewpoint of your study.

The purpose of an Architecture is to arrange the component parts that make up your system of study in a manner which puts those that have the highest level of interaction with the topic at the crux of your question at the centre of the concentric circles in the specific system. You then move outwards through the ecosystem and global system until you have categorised all the factors and actors you wish to include using the following logic:

For a system of study with an **organisational viewpoint**:
'The future of an alliance of NGOs in 2030': Specific system – the activities and operations that the organisation can influence/change (including any internal dynamics you want to include as well as the kinds of activities the organisation engages in); Ecosystem – the factors and actors that shape the system in which the organisation

102 *A toolkit for humanitarian action*

operates (e.g. if it is an organisation working on food insecurity, then you would consider the factors and actors of food systems in your ecosystem); Global system – the dynamics which are changing the world in which we live (e.g. demographic growth, urbanisation, climate change).

For system of study with a **contextual viewpoint**:

'An outlook for Kenya in 2030': Specific system – factors and actors in the contextual area (e.g. country; Kenya); Ecosystem – factors and actors in the region surrounding the contextual area of your study (e.g. East Africa); Global system – factors and actors which are changing the world in which we live (e.g. global phenomenon/actors such as urbanisation, climate change, United Nations).

'LGBTIQ exclusion in Uganda in 2030': Specific system – factors and actors that are central to the topic you are exploring in the defined geographic area (e.g. LGBTIQ communities and their lived experience in Uganda); Ecosystem – factors and actors that are in the environment which your system of study is embedded in (e.g. social and political structures such as human rights legislation); Global system – factors and actors which are changing the world in which we live (e.g. demographic growth, urbanisation, climate change etc.)

Step 3 Place the PESTLE components on the Architecture

With the template of your Architecture and the logic of how you are going to fill it, you can begin to place all the components you have listed in your PESTLE on your Architecture. You should do this using the abbreviations in your PESTLE table to label each one and follow the logic of the viewpoint of your system of study. The reformulating of your PESTLE into an Architecture allows you a different graphical representation of your system, and seeing your work in this new format can flag any points that are missing. If after completing your Architecture you find that there are some components that were not included in your PESTLE, you can add them at this stage, ensuring that you enter any new actors or factors in both the Architecture and the PESTLE table to maintain coherence.

Your finalised system map should look something like Figure 4.8 and Figure 4.9 (please note that, for clarity, we have not used abbreviations for labels here but you should where necessary).

A toolkit for humanitarian action 103

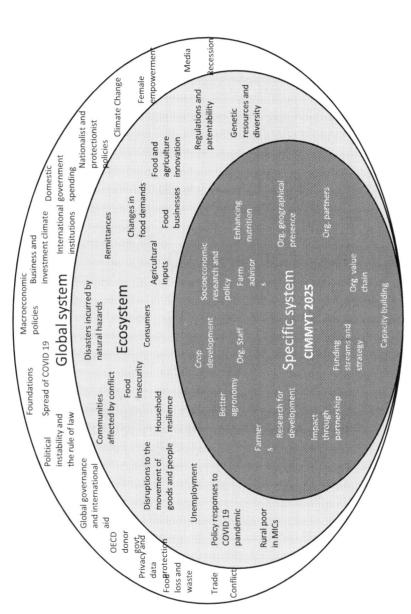

Figure 4.8 Example of an organisational Architecture, 2025: Agri-food systems in a plus COVID-19 world – Global perspective (CIMMYT 2021)

104 *A toolkit for humanitarian action*

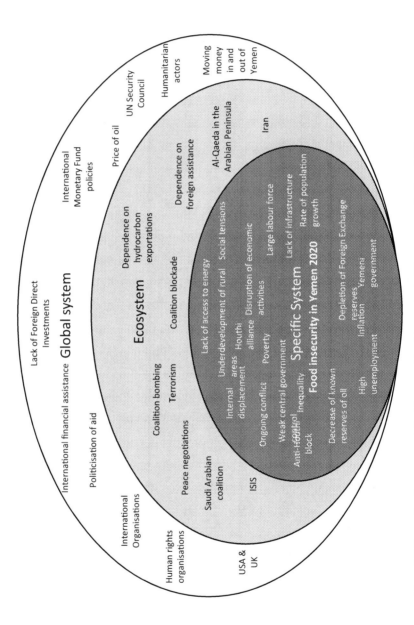

Figure 4.9 Example of a contextual Architecture, Food insecurity in Yemen: an outlook to 2020

Step 4 Reviewing

When you have a draft version of an Architecture, it should be shared with colleagues and external experts for validation. During the validation you should ask for input on the placement of the actors/factors on the Architecture. Once your Architecture is validated and you have progressed to the next step of your study it will be difficult to revise it, so it is worth spending time to ensure that it is a considered and robust piece of analysis.

Frequently asked questions

What if a component is on the boundary between two different levels of the Architecture?

If you are undertaking a contextual study and feel that a component sits between two different levels (e.g. between the specific system and the ecosystem) you can place it on the boundary line between them to demonstrate this. While this is an option, you should endeavour to place components within one of the three levels wherever possible. If you are conducting a study with an organisational viewpoint, then you may place components on the boundary line between the ecosystem and the global system but not in between the ecosystem and the specific system. This is because in an organisational study you will treat the components of the specific system slightly differently and so you cannot combine them with those on the ecosystem.

Facilitation notes

You can draft your Architecture yourself or you can host a workshop (physical or virtual) to complete it with colleagues. The approach you choose will likely be determined by your time constraints and the level of interest of the colleagues you are engaging. Regardless of how you create your Architecture it should be reviewed and validated by people who can challenge your thinking and provide a different perspective (Step 4).

If you choose to conduct this exercise from start to finish in a physical workshop, it should take 1–1.5 hours (time with no breaks) depending on the system of study and number of participants.

Virtual workshop (1–1.5 hours for creating the Architecture)

There are several ways that you could approach an online workshop, but we present a step-by-step guide of one potential option using a virtual whiteboard.

106 *A toolkit for humanitarian action*

Preparation

   i. Create an online virtual whiteboard and preload your it with a template of an Architecture (see Figure 4.7). Then add sticky notes/text boxes to the side of the Architecture frame, each one with the name of one of the actors and factors from your PESTLE. You should use one colour for actors and one colour for factors.

  ii. Invite participants to a group call, ensuring that they will have access to the virtual whiteboard during the call.

Workshop

 iii. On the call introduce the exercise, explain the process – detailing the logic of the Architecture and different system levels – and give guidelines for how the exercise will unfold. You should allow some time for participants to learn to manipulate the software. (15–20 minutes)

 iv. Begin by facilitating the placement of the first few components on the map. We advise you do this by selecting one Post-it note and asking the group on which level they would place it (they can write it in the chat or you can do this by conversation). Once you have consensus move the Post-it note into the corresponding ring. (3–5 minutes)

  v. Complete Step iv three more times before you nominate someone else in the group to take over, facilitating the placement of at least three components each time. (6–10 minutes)

 vi. Continue with the exercise until all the factors and actors have been placed on the Architecture frame and you have a completed map. (30–50 minutes)

Note: You will find that the process speeds up with each component you place on the Architecture as the participants become more familiar with the process and the logic you are applying.

Follow-up

 vii. Share the final output with participants and experts for a final review.

viii. Finalise the Architecture.

Resources: pre-prepared polls loaded on an accessible online platform and access to an open, virtual workspace.

IMPORTANCE/UNCERTAINTY MATRIX (MIU)

The Importance/Uncertainty Matrix (MIU) gives you a frame to begin to categorise the components that you identified in your Architecture by considering each one in two dimensions (their importance in your system of study and the uncertainty of their evolution). By doing this you can reduce the complexity of the system you are exploring, focusing your attention on the factors/actors that are going to be most influential in shaping how it evolves.

While the output of this exercise is a consolidated list of scenario drivers, this is a useful tool even if you don't intend to exploit the output to write scenarios. The MIU provides you with an idea of what components in your system are important and an indication of how dynamic your system of study is. It can be the basis of important discussions about the context that you are navigating within organisations and between partners by providing a platform of shared analysis.

It is important to note that the components you consider in this exercise depend on the viewpoint of your system of study. If you are working on a system of study with a contextual viewpoint, then you need to treat all the factors in the specific system, ecosystem and global system of your Architecture. If you are working on a system of study with an organisational viewpoint, then you need only take the factors in the ecosystem and global system. The factors in the specific system of the organisational map will be reintegrated later in the strategic planning process.

Prerequisites

Before you begin the MIU you must have already identified and defined all the components of your system through the PESTLE and finalised your Architecture.

How to do it

Step 1 Preparation

Create an empty matrix. Such as in Figure 4.10.

Step 2 Place actors and factors on the matrix

Select one actor or factor from your list and determine where it falls on the scale of each axis, importance and uncertainty. First, consider the importance (y axis) and then the uncertainty (x axis). Note the placement of each actor/factor on your matrix (usually the abbreviation listed in

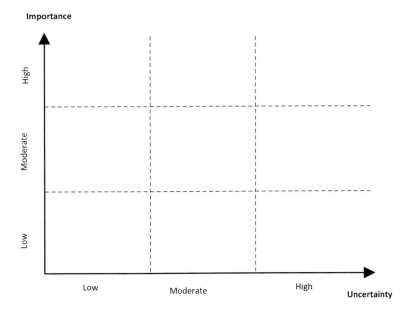

Figure 4.10 Empty Importance/Uncertainty Matrix

your PESTLE and used in your Architecture). When considering where each component falls on your matrix ask yourself the following questions:

For **importance**: How influential could this actor/how impactful could this factor be in determining the way your system of study will evolve between the present and the end of your outlook?

For **uncertainty**: What is your level of certainty in accurately predicting the behaviour of this actor/evolution of this factor over the course of the outlook?[1]

Note: It is useful to note all your actors on the matrix in one colour (e.g. green) and all your factors in another (e.g. black) so that you can more easily distinguish them when you interpret your findings.

Repeat this process until you have treated all the components that were identified in your Architecture (see Figure 4.11 for an example). For clarity it can be helpful to include your PESTLE table (Table 4.3) underneath the matrix.

A toolkit for humanitarian action 109

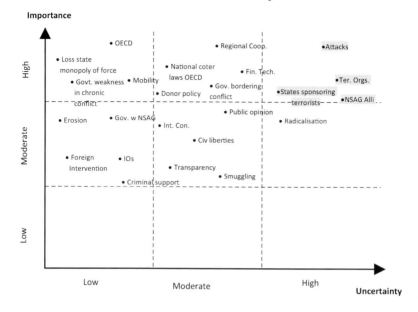

Figure 4.11 Abbreviated example of a completed Importance/Uncertainty Matrix used for a study on counterterrorism

Table 4.3 Sample of a PESTLE table for a completed Importance/Uncertainty Matrix used for a study on counterterrorism (components in top-right box of Figure 4.11)

Actor/factor	Abbreviation	Full name	Definition
Factor	Attacks	Attacks	The increased prevalence of deadly terrorist attacks in countries outside conflict zones (e.g. France) claimed by terrorist groups.
Actor	Ter. Orgs	Actors classified as terrorist organisations	Organisations that are declared by legitimate governments and international organisations to be 'terrorist' organisations according to their respective definitions of the term (e.g. ISIS, Al Qaeda, Al-Shabaab, Boko Haram).
Actor	States sponsoring terrorists	States sponsoring terrorists	States that openly or covertly finance terrorist organisations.
Actor	Govt. w NSAG	National governments in states with NSAG presence and law enforcement	The national governments in states with non-state armed groups (NSAGs) present.

110 *A toolkit for humanitarian action*

Step 3 Interpretation

To interpret the output of your MIU you must consider the actors and the factors separately.

To interpret your findings for the factors on your MIU, you need to classify them based on where they fall on your matrix.

Group the factors on your matrix according to the boxes represented in Figure 4.12. These are broad groupings and you should allow yourself some licence to interpret where to place factors that are on the boundary between two groups according to your own understanding of the system you are exploring.

Using this interpretation, you can begin to categorise your list of factors into heavy trends, important scenario drivers, critical scenario drivers and those which you need to continually monitor and reassess. Each group of factors is treated differently.

Heavy trends: Heavy trends are factors which have varying levels of importance but have a low level of uncertainty. You can more confidently predict how heavy trends will evolve (if they evolve at all) over the course of your outlook. We will not include heavy trends in framing our matrix or Morphological Scenarios, but they should be considered as

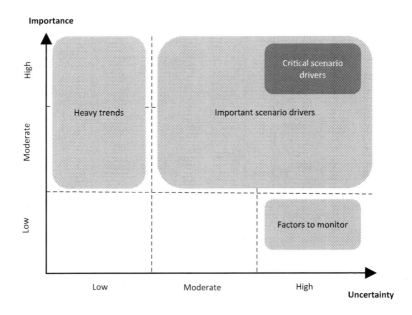

Figure 4.12 Interpretation factors in an Importance/Uncertainty Matrix

setting the character of the system that you are exploring. Some could be added to the list of assumptions on which you are basing your study, as they will remain consistent for all of the scenarios that you develop, e.g. climate change in a study with a 1-year outlook.

Important scenario drivers: Important scenario drivers are those factors which are moderately or highly important and uncertain. Each of these factors could evolve in multiple different ways. To understand this complexity, all the potential evolutions of these factors must be explored, as how they behave will determine the way your system of study will change over the course of the outlook. It is from this group of factors that you will select the drivers that will form the basis of your scenario analysis.

Critical scenario drivers: Critical scenario drivers are a subset of important scenario drivers. They are the most important and uncertain in your system and as such are the factors which require the most attention.

Factors to monitor: The factors which have a low level of importance but a high level of uncertainty will not be included in the scenario analysis but should be monitored in case a significant shift occurs which could increase their relevance in the system you are exploring.

How you select the drivers for your scenarios (from the important and critical scenario sections of the matrix) depends on the scenario method that you are using. Driver selection for Morphological and Matrix Scenarios are explored in detail in their respective sections (see Morphological Scenarios, pp. 117–125, and Matrix Scenarios, pp. 126–136, for more on the selection of scenario drivers).

To interpret the actors in your MIU: All actors included in the high and moderate importance areas need to be considered. Again, you should allow yourself some freedom to assign actors which fall on the boundary of two areas to different categories depending on your analysis of the system you are studying (Figure 4.13).

Actors to be considered for an actor analysis (using the Influence/Dependency Matrix, pp. 146–162, and Actor/Objective Matrix, pp. 181–194): The actor analysis or game of actors' analysis is a fundamental tool in your structural analysis and strategy development. The MIU enables you to focus your attention on only the most important (influential) actors in your system of study, and taking this one step further, the actor analysis allows you to identify the most strategic ones within that group.

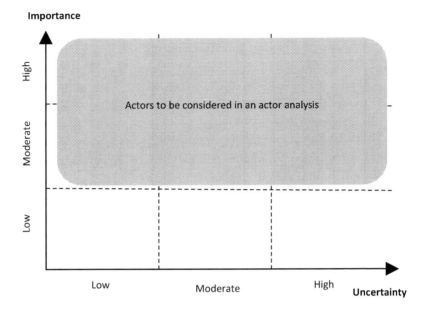

Figure 4.13 Interpretation actors in an Importance/Uncertainty Matrix

Step 4 Reviewing

Invite colleagues and external experts to review your matrix for comments, integrating their feedback before you finalise the output.

Frequently asked questions

What if I have very few critical or important scenario drivers?

This means that your system is quite stable; it is not highly changeable as the evolution of the majority of your important factors are not uncertain. If you have less than three factors in the four top, right-hand boxes of your matrix, then it would not be worth creating scenarios. Rather you could take your analysis forward by doing in-depth analysis into the most important heavy trends and the important/critical scenario drivers and make some inferences about how they will interact over time in a less structured way.

Facilitation notes

A physical or virtual workshop to complete an MIU usually takes between 2 and 3 hours depending on the number of components that you are considering. You must ensure that participants understand what is meant by importance and uncertainty before you begin placing the components on the matrix, as it is necessary to have both dimensions represented. As with most analytical tools, your MIU will be more robust with increased participation. Therefore, if you are not able to run a workshop it is highly recommended that you launch a survey to gather input. If you have to conduct this analysis alone, then you should ensure that your output is validated by colleagues and experts (Step 4).

Tip: If you are hosting a workshop ensure that you allow enough time at the beginning to review the Architecture with all the participants so that the definitions of the actors and factors are clear for everyone before you begin.

Virtual workshop

There are two options to running this workshop virtually. One is through a survey and the other can be run as a seminar with live polling. With a survey, though there is no discussion in this format, it does allow you to integrate as many perspectives as you can by asking people to quantify importance and uncertainty.

With a survey (allow at least 1 week for responses)

Prepare a validated Architecture which includes the list of well-defined factors and actors to circulate to the group of participants along with the survey. Your survey should include an introduction where you explain the purpose of the exercise and make clear the definition of importance and uncertainty that you are using.

Preparation

i. Create a survey in which participants are asked to rank each factor's and actor's importance and uncertainty on the system you are exploring on a scale of 1 to 9 (where 1 is the lowest level of importance/ uncertainty and 9 is the highest). The questions on importance and uncertainty should be separate, i.e. one question on importance and one question on uncertainty for each factor and actor (for guidance,

114   *A toolkit for humanitarian action*

see the questions about importance and uncertainty presented in Step 2).

If you prefer, you could do this in a spreadsheet instead of a survey. To do so, create three columns, filling the first with the name of each component and leaving the second two blank. Title the columns (Actor/Factor, Importance, Uncertainty) and ask all participants to enter a whole number between 1 and 9 (where 1 is the lowest level of importance/uncertainty and 9 is the highest) to rate the importance and uncertainty of each component.

Survey

ii. Distribute survey

Follow-up

iii. Your survey platform should provide you with an output report which combines the feedback from all participants. If you have used a spreadsheet you should take an average of all the entries that you received, review the combined scores from all participants for each factor/actor, then enter both dimensions into a spreadsheet. For example, see Table 4.4.

iv. Once you have your collated results in a spreadsheet, create a scatter plot using the importance value for each component as the y variable and the uncertainty value for each component as the x variable.

v. Interpret your grid: Group the factors on your grid into heavy trends, important scenario drivers, critical scenario drivers and factors to monitor.

vi. Circulate the final matrix and validate it with the participants.

Table 4.4 Example of a spreadsheet with combined inputs from an Importance/Uncertainty survey

Factor	$y = Importance$	$x = Uncertainty$
Agricultural inputs	41	31
Business and investment climate	46	65
Changes in food demands	64	46
Etc.		

A toolkit for humanitarian action   115

With a seminar and live polling (approximately 1.15–1.5 hours)

The process for a seminar with live polling presented here is one we have found to be very user-friendly, which makes it easy to run and more fun for participants to engage with. However, it does give you less nuance results, as you are not asking participants to answer questions about the importance and uncertainty of each individual component but rather you are asking them to choose the five or so most important factors and actors and the five or so most uncertain factors and actors. As a result, you may end up not plotting every component on your matrix if some factors or actors were not selected by any participant for any question – these would then be clustered at 0,0 on your matrix.

Preparation

i. Invite participants to the online seminar.
ii. Circulate the validated Architecture, which includes the list of well-defined factors and actors, to all participants before the session so they have time to review it.

Seminar

iii. Give a presentation explaining the methodology of the study, the purpose and expected outputs of the MIU exercise and explore the validated Architecture. You should allow for questions and run one poll during the introduction session to ensure that everyone is logged on and can use the software. (15–25 minutes, plus time for questions)
iv. Using a platform that allows for live polling. Run two polls based on the questions about importance and uncertainty presented in Step 2 in the 'How to do it' section. The first poll should ask participants to select the five or so factors (you could ask them to select more or fewer, but the range should be between three and eight) that they believe are the most important. The second poll should ask participants to select the same number of factors as they did for the first poll, but this time assessing their uncertainty. You should structure the polls to hide the results until voting is complete to ensure that people are not biased by the feedback of their colleagues. Once the voting is complete, have a discussion about the ranking that has been created. (30 minutes)

116 *A toolkit for humanitarian action*

   v. Rerun Step iv, asking participants to select the most important actors and the most uncertain actors. (30 minutes)

  vi. Close the seminar by outlining the next steps. (5 minutes)

Follow-up

vii. Extract the rankings from your online platform (it should give you one value for the importance and uncertainty of each factor according to how many votes it received from each poll) and follow Steps iii–vi (the 'Follow-up' section) from the 'Virtual workshop' using the preceding survey.

Resources: presentation; survey or preprepared polls loaded on an accessible online platform

MORPHOLOGICAL SCENARIOS

General morphological analysis, conceived by Fritz Zwicky, is an approach to analysing relationships in a multidimensional, complex problem where the elements are unquantifiable and have a degree of uncertainty, e.g. sociopolitical components (Ritchey 2018). This approach has been applied to a variety of fields but began to be used in futures studies for developing scenarios in the 1990s (Godet 1994).

Morphological analysis gives you the structure to outline the important uncertainties in your system of study, summarising them in a set of scenarios in a clear and concise way while not losing the complexity you seek to understand. It is a transparent process whereby the construction of the scenarios and the hypotheses on which they are predicated are presented for scrutiny and revision. It is with this tool that we move from discussing factors in your system of study to scenario drivers. Morphological analysis is a very useful process, as it condenses the result of your research and analysis into a manageable format and supports you in translating that analysis into scenarios.

The output of the morphological analysis is a framework for creating multiple different scenarios that encapsulate the range of uncertainty in your system of study.

Prerequisites

Before you begin creating Morphological Scenarios you will need to have a validated MIU, which you have built up from your Architecture.

During the process of creating your Morphological Scenarios you will need to write your Driver Files (please see the guide on Driver Files, pp. 137–140, to support with this).

How to do it

Step 1 Selecting scenario drivers from your MIU

Morphological Scenarios are extremely robust in their analysis of complexity, as they allow you to consider a greater number of drivers than other methods. For Morphological Scenarios you should select between five and ten scenario drivers. You can do this in a number of ways depending on the structure of your MIU.

A) *If you have between five and ten factors in your critical scenario drivers group*, then you can select all of those to take forward as your scenario drivers (all the factors in the top-right cell of your matrix).

118 *A toolkit for humanitarian action*

B) *If you have a combined total of less than ten drivers in your important and critical scenario driver groups*, then you can take them all forward as your scenario drivers (all the factors in the four cells which are marked as both moderate and high in terms of both importance and uncertainty).

C) *If you have a combined total of more than ten drivers in your important and critical scenario driver groups*, then you must narrow them down further. To do so, draw a diagonal line across the top right-hand cell (critical scenario drivers) and move it towards the centre of the matrix until there are five to ten drivers above it.

The drivers selected from the map in Figure 4.14 would be (1) Attacks, (2) Public opinion, (3) Regional Coop., (4) NSAG Alli, (5) National COTER laws OECD, (6) Radicalisation, (7) Fin. Tech.

The number of drivers that you select will depend on how uncertain the system you are exploring is and how much time you are able to dedicate to research. In a more dynamic system, it is likely that you have a larger number of highly important and uncertain factors, and as a result you may need to include more in your study to properly explore the

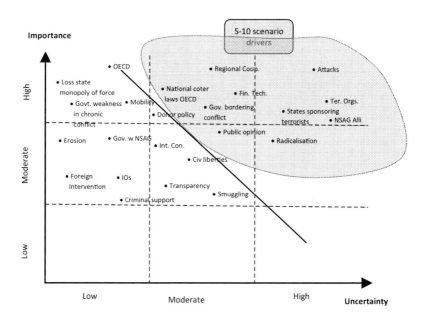

Figure 4.14 Selecting scenario drivers from the MIU – Morphological Scenarios

dynamics of your system. However, the more drivers that you include, the more time you will have to dedicate to researching each of them. As a result, you may wish to limit the number of drivers that you take forward in the study if you have a time constraint.

The selection of drivers is not a rigid process, but it is important to respect the logic of the exercise. You may find that by changing the slope of your line you are able to include or exclude different drivers on your matrix. You can explore this and how it changes the scenario drivers you will be working with, but you should do so within reason. You cannot select drivers randomly from the important or critical scenario groups; you should respect the logic of focusing on the factors that your analysis shows are the most important and uncertain. For example, in the matrix shown in Figure 4.14, you should not arbitrarily decide to include Smuggling in your study (which is below the line) but exclude Public opinion (which is above it).

Step 2 Write your Driver Files and create hypotheses

Once you have selected your scenario drivers you need to conduct research into each one. These should be structured in Driver Files (please see the guide on Driver Files, pp. 137–140, for how to construct these).

For Morphological Scenarios, you can use the structure which is presented in the Driver Files section of this toolkit; however, you must also include a set of hypotheses (usually between two and five) for each driver.

A hypothesis is a statement which postulates a potential evolution for your driver over the course of your outlook. In foresight we use hypotheses to outline the different ways a driver may evolve, and then monitor those hypotheses to better understand how the system of study is changing. Hypotheses frame your investigation, and as a result are a crucial step in creating Morphological Scenarios. They must be tested, validated and agreed by a panel of experts.

To create a set of hypotheses you can first begin by considering how the driver would evolve if it continued along the same development path that it has exhibited in the past. This is called a trend hypothesis, as it follows the trends that you have observed (and already explored in your driver file).

You then need to create alternative hypotheses to cover the spectrum of uncertainty which you are endeavouring to capture. For inspiration you could consider the affect the uncertainties you listed in your driver file may have, e.g. what would happen to this driver there was an economic shock. There are also several different approaches to developing

120 *A toolkit for humanitarian action*

hypotheses that you can draw on. Hypotheses can be situational, historical, theoretical or a mix of all three.

A *situational hypothesis* looks at facts and underlying forces. For example, rural poverty increases as a result of prolonged drought, which has severely impacted the livelihoods of farmers and pastoralists.

A *historical hypothesis* considers how similar dynamics have played out in the past. For example, as was demonstrated during the last economic crisis, rural households see greater increases in poverty than their urban counterparts, as there are fewer economic opportunities to supplement their income when their livelihoods are affected.

A *theoretical hypothesis* draws on theories or concepts such as fragility, conflict theory, ecology, etc. For example, investments in an agroforestry system have resulted in a decrease in rural poverty, as the improvements in agricultural results increase household income.

Ultimately a hypothesis should:

- Be a definitive statement
- Be based on observations and knowledge
- Postulate results clearly
- Express a different potential evolution of the driver; they should be mutually exclusive, i.e. if one is true the others cannot be

An example of a set of hypotheses:

Hypothesis 1: The number of people in poverty increases as a result of a severe economic shock, which forces millions of people into unemployment.

Hypothesis 2: The number of people in poverty decreases as economic growth continues at projected high levels resulting in a sustained reduction in unemployment and an increase in wages.

Hypothesis 3: Poverty levels stay more or less the same, but the demographics of people living below the poverty line shifts as an increasing percentage of people living in poverty are living in cities.

Once you have created your set of hypotheses you should review them by asking yourself the following:

A) **Are they mutually exclusive?** If not, discard the ones that are contradictory.

B) **Seek contrary evidence.** Consider what evidence would prompt you to remove a hypothesis from your study because you no longer

A toolkit for humanitarian action 121

think it is a viable option. Try to find that evidence, and if you find it, decide if it can be reconciled or if you need to discard the hypothesis. You do not automatically need to discard a hypothesis if you find contrary evidence, the system of study will change over the course of the outlook so something that seems unbelievable today may not be in 2 years. As a result, you should only disregard the hypotheses that you think are not valid for your study throughout the whole outlook.

C) **Look for any alternatives you have not yet included** by questioning whether you have limited your alternatives to those which are typical and familiar.

Step 3 Build a hypothesis grid

Based on the research in your Driver Files, you must now construct your hypothesis grid. To do this you need to take each set of hypotheses from your Driver Files and enter them into a table. You do not need to have the same number of hypotheses for each driver. You should have one row for each driver, as is shown in Table 4.5.

Step 4 Building scenarios

Using this grid, you can now link together one hypothesis from each driver to create the framework of a scenario. Be sure to consider how each hypothesis connects to the others (e.g. 'if hypothesis 1 for driver (a) occurs, then that will result in hypothesis 3 for driver (b), etc.'). You must ensure that the interplay of drivers you are connecting is logical, trying to avoid contradictions between the hypotheses that you are selecting.

You will then repeat this process multiple times until you feel that the scenarios you have created explore the full spectrum of ways that the system could evolve over your given time horizon.

Lighter-shaded scenario: Role of governments (hypothesis 2), Mobile technology/internet access (hypothesis 1), Use of financial services (hypothesis 5), Role of the private sector (hypothesis 5).

Darker-shaded scenario: Role of governments (hypothesis 4), Role of the private sector (hypothesis 3), Mobile technology/internet access (hypothesis 2), Use of financial services (hypothesis 4).

How to choose a starting point: You can begin constructing your scenario from any cell in your hypothesis grid.

It could be that you feel one driver is particularly determinant in your system of study and as a result you will begin each of your scenarios from the hypotheses that you have created for that particular driver. For example,

Table 4.5 Example of a hypothesis grid using selected drivers looking at the future of financial assistance – multiple scenario paths

	Hypothesis #1	Hypothesis #2	Hypothesis #3	Hypothesis #4	Hypothesis #5
Role of governments	Governments create a regulatory environment that enables financial access and use.	Governments are increasingly able to raise the funds (internally or externally) to provide for financial assistance to their domestic population, including IDPs	Governments will exert greater control over the means, methods, and recipients of financial assistance, in particular through greater use of data	Governments will become greater providers of social safety nets.	Governments are unwilling to facilitate or directly deliver financial assistance.
Role of private sector	Private sector actors will become more influential as donors for in financial assistance to people in need.	Private sector actors will become nearly as more influential as delivery agents in financial assistance to people in need.	Private sector actors will become an even greater service providers to traditional humanitarian actors, contracted to perform specific functions.	Private sector actors will increasingly become substitutes to traditional humanitarian actors performing functions across the programme cycle	The private sector and traditional humanitarian actors will predominantly partner through global partnerships
Mobile technology / Internet access	Internet access will continue to expand through increased access to mobile technology, particularly smartphones.	Internet access will be increasingly government-controlled	Internet access rates (including mobile) will plateau due to poverty (financial accessibility of smartphones and service plans), lack of infrastructure (mobile coverage, service providers, etc.) and the urban/rural divide		
Use of financial services	Financial services will become increasingly digital.	Tech companies will have a greater influence over financial services than banks	Access to financial services will increase but use will remains low among vulnerable people	Financial assistance programs will become more coordinated into single accounts, which enable control and management of money.	Financial assistance will be transferred digitally but recipients will continue to predominantly make cash payments

in a conflict setting you may feel that your hypotheses of (1) continued conflict, (2) temporary ceasefire, (3) victory for one party and 4) entry of another actor will set the tone for each scenario you choose to explore and, as a result, you have the starting points for the four scenarios you will create.

Alternatively, you can choose hypotheses from different drivers to start your scenarios to allow you to consider a more varied set of dynamics. In this instance you might feel that the economic conditions may be the engine of one scenario, but the relationship between civil society and the government is the most important dynamic in the second.

If you are finding it difficult to get started, it can be useful to focus on creating the 'base case' or 'trend' scenario. This is a scenario where you are considering what will happen if there is no major change in any of the drivers; they evolve in line with what is expected and so the system continues on the same development path that it is on today.

Things to be aware of:

- Your scenarios must be logical; you should avoid having contradictory dynamics within a scenario
- You must use one, and only one hypothesis for each driver
- You can use the same hypothesis more than once
- You should try to make your scenarios as different as possible
- You should avoid having scenarios which are all good or all bad, as this is rarely a reflection of reality

Ideal number of scenarios

How many scenarios you will create will be dictated by the complexity and dynamism of the system you are exploring. You should endeavour to capture the full spectrum of uncertainty.

Note: In our experience it is best to try and have more than three scenarios to avoid falling into the trap of having best/middle/worst case scenarios. We try to avoid these, as they insert the perspective of the author into the analysis; what is best for one actor is not necessarily best for all. It can also encourage decision makers to only consider one scenario rather than examine the full spectrum of uncertainty. In most cases, the middle case scenario is the base case and the scenario that people think is most likely, but looking exclusively at this one future means you are open to surprises.

Step 5 Reviewing

Once you have completed your table and identified your scenarios, you should share the table with experts and colleagues for their feedback.

124   *A toolkit for humanitarian action*

Frequently asked questions

Should I use all the hypotheses in the grid?

No, you do not need to use them all. However, remember that the hypotheses that you do not include will not be represented in your scenarios so you should try to use as many as possible and make sure that you are not omitting any dynamic that you think is critical to explore.

How to measure the likelihood of a scenario?

At this point, we are not interested in the likelihood of scenarios. You want to ensure that the scenarios you are creating are not impossible, but this is a very high bar. Part of the value of foresight is exploring scenarios that are possible but unlikely, as that is where strategic surprises can happen.

If I can use the same hypothesis more than once, how can the scenarios be different?

It is the combination of your hypotheses that should make the scenarios distinct. You should avoid using the same set of hypotheses more than once to avoid duplicating scenarios.

Facilitation notes

There are two steps in building your Morphological Scenarios: the selection of your drivers and the analysis of your hypotheses grid. In between these two steps you must take time to write your Driver Files. Reading the MIU you can easily select the drivers alone. However, it is worth validating your output with colleagues before you move on to the next step. Alternatively, if you are hosting an MIU workshop, you can confirm the drivers that will be selected to close the exercise.

The subsequent step, the analysis of your hypotheses grid, can be done either alone or in a physical or virtual workshop (workshops take between 1 and 2 hours). If you are hosting a workshop you should ensure to circulate the Driver Files and hypotheses grid prior to the workshop to give participants the chance to comment, edit or suggest alternative hypotheses which they feel have not been included.

During the workshop you should encourage participants or groups of participants to try to create scenarios which maximise the difference between the futures you are creating. It can be useful to challenge your

A toolkit for humanitarian action 125

participants by giving them different starting points, such as either giving each group a different driver to work from or assigning each group one hypothesis from a single driver. If participants present scenarios which are too similar, you can either brainstorm a cogent way to make them more divergent or eliminate one. Your scenarios should always be validated with a group of experts.

Virtual workshop (approximately 1–1.5 hours)

Preparation

   i. Distribute the hypotheses grid and Driver Files to the participants and circulate a list of instructions explaining the process of creating scenarios using the morphological approach.
  ii. Create a few scenarios and represent each one on a slide/document to present on the call.

Seminar

 iii. Host a call with the participants, presenting each of the scenarios that you have identified – be sure to describe them as preliminary. (15 minutes)
 iv. Talk through each scenario and ask the participants the following: (30–60 minutes)
      Are there are any inconsistencies in the logic of this scenario?
      Is this scenario sufficiently different from the others to be worth including?
      Ask if there is a path that you have missed and begin to craft other scenarios to complement the few that you brought to the workshop. (If you have more than eight people you will want to do this in breakout groups, asking each group to identify a few additional scenarios to represent the uncertainty that you are seeking to explore. Get the groups to present back to the full team.)
  v. Discuss if there are any scenarios people would disregard. (15 minutes)

126 *A toolkit for humanitarian action*

MATRIX SCENARIOS

Matrix Scenarios are a scenario method that is exploited by many sectors. It is credited with being inspired by the Shell approach to scenario building, popularised by Peter Schwartz in *The Art of the Long View* (Schwartz 1996). Matrix Scenarios are a relatively quick and intuitive way to build a set of scenarios for exploring the future.

The Matrix Scenario method gives you the opportunity to create scenarios in a different way. The frame for the scenarios can be developed in workshop in an afternoon, which you can supplement with further research as you write them making it a more accessible approach. In some senses, Matrix Scenarios do not consider as wide a range of complexity as Morphological Scenarios, as they reduce the system you are exploring to two dimensions. However, the matrix approach has several benefits: it is quicker to develop, it is easy for participants to engage with and Matrix Scenarios can be communicated effectively.

Prerequisites

Before you begin creating Matrix Scenarios you will need to have a validated MIU which you have built up from your Architecture.

During the process of creating your Matrix Scenarios you will need to write your Driver Files (please see the guide on Driver Files, pp. 137–140, to support with this).

How to do it

Step 1 Select the drivers

Begin by selecting your drivers from your MIU. Similar to the interpretation which is used for Morphological Scenarios, we are looking to identify drivers that are the most impactful and uncertain. However, unlike with Morphological Scenarios, we are not looking to capture between five and ten drivers but rather to select two drivers, or create two groups of drivers, which can be used as the axes of a 2×2 matrix.

As with your Architecture, the way that you select your drivers will depend on what kind of study that you are doing (organisational or contextual).

If you are conducting an organisational study, then you should have one group of drivers which is selected from the factors at the ecosystem level of your Architecture and the other group which is comprised of factors from your global system. To do this, you should refer back to your Architecture and mark on your matrix which drivers belong in which system so that you can clearly see the ones you are going to select from each level.

A toolkit for humanitarian action 127

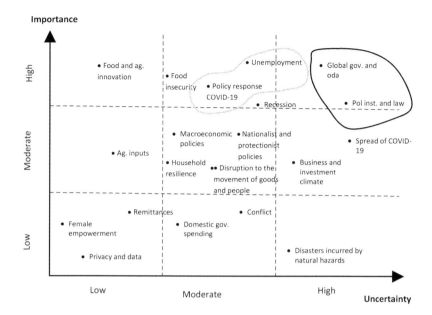

Figure 4.15 Abbreviated and adapted MIU for Matrix Scenarios, 2025: Agri-food systems in a plus COVID-19 world – Global perspective (CIMMYT 2021)

In the example in Figure 4.15, two groups of drivers have been created.

The drivers encircled in grey – 'Unemployment' and 'Policy response COVID-19' – create the group of drivers pulled from the ecosystem level of the Architecture.

Unemployment – 'Unemployment rate'. "The unemployment rate expresses the number of unemployed as a percent of the labour force (which includes persons in unemployment plus those in employment). The unemployed are persons of working age who were not in employment, carried out activities to seek employment during a specified recent period and were currently available to take up employment given a job opportunity" (International Labour Organisation, n.d.).

Policy response COVID-19 – 'Policy responses to the spread of COVID-19'. The restrictions and regulations which are put in place by governments in an effort to suppress or mitigate the impact of the virus on the population. Including social distancing, lockdowns, closure of schools and businesses, etc.

128   *A toolkit for humanitarian action*

In selecting these drivers, we have given a slight weighting to the level of uncertainty over the level of importance. This is because, for scenarios, our focus is on managing uncertainty and, therefore, while 'Food insecurity' for example is slightly more important than 'Policy response COVID-19' it is less uncertain and as such has not been selected. Though you could easily include all three drivers of 'Unemployment', 'Policy response COVID-19' and 'Food insecurity' if you wish, for Matrix Scenarios the fewer drivers you use to make your matrix, the clearer and more cogent your scenarios will be. Drivers such as 'Food insecurity' are not disregarded; they will be re-integrated later.

In the black circle are the two most important and uncertain drivers from the global level of the Architecture.

Global gov. and oda – 'Global governance and international aid'. The extent to which governments subscribe to, and support, international coordination through extant global institutions, predominantly the United Nations, the World Bank, etc. This includes the politics of international aid and the allocation of overseas development assistance (e.g. domestic COVID-19 response vs. commitments on international poverty) and the reduction in available funds for international non-governmental organisations (INGOs) and international organisations, which leads to increased competition for resources and the pursuit of alternative funding strategies.

Pol inst. and law – 'Political instability and the rule of law'. "Sustained civil disobedience or protests [which could rise to the level of civil unrest] resulting in a weakening of a government's legitimacy, the potential loss of trust in governance structures or processes, and the propensity for irregular regime change (e.g. assassinations or coups)" (IARAN 2016, p. 107). This is often coupled with sustained challenges to the rule of law, for example, by organised crime.

If you are doing a contextual study you do not need to consider the differing levels of your Architecture (though it can still sometimes be helpful to do so if you are struggling with grouping drivers). However, you should ensure that the two groups of drivers you are selecting consider different dynamics in your system. For example, if you have one group of drivers that is examining a country's economic growth and inequality and the other group is considering rates of poverty in that country, your scenarios are going to be quite one dimensional. While you do not need to consider the levels of the Architecture, it can be useful to return to your PESTLE and create your groups of drivers based on different PESTLE dimensions. For example one group could focus on factors

A toolkit for humanitarian action 129

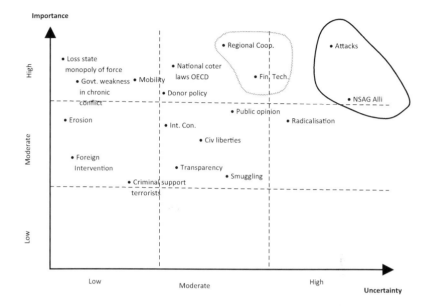

Figure 4.16 Abbreviated and adapted MIU (actors removed for clarity) for a system of study with a contextual viewpoint to build Matrix Scenarios examining the future of counterterrorism

from the political and social dimensions, and the other group on factors in on the economic and technical dimensions.

In the example in Figure 4.16, the two axes would be made up of the four drivers that are circled.

The grey circle is comprised of two drivers that are within the legal and technology categories of the PESTLE.

Regional Coop – 'Regional Cooperation', i.e. regional coherence/cooperation on counterterrorism legislation and information sharing.

Fin. Tech. – 'The international banking system', i.e. the international banking system that can facilitate the financing of terror activities on an international scale.

The black circle is comprised of two drivers that are in the political and social categories of the PESTLE.

Attacks – 'Rise in terror attacks outside conflict zones'. The increased prevalence of deadly terrorist attacks in countries outside conflict zones (e.g. France) claimed by terrorist groups.

130 *A toolkit for humanitarian action*

NSAG Alli – 'International alliances of NSAGs'. Formal (Al Qaeda) and informal (swearing of allegiance to ISIS) international terrorist networks.

Note: You do not need to have an even number of drivers for each axis (you can, for example, have one group with two drivers and the other with just one or three).

From this step, the steps to create Matrix Scenarios are the same for both organisational and contextual studies.

Step 2 Write Driver Files

Once you have your created your drivers you can write Driver Files for each one (see Driver Files, pp. 137–140). You should research each driver individually rather than the group that you have created to ensure that you have a comprehensive understanding of the dynamics you're studying. However, for Matrix Scenarios, if you do not have time to make dedicated Driver Files, you can continue on to Step 3 and conduct research into the dynamics you are exploring while you're writing your scenarios.

Step 3 Identify two matrix dimensions

Begin clarifying how you are defining the groups that you created from the MIU and create two opposing hypotheses for each one. Take each group of drivers and create a new name to describe it as well as a coherent explanation of what this group encapsulates.

For example, the global-level drivers in the organisational MIU in Figure 4.16, 'Global governance and international aid' and 'Political instability and the rule of law' could be combined to become a driver on 'Efficacy of governance and political stability'.

'Efficacy of governance and political stability' – This group includes dimensions of international politics (including aid) as well as global and regional trends of political instability (driven by either uncertain elections, increasing civil unrest or a loss of government legitimacy) and challenges to the rule of law.

The drivers of 'Unemployment rate' and 'Policy responses to the spread of COVID-19' from the ecosystem level could be combined and renamed as 'Disruption to economic processes'.

A toolkit for humanitarian action 131

'Disruption to economic processes' – This group focuses our attention at the national level. It looks at the policy responses to COVID 19 and their economic and social consequences, especially the dynamics of unemployment (both formal and informal).

Once you have clarified what is contained under each title, you need to create two opposing hypotheses for each group. Unlike with Morphological Scenarios, you are not trying to encapsulate the full spectrum of uncertainty in your two hypotheses but rather you are exploring the two potential pathways that you believe are the most relevant, interesting and divergent. Unlike with Morphological Scenarios, you do not create hypotheses in your Driver Files, but rather at the level of the group.

Though you only need two hypotheses, you may find it easier to brainstorm a longer list of hypotheses and then select two to take forward. Or you may choose to use the trend hypothesis at one end of the axis and the most disruptive alternative at the other.

Remember a hypothesis should

- Be a definitive statement
- Be based on observations and knowledge
- Postulate results clearly

For Matrix Scenarios it is especially important that each hypothesis expresses a very different potential evolution of the driver. The hypotheses should be mutually exclusive ,i.e. if one is true the other cannot be.

For example, considering the 'Efficacy of governance and political stability' two sets of potential hypotheses could be:

Set 1

- Decreasing efficacy of governance reinforced by challenges to political stability
- Resurgence of regional governance, stabilisation of political structures and the rule of law

Set 2

- Increased legitimacy of global governance institutions as international bodies promote political stability and the rule of law
- Withdrawal of states from international governance institutions as instability rises at home and the rule of law is flouted

132 *A toolkit for humanitarian action*

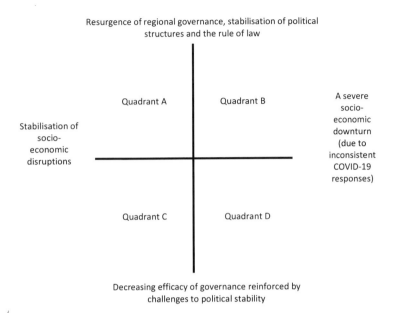

Figure 4.17 Frame for Matrix Scenarios for a system of study with an organisational viewpoint, 2025: Agri-food systems in a plus COVID-19 world – Global perspective' (CIMMYT 2021)

Step 4 Create the matrix

Create your scenario matrix by placing the hypotheses for one driver on each end of the y axis, then do the same for the x axis (see Figure 4.17 for an example).

Step 5 Write the scenarios

Consider the scenario the combination the two hypotheses would create in each quadrant of the matrix.

For example, in Quadrant A of Figure 4.17 you are creating a scenario which explores a future where there is a 'resurgence of regional governance, stabilisation of political structures and the rule of law and stabilisation of socio-economic disruptions'. You need to brainstorm what the confluence of these two dynamics might look like, how it could come about and what the implications of it are. In doing this you should consider what the other drivers which were highly important in your MIU might look like in this scenario. For instance in our organisational study example food security was a very important driver (see Figure 4.15), and so you should consider what it would look like in all four futures. You can use the other drivers in your matrix to add detail to your scenario. For example, in quadrant A there is political instability, so how would that affect the macroeconomic policies a government could explore?

At the end of this exercise, you should have four distinct scenarios. Each of them should be named with a descriptive title that helps to evoke the image of that particular future. In your matrix you should try to summarise the scenario that you have created into a few lines. Later, this graphical summary becomes a useful communication tool (see Figure 4.18).

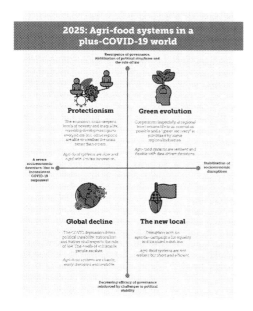

Figure 4.18 Matrix Scenarios for a system of study with an organisational viewpoint, 2025: Agri-food systems in a plus COVID-19 world (CIMMYT 2021)

Validate the matrix with a panel of experts. Send your scenario matrix and summary of the dynamics of each of the scenarios you have explored to a panel of experts and ask them to consider:

- Do the hypotheses at each end of the axis make sense?
- Are the hypotheses mutually exclusive?
- Are the scenarios sufficiently different?

134   *A toolkit for humanitarian action*

- Are there any dynamics or characteristics missing from any of the scenarios?

Step 6 Reviewing

Collect feedback and make the required amendments to finalise the matrix.

Frequently asked questions

Are the scenarios created using this method not overly simplistic?

In short, no. This is because while the matrix provides you with a framework through which to consider the evolution of your context, it is not intended to be limiting. You can and should delve back into your structural analysis and consider how the other important and uncertain factors (those that were not selected to be part of your drivers) would behave in each of the futures that you are creating. You should also include analysis on how the heavy trends of your system will shape all four of the images of the future that you are creating. While the matrix scenario approach allows you to create a simpler frame, it also gives you the scope to add significant amounts of nuance and detail while drafting your narrative.

What if I want to include more than two dimensions to frame my scenarios?

If when analysing your MIU you do not feel that your most important and uncertain drivers could be grouped coherently or you feel that you want to explore each as a particular dimension of your system, then you should use the morphological scenario approach (please see the morphological scenario guide on pp. 117–125).

Facilitation notes

Provided you are seeking input at each step where you can (selection of drivers, creation of hypotheses for either end of the matrix, preliminary picture of the four scenarios that are created by your matrix), a substantial portion of this tool can be done as a solitary exercise. However, particularly from the point of creating your hypotheses (Step 3), it can be useful to run the rest of the Matrix Scenarios exercise in either virtual or physical workshops. These should be structured to encourage discussion among participants and they should try to fully immerse themselves in each future as they explore it. It can be useful to provide guiding

A toolkit for humanitarian action 135

questions during the discussion about what each scenario might look like to prompt participants to consider all the key dynamics that were raised during the structural analysis phase. Ensure that participants leave sufficient time to consider the implications of each scenario for the actor that you are delivering your study to.

Tip: If you are writing Driver Files and using a workshop for the whole exercise, you will need to complete this exercise in two iterations. First, you should select the drivers and send your results to participants, asking them to comment on and validate your approach. Once you have agreed on the groupings, you can then write the Driver Files for all the relevant drivers and share them with your participants as preparatory material for the second part of the workshop, where you will then consider the hypotheses you are proposing for each grouping and the scenarios that they create.

Virtual workshop (2–2.5 hours, with no breaks)

To run a virtual workshop, you should first identify the two drivers or groups of drivers that you will be using to frame your scenarios from your MIU and validate this selection with participants. If you have time, you should then write your Driver Files (Steps 1 and 2 of this guide).

Preparation

i. Based on the analysis in your Driver Files or your analysis of your groups of drivers as a whole, draft two hypotheses for each driver (Step 3 of this guide).
ii. Circulate the MIU, Driver Files and the draft hypotheses to participants.
iii. On a virtual whiteboard, create your matrix frame (see Step 4 of this guide and Figure 4.17 for an example). Adjacent to each quadrant, add a selection of blank sticky notes/text boxes with one colour for each quadrant (e.g. Scenario A, red; Scenario B, blue; Scenario C, green; Scenario D, yellow). Ensure that all participants have access to this platform.

Seminar

iv. Present the MIU, review the groupings that have already been validated by the participants and summarise your research into your drivers (if you have Driver Files you can share these with the

136   *A toolkit for humanitarian action*

participants directly). During your introduction you should also ensure that all participants are comfortable using the virtual whiteboard software. (30 minutes plus time for questions; 45 minutes total)

v.   Present the hypotheses that you have drafted and divide your participants into two groups. Assign each group one driver and ask them to discuss the two hypotheses that you have prepared, encouraging them to make any amendments they think are necessary to make the hypotheses as relevant as possible. (15 minutes)

vi.   Have one member of each group present the final hypotheses that they have created (there may be no change). During this presentation, if necessary, you should update the matrix frame that you created on the virtual platform to reflect any changes to the hypotheses you proposed. (15 minutes)

vii.   Guide everyone to the virtual whiteboard. Divide the participants into four groups. Assign each group to one scenario and ask them to consider what a future defined by the combination of the two hypotheses they are working on would look like, taking notes on the pre-provided Post-it notes and adding more when necessary (for more guidance, see Step 5 of this guide). If you have fewer than three people in each group, then create two groups and ask each group to look at two scenarios. Once you have given instructions, go into breakout groups to complete the exercise. (30–40 minutes)

viii.   Have each group present back on the scenario that they have been working on. (30 minutes)

Follow-up

ix.   Summarise the input on the virtual whiteboard into bullet points for each scenario, and circulate those and the final scenario matrix to all participants for validation.

Resources: validated MIU with driver groupings and (if writing) Driver Files for each of the selected drivers; an empty matrix frame on a virtual whiteboard on which you can put your hypotheses and enter the details of each scenario as it is created.

DRIVER FILES

Driver Files are a way to structure your research into the most important and uncertain factors in your system of study, i.e. your scenario drivers. For each of the scenario drivers that you have identified depending on the type of scenarios that you are building (morphological or matrix), you need to create a Driver File. This is a short report that explores the history, current situation, trends and uncertainties of the driver you are researching. If you intend to write Morphological Scenarios, you will conclude each Driver File with a set of hypotheses which explore several different potential evolutions of the driver over the course of your outlook.

In futures studies you have to engage with information that is typically incomplete, unverifiable and vague. You must manage that uncertainty by being as robust as possible with your analysis and as transparent as possible with the hypotheses you are making about the different ways in which the driver may evolve. As a result, you must endeavour to gather and integrate all the information that is available to you and consult as many actors as possible who could share different perspectives and challenge any preconceived notions you have about the way your drivers may behave.

The output of building the Driver Files is a library of research into the most important uncertainties in your system of study. These documents should be well researched and well referenced. If these documents are kept up to date, they can provide the framework for a monitoring system for you to track changes in your system of study. Researching and writing Driver Files is often the most time-consuming part of a project, but it is worthwhile. You should allow at least 3 days for each Driver File and ensure that you have a pool of experts who can review them.

Prerequisites

Before you begin writing your Driver Files you need to have identified your critical drivers from your MIU. The way in which you will identify these drivers depends on the type of scenarios that you are building. You can find information on how to do this in the Morphological Scenarios (please see pp. 117–125) and Matrix Scenarios (please see pp. 126–136) sections of the toolkit.

How to do it

Step 1 Introduction

Driver Files can take many different formats, but they usually include the following key components:

138 *A toolkit for humanitarian action*

- Definition
- Overview
  History
  Current situation
  Trends exhibited in this driver
  Uncertainties over the course of the outlook
- Indicators
- Hypotheses (for Morphological Scenarios)
- Conclusion

This structure can be used as an outline for each report.

Step 2 Write the definition

Using the definition that was identified in your PESTLE to define the scope of your Driver File, begin researching the factor in-depth based on the outline in Step 1.

Step 3 Compose the overview

In the overview section you should focus on identifying and exploring the trends (both established and emerging), weak signals of change, major uncertainties and disruptive innovations (Lamblin 2017). The following subheadings can useful for organising your research.

History. Looking back at the dynamics of this driver for at least double the length of your outlook (i.e. if the time horizon for your study is 10 years, you should look back at least 20 years) to explore how it has changed over time. For example if your driver is poverty, How has the rate of poverty changed over time? Has the change been consistent/accelerating/slowing down? Which groups within a population have been most consistently at the lower end of the income scale? How dynamic is the change in poverty; are levels of social mobility high?

Current situation. Provide a summary of the current state of this driver. For example if your driver is poverty, What is the current percentage of the population living below the poverty line? Does looking at the multidimensional poverty index tell a different story? Is poverty equally distributed across a country/region, or is it concentrated in particular pockets either geographically or in society? Is there a social safety net?

Trends exhibited in this driver. Reviewing the history and current situation which you have already written, outline the general directions that you see the driver changing in. For example poverty has declined for the last decade and is continuing to do so; inequality between rural and urban communities has been intensifying and will continue to do so as economic growth is concentrated in cities.

You should also try to identify emerging trends and weak signals. These are shifts which are more uncertain or appear to be insignificant, as they have not been observed for very long, but your research suggests could become a trend over the course of the outlook.

Uncertainties. In your analysis, what are the major uncertainties in this driver over the course of the outlook? Here you could consider how shifts in the environment could affect your driver as well as potential new technologies or disasters. For example if poverty is your driver, How robust is the economy? Is the economy highly susceptible to shocks? Is there a chance of conflict/worsening conflict? Is there potential for economic transformation through the advent of new technology or increased connectivity?

Step 4 Determine the indicators

You should identify between four and six indicators for each of your drivers. Indicators are "observable phenomena that can be periodically reviewed to help track events, spot emerging trends, and warn of unanticipated changes" (Heuer 2014, 6.2 Indicators). Including indicators in your Driver Files can provide a snapshot of the state of your driver and help you to track how it is changing. They can be 'soft' indicators, which are more intangible but, where possible, these should be quantified. You should critically evaluate the source of your indicators and endeavour to ensure that you can easily track changes. Where possible, try to avoid composite indicators (such as the human development index (HDI)) as the change in the HDI score could be attributed to any of its composite factors, some of which may not be relevant for your driver (see Table 4.6 for an example of indicators).

Step 5 Formulate the hypotheses (for Morphological Scenarios)

If you are going on to write Morphological Scenarios, then you should include a section on hypotheses here (see Morphological Scenarios, pp. 117–125, for more details).

Step 6 Concluding

If you are not building Morphological Scenarios, then you do not need to create hypotheses in your Driver Files. Rather you can conclude by summarising what the debates and controversies are on this topic.

140   *A toolkit for humanitarian action*

Table 4.6 Example of indicators for a Driver File

Indicator	Definition	Source
Increase in social safety net allowance	The government passes new legislation which increases the monthly allowance provided to households below a certain threshold of income.	Government websites; think tanks that review government policy
Percentage of population living below the national poverty line	"National poverty headcount ratio is the percentage of the population living below the national poverty lines" (World Bank n.d. (a)).	National offices of statistics, World Bank
GDP growth rate	"Annual percentage growth rate of GDP at market prices based on constant local currency" (World Bank n.d. (b)).	National offices of statistics, World Bank

Step 7 Reviewing

Share your Driver Files with colleagues and experts for their review and comments.

Frequently asked questions

How long should my Driver Files be?

This depends on the complexity of the driver that you are researching and the amount of information that is available. However, we recommend that Driver Files be between three and eight pages long to ensure that they are sufficiently detailed but still easy to read and engage with.

Do I need to have quantitative information in my Driver Files?

You do not need to include quantitative information, but if there are useful metrics available for tracking the evolution of your driver in your indicators, then this can be incredibly useful data to include in your analysis. Please be sure to scrutinise the source of any quantitative information that you are including.

Facilitation notes

The writing and research of Driver Files is usually led by a single person, charged with conducting the research and gathering expert input. However, you should endeavour to validate the Driver Files with as many experts as you can, especially your hypotheses. The review process usually takes approximately 2 weeks.

ACTORS FILE

In a system of study, actors have different levels of freedom which they can exercise through operations, tactics and strategies to achieve their agenda. Some actors are very constrained by their circumstances or resources; others have fewer limitations which can increase their ability to act independently or have influence in your system of study. Analysing the actor's identity, their agenda and examining the potential role they might have in the system of study is a precondition for an actors game analysis and/or to develop your strategy.

The Actors File is a way to structure your research into the most important actors identified in your MIU. It is a document that summarises the identity, the agenda (hidden and/or public) and the potential role of the actor in your system of study. All actors included in the high and moderate importance areas of the MIU need to be integrated into your Actors File.

Building an Actors File will force you to engage with information that is incomplete, ambiguous and mostly hypothetical. You must manage these difficulties by being as robust as possible with your analysis and by being clear about any inferences or assumptions you are making, i.e. about the hidden agenda and the role of each actor in the system of study. As a result, you must endeavour to gather and integrate all the information that is available to you, consult as many actors as possible who could share different perspectives and challenge any preconceived notions you have about the way your actors may behave.

The output of building an Actors File is a spreadsheet summarising the research into the most impactful actors in your system of study. This file should be built with substantial research, and unverified information must be visible/highlighted (written in italic or/and in red colour).

Prerequisites

Before you begin your Actors File you should already have built up your knowledge of your system of study through the other structural analysis exercises; the PESTLE, Architecture and MIU should already have been completed by this point.

How to do it

Step 1 Identify the actors

First, you need to identify which actors you are going to include in your Actors Files. To do this, you should look at your MIU (please see the MIU in the toolkit section, pp. 107–116) and select the most important

142　*A toolkit for humanitarian action*

actors (those that are of high and middling importance, regardless of their level of uncertainty).

Step 2 Create the Actors File

Then you need to create an Actors File. This is a spreadsheet which can have many different columns to host the information you think is most relevant, but they usually include the following key areas:

- Identity
  Name
  Acronym
  Definition
- Agenda
  Public
  Hidden
- Role

In the identity column you should introduce the actor, listing their name, the acronym or abbreviation, and the definition as it was given in your PESTLE and Architecture. It is important to have this continuity throughout your research.

You can create more columns with more information, for example you can detail the actors grouping done during the Architecture and the Impact/Uncertainty Matrix and attribute different acronyms to a group of actors if relevant for your game of actors analysis.

Remember that an actor could be an individual, a group of people, an institution, a business or an organisation included in the high and moderate importance areas of the MIU. They all are influential actors of your system of study and as such merit further investigation (see Table 4.7 for an example).

Step 3 Describe the actor's agenda

In the agenda column you should focus on the hidden and public agenda of each actor and try to clarify the any ambiguities: what they say they want (public agenda) and what they really want (hidden agenda).

The *public agenda* is an underlying (often ideological) plan or programme about which the actor is very open. It depends on the type of actor (i.e. an individual, a group of people, an institution, a business or an organisation), but the public agenda is usually easy to research. You can do so by analysing the actor's official documents (i.e. public strategy documents and stated aims), reviewing its programme/mission, drawing

Table 4.7 Example of an Actors File

Identity			Agenda		Role
Name	*Acronym/abbreviation*	*Definition*	*Public*	*Hidden*	
Government of Iaransia	GoI	The national government including the presidential and legislative branches as well as the civil service	Protection, security, well-being and wealth of the Iaransia population	Preserve the power leadership of the Cara ethnic group	National Authorities which set the rules and structures for interactions of many other actors in the system.
Min Ethnic Group	MEG	Those in the Iaransia population who define themselves as part of the Min Ethnic group	Government Opposition	Support external and multinational influence to increase their political power	A subset of the population who are a majority in the western region but have limited national representation
Multinationals	Multinat.	Multinational corporations which are headquartered in other countries but operate in Iaransia	Mining prospection and business development in Iaransia	Profits for stakeholders	An external actor that holds significant influence in Iaransia as they have massive resources to leverage in the country

Example using ficticious country of Iaransia.

144   *A toolkit for humanitarian action*

content from public interviews and/or statements to the media, or simply by asking the actor directly or indirectly (via surveys).

The *hidden agenda* is the real agenda the actor pursues in the system of study. It is fundamental that you put effort into identifying the hidden agenda of an actor, as many actors may not be completely transparent in their public aims and statements and you do not want to overlook this nuance in your analysis. For example, while most armed groups have a stated public agenda outlining their political aims (e.g. independence/ power sharing), they often have a hidden agenda which is motivated by the economic gains they are able to make in a lawless environment (e.g. the ability to continue to manufacture and traffic drugs). Some hidden agendas are hard to reveal, others are more obvious. As with the public agenda, you should cast a critical eye over any documented sources and interviews both by and about the actor.

Step 4 Envision the actor's role

The role column should describe how you see the actor 'playing' in the system of study. Your assessment here of what to include here is based on your understanding of the identity of the actor, its position in the impact/uncertainty matrix and the Architecture, its public and hidden agenda, and its relationship to the other actors and the system of study.

The role of an actor can change across your time horizon and so you should be prepared to continually update your Actors File as these shifts occur. The analysis of the role of your actors and the iterative process of updating your assessments can help you to identify potential partners, allies, champions, facilitators and targets for your work.

Step 5 Reviewing

Validate your Actors File with colleagues and experts who may have a different perspective or new information to add.

Frequently asked questions

How many actors should I be taking from my MIU?

Generally, you should not select more than 20–25 actors from your MIU, starting from those that are of the highest importance down to the ones that are of middling importance, regardless of their level of uncertainty. If you have fewer than 20–25 actors in these two areas of your MIU, your workshop will be quicker. If you have more than 25 actors in the middle and high importance areas of the MIU, you should take the 25 that are of the highest level of importance.

If I cannot find sufficient evidence to define the hidden agenda of an actor, can I state my hypotheses?

You may be unable to fully confirm your hypotheses about an actor's hidden agenda and as such it might stay hypothetical in your Actors File. In this case, fulfil that cell in italic or/and in red colour to flag that uncertainty to all readers.

Facilitation notes

The writing and research of an Actors File is usually led by one person, coordinating the research (you can split the actors among team members) and gathering expert input. Researching and writing an Actors File is an ongoing project; you should never consider it to be final, as dynamics of the actors in your system are probably highly changeable and so your analysis should be continually updated to remain useful.

You should allow at least 2 days for an Actors File to be filled for the first time and ensure that you have a pool of experts who can review it before engaging in an actors game analysis (you can combine this step with the process of reviewing your Driver Files). The review process usually takes approximately 2 weeks.

146 *A toolkit for humanitarian action*

INFLUENCE/DEPENDENCY MATRIX (MID)

The Influence/Dependency Matrix (MID) and Actor/Objective Matrix (MAO, see pp. 181–194) are the two complementary tools of the MACTOR[2] method. Though this method was originally intended for strategic foresight, it has been successfully applied to a variety of situations, such as to support decision makers to enhance existing strategies by considering how to be more effective in a complex or volatile system where there is a highly dynamic game of actors.

The MID is a workshop which gives you a frame to analyse the role, ambition and relationships (or game) of all the actors in your system. The game of actors analysis is an important step in building your scenarios and designing your strategy. A detailed analysis of the role and agendas of the actors in your system can bring added nuance and robustness to your scenarios. The game of actors analysis is even more crucial when developing your strategy. It adds a degree of sophistication to the strategy development process by providing you with a comprehensive analysis of the actors operating in your space against which you can refine your strategic objectives or identify successful tactical moves to achieve your goals.

The MID workshop is structured to enable you to analyse the role of the actors, unpack their agenda, examine the balance of power between each of them, and visualise the degrees of freedom and power of the actors in your system of study. Through the process, you will create a collective representation of the game of actors, and identify influential actors and game changers, as well as potential alliances.

The output of the MID is a captivating chart where you can easily identify the roles of key actors in your system of study where the x variable represents the actor's dependency on other actors' decisions or actions, and the y variable represents the actor's influence over others.

Prerequisites

Before you begin to plan your MID workshop, you should already have built up your knowledge of your system of study through the other structural analysis exercises; the PESTLE, Architecture, MIU, Driver Files and Actors Files should already have been completed by this point.

The finalisation of the MIU and the Actors File are especially important to complete before the game of actors analysis. The MIU will allow you to focus on only the most important actors (please see the MIU in the toolkit section, pp. 107–116), while the Actors File will enable you to draw on your analysis of the actor's identity, their agenda, and their role throughout the MID workshop.

How to do it

To start, you need to build a representative panel where all participants have a detailed knowledge of your system of study. To build your panel you need to select the workshop participants according to the viewpoint of your system of study.

For an organisational study: you should engage the senior leadership team of the organisation. They will constitute three-fifths of the panel, and they should identify one-fifth of participants from among the mid-management and junior staff and the remaining one-fifth from their key partners or/and external experts.

For a contextual study: you should engage with a selection of internal and/or external experts, with a high level of understanding of the geography and/or thematic area and an interest in building a collaborative vision.

The quality of the participants is critical not only for the validity of the MID output, but also for getting buy-in and building consensus and consistency for the overall strategic process. The number of attendees has an impact on the performance of the workshop. Where possible, try to have an odd number of participants for a smart workshop so that you are never in the position of having a tied vote.

Step 1 Preparation

To prepare for your workshop, the attendees need to do some light preparatory work. You should share a brief introduction, in which you explain the purpose of the MID exercise and provide a summary of the Actors File. In the summary, you should highlight the hidden agenda of the actors (or their public one if the it is not available). Remember: the agenda of an actor describes the strategy that the actor is implementing or intends to implement in your system of study (please see the Actor File in the toolkit section, pp. 141–145).

You then need to prepare an MID table by building an Actor × Actor table in a spreadsheet (see Table 4.8). You should populate this grid with the actors selected from your MIU and represented in your Actors Files (so there should be no more than 25). Then fill the cells, which represent the intersection of an actor with itself, with a short note on the actor's agenda using the information in your Actors File. In a spreadsheet, you cannot easily include a substantial amount of text without distorting the table, therefore you may want to summarise the

148 *A toolkit for humanitarian action*

Table 4.8 Example of an MID table with actors' agenda cases

	Actor 1	Actor 2	Actor 3	Actor ..	Actor N	Influence (Y)
Actor 1	Actor 1 Agenda					
Actor 2		Actor 2 Agenda				
Actor 3			Actor 3 Agenda			
Actor ..				Actor .. Agenda		
Actor N					Actor N Agenda	
Dependency (X)						

actor's agenda with a very short sentence and refer people to the Actors File for more detail.

Finally, build an Influence (y) column and a Dependency (x) row, and fill it with a formula summing all the entries of each row (influence) and each column (dependence) of the Actor × Actor table.

This spreadsheet will be used as a base for your workshop. The remaining empty cells need to be filled during the group discussion.

Step 2 Introducing the workshop

At the beginning of the workshop, after a short introduction of the participants, you should share the MID table with the prefilled actors' agenda cells (Table 4.8). You should assume that all the attendees have done their homework and they have a good knowledge of the Actors File that you have created. However, it can be useful to provide a copy of the Actors File for reference during the session. If they haven't done their homework, give the attendees 20 minutes to read and discuss the Actors Files summary prepared in Step 1.

After you introduce the participants you should outline the purpose of the MID workshop and explain, in detail, how the MID table will be filled by a swift group discussion and vote. Particular attention needs to be paid to how you will define the values in the empty cells. Each cell represents your analysis of the relationship between two actors, that is the level of influence of one actor over another. The group will be tasked with assessing the strength of the relationship of influence using a numerical value (0 to 4).

This is best demonstrated by an example. Table 4.9 and the following list show how to fill the highlighted cell 'actor2 × actorN':

- If actor 2 has no influence on actor N, the value to fill is 0.
- If actor 2 has an influence on (or jeopardises) the operations of actor N, the value to fill is 1.
- If actor 2 has an influence on (or jeopardises) the tactics of actor N, the value to fill is 2.
- If actor 2 has an influence on (or jeopardises) the strategy of actor N, the value to fill is 3.
- If actor 2 has an influence on (or jeopardises) the existence of actor N, the value to fill is 4.

Note: It is important to verify that your group is familiar with the meaning of 'strategy', 'tactics', 'operations' and their differences. A good,

Table 4.9 Example of an MID table with Actor × Actor cases

	Actor 1	Actor 2	Actor 3	Actor ..	Actor N		Influence (Y)
Actor 1	Actor 1 Agenda	actor1 x actor2	actor1 x actor3	actor1 x actor..	actor1 x actorN		=sum(actor1 x actor2; actor1 x actor3; actor1 x actor..; actor1 x actorN)
Actor 2	actor2 x actor1	Actor 2 Agenda	actor2 x actor3	actor2 x actor..	actor2 x actorN		etc.
Actor 3	actor3 x actor1	actor3 x actor2	Actor 3 Agenda	actor3 x actor..	actor3 x actorN		etc.
Actor ..	actor.. x actor1	actor.. x actor2	actor.. x actor3	Actor .. Agenda	actor.. x actorN		etc.
Actor N	actorN x actor1	actorN x actor2	actorN x actor3	actorN x actor..	Actor N Agenda		etc.
Dependency (X)	=sum(actor2 x actor1; actor3 x actor1; actor..x actor1; actorN x actor1)	etc.	etc.	etc.	etc.		

A toolkit for humanitarian action 151

collective understanding of these terms is critical for the success of the exercise. If you need to explain these concepts further, you will find more explanation in Chapter 3 (p. 52).

The Influence column and the Dependency row will be automatically computed as the exercise progresses with the sum of the Actor × Actor cells of the MID table (influence is the sum of each row, dependency is the sum of each column).

It is very important to recognise that the influence of actors in any system of study has two directions. Using our current example these are (a) the influence of actor 2 over actor N and (b) the influence of actor N over actor 2. They may have the same value, for example if the actors share a reciprocal relationship, but they represent two different sides of the question and so each interaction must be analysed discretely. Each Actor × Actor question is specific to one direction of influence. To fill the MID table you are always asking yourself what the influence of the actor in the row you are examining is over the actor in the column (Table 4.10).

Step 3 Plotting the MID chart

After you have introduced the workshop, explained the mechanics of how to fill the table and responded to any questions, you can start the exercise. First, you need to set some facilitation rules:

Voting and timekeeping. Apart from the facilitator, all the attendees should vote by expressing a value between 0 and 4 according to the level of influence of one actor over another, i.e. one value for each cell. To fill the relative Actor × Actor cell, the facilitator will input the mathematical mode or modal value, which is the value expressed most often by the votes of the attendees (if eight attendees vote, respectively, 0, 0, 1, 3, 1, 0, 0, 0, then the facilitator will input 0). In the case of a tie, e.g. 0, 0, 1, 1, 1, 1, 0, 0, the facilitator should allow a discussion of no more than 5 minutes where each side of the tie (in this example those who voted 1 vs. those who voted 0) to present their rationale and then run a new voting session to see if anyone has changed their minds. In case of a tie that cannot be broken through discussion, the facilitator should cast the deciding vote.

Facilitation. The role of the facilitator should rotate among the attendees. Each attendee should complete at least one row (i.e. the inputs for one actor). The facilitator is the timekeeper, the mediator in case of a tie and the tie-breaking vote if necessary. The facilitator manages the input into the MID spreadsheet and fills it in according to the outcome of the voting.

You should start with the first row or two to show an example of how the facilitation works and then you can hand it over to another member

Table 4.10 Example of an MID table with directions of influence

	Actor 1	Actor 2	Actor 3	Actor ..	Actor N	Influence (Y)
Actor 1	Actor 1 Agenda	actor1 x actor2	actor1 x actor3	actor1 x actor..	actor1 x actorN	=sum(actor1 x actor2; actor1 x actor3; actor1 x actor..; actor1 x actorN)
Actor 2	actor2 x actor1	Actor 2 Agenda	actor2 x actor3	actor2 x actor..	actor2 x actorN	etc.
Actor 3	actor3 x actor1	actor3 x actor2	Actor 3 Agenda	actor3 x actor..	actor3 x actorN	etc.
Actor ..	actor.. x actor1	actor.. x actor2	actor.. x actor3	Actor .. Agenda	actor.. x actorN	etc.
Actor N	actorN x actor1	actorN x actor2	actorN x actor3	actorN x actor..	Actor N Agenda	etc.
Dependency (X)	=sum(actor2 x actor1; actor3 x actor1; actor.. x actor1; actorN x actor1)	etc.	etc.	etc.	etc.	

A toolkit for humanitarian action   153

of the group take forward, switching facilitators every row or every other row.

Once your Actor × Actor cells are filled, the Influence column and the dependency row will have been automatically computed, giving you an (x,y) value for each actor, where y is an actor's influence in the system of study and x is their dependency in the system of study (Table 4.11).

Once each actor has a specific (x,y) value, you can then plot them on a chart (a scatter plot). Scatter plot functions are embedded in most of the available spreadsheet software and plotting it should be relatively straightforward from a completed MID spreadsheet.

The MID chart represents the game of actors in the system of study. Once it is built, you can show attendees the fruits of their long labour by visualising the game of actors on the MID chart. If you wish, you can show a visualisation at the start of your session but you should not explain its interpretation until after the exercise is complete or it may bias their input.

Step 4 Interpretation

After the MID chart is plotted and shared, it is time to share the MID interpretation. You will use the MID chart to do this.

First, divide the MID chart in nine equal areas (divide the influence and dependency axis by three and plot two perpendicular dotted lines at one-third and two-thirds of the two axes).

Then, plot two diagonal lines crossing the MID chart, a grey one that you will call 'Control', going from the top of the influence axis to the top of the dependency one, and a dashed line that you call 'Implication', going from the 0,0 intersection to the top right of the plot area (Figure 4.20).

You now need to share the MID interpretation. Each area in the MID chart is labelled and named, corresponding to precise behaviours or roles in the game of actors for your system of study. You can use of chess game pieces to explain them (Figure 4.21).

Kings: If your system of study has one or more kings, they will be represented in the top-left area of your MID chart. Kings are highly influential in your system of study, however, they have a low level of dependency on other actors within your system. This means they operate very autonomously (which can also make them less agile and create structural inertia in your whole system). Kings are the most dominant player in your system of study, they heavily influence or control the game of all the actors situated under the line of control.

154 *A toolkit for humanitarian action*

Table 4.11 Example of an MID table with filled Actor × Actor cases

	Actor 1	Actor 2	Actor 3	Actor ..	Actor N	Influence (Y)
Actor 1	Actor 1 Agenda	0	2	1	0	3
Actor 2	1	Actor 2 Agenda	3	3	1	8
Actor 3	2	2	Actor 3 Agenda	0	1	5
Actor ..	3	0	0	Actor .. Agenda	1	4
Actor N	0	0	1	0	Actor n Agenda	1
Dependency (X)	6	2	6	4	3	

A toolkit for humanitarian action   155

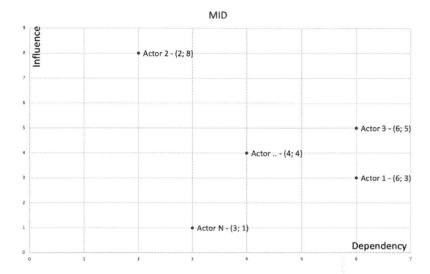

Figure 4.19 Example of am MID chart

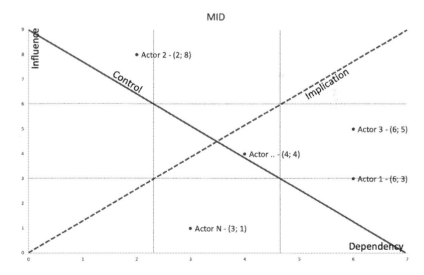

Figure 4.20 Example of an MID chart with nine areas and two diagonal lines

156 *A toolkit for humanitarian action*

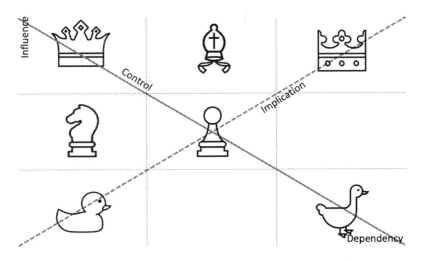

Figure 4.21 Example of an MID chart with all the roles and behaviours

Queens: If your system of study has one or more queens, they are in the top-right area of your MID chart. Queens are highly influential on the system of study but also have a strong dependency on most of the other actors. This high dependency gives the queens a certain agility – they can vary their operations, tactics and strategies, which, coupled with their influence, makes them true game changers in your system of study. Queens can be influenced by all the actors distributed along the implication line above the line control.

Bishops: If your system of study has bishops, they are in the top-middle area of your MID chart. Bishops are highly influent on the system of study, especially if you do not have kings or queens in your game. In the presence of both kings and queens, bishops usually play a role of intermediary and add fluidity to the system of study. In absence of a king, the bishops control the game of all the actors situated under the control line.

Pawns: Pawns are at the centre of your game of actors and they are in the middle area of your MID chart. Pawns are dynamic and can change their position over the course of your outlook if your system of study is sufficiently fluid. Pawns below the line of control are influenced by the king or the bishop (if there is no king). Pawns distributed above the line of implication and above the line of control are potential allies in any game to influence the queens in your system or even could become a queen themselves.

Knights: Knights are in the middle-left area of your MID chart. They are under the control of the king or the bishop (if there is no king). They reinforce the system of control in your game of actors though they are very autonomous players.

The out-of-games and dominated actors: The actors in the lower areas of your chart can be ignored. Those in the bottom-left area of your MID chart are 'out of game' in your system of study. This means that they have a very low level of both influence and dependence implying that they have a limited stake in your system and so are not relevant to your inquiry. Those in the bottom-middle and bottom-right areas are dominated by the other actors. If needed, you can use the allegory of a 'duck' to explain it and add a note of humour at the same time.

Step 5 Game of actors analysis

After presenting each of the different groupings, you should begin attributing the behaviour/role to the actors identified on your MID chart and visualise the game of actors analysis in your system of study.

In our example you would identify Actor 2 as a king, Actor 3 as a king, Actor. as a pawn while discarding Actor 1 (as a dominated actor) and Actor N (as an out-of-game). You can continue your explanation by outlining that the game of actors in this specific system of study is dominated by Actor 2, while Actor 3 might play the role of a game changer, especially if it allies with Actor. etc. (Figure 4.22).

For more detail, in Figure 4.23 you will find an example of an MID chart with game of actors analysis on a system of study 'Sudan 2027'. The working group was mainly composed of the national staff from an INGO based in Sudan and engaged in a process of strategic foresight to design their 2027 country strategy.

In this case study the transitional government plays the role of a powerful game changer in a system without a king but with a relatively influential army. Given its position of influence, the army represents the main obstacle to the transitional government to take overall control of the game (to become a king) and could in fact, move into that position itself. The US plays a powerful knight role in a system without a king and the army is not independent enough to have any influence on the US.

With this analysis we can start to make speculations such as an alliance between the transitional government, the business actors and the citizens, supported by bilateral donors, might open the way for the transitional government to become a king in Sudan in 2027. This could potentially

158 *A toolkit for humanitarian action*

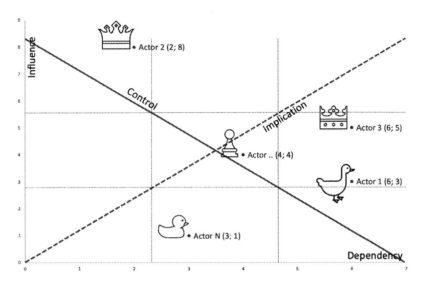

Figure 4.22 Example of an MID chart with game of actors analysis

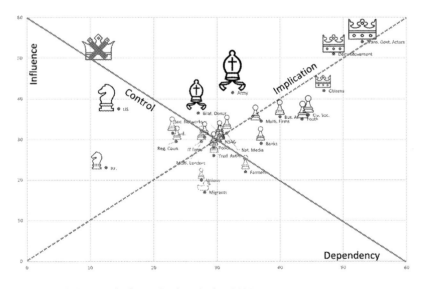

Figure 4.23 Case study for MID chart Sudan 2027

A toolkit for humanitarian action 159

be achieved by leveraging the US to exploit the army's dependencies in the system of study.

To begin to make such inferences and explore how these relationships could change, it is important to go back to the MID table to look at the specific relationship between the critical actors to confirm the hypotheses you are making.

The value of the MID is fully realised when its outputs are combined with your scenarios. The game of actors analysis adds to the storyline and enhances the overall quality of each scenario by exploring how each of your influential actors would behave in different potential futures.

Frequently asked questions

How long should a MID workshop take?

This depends on the number of actors that you are putting in your MID table. The rules suggested in Step 3 are very useful to make the workshop as efficient as possible. Usually, the first two rows of the MID table are very time-consuming; this is when the group is learning and adjusting to the rules as well as becoming better acquainted with the actors. However, the speed with which you can fill the table increases as you go and a row of actors with 25 actors can be performed in approximately 12 minutes. Under these conditions, an overall MID table of 25 actors × 25 actors can be done in approximately 5.5 hours. Twenty-five actors is the maximum number of actors that we suggest to select for your Actors File, so your workshop will often be shorter than this.

Is the quality of the MID affected by the rules of voting and the timekeeping?

It is not uncommon for participants to be frustrated by the approach of MID facilitation and for them to feel that the value of the output is compromised by the lack of consensus and extensive discussions. The process explained in Step 3 is the result of years of experience and lessons learned; the overarching methodology is based on the theory that a snap judgement of 'informed' people (or experts) can be as good or better than reasoned conclusions. This concept is elaborated and demonstrated by Malcom Gladwell (2005) in his book *Blink*. The key part of this concept is that you are engaging informed people, which is why it is strongly recommended that attendees have access to the Actors File and do some homework to internalise that analysis information prior to the workshop.

160 *A toolkit for humanitarian action*

***If my actor is not exactly in the specific area for a behaviour/
role, can I still attribute a designation to it?***

The areas presented are indicative. If your actor is close to a particular area, you can still attribute it the specific behaviour/role. As in Figure 4.22, the queen is not really in the queens area, however, because there are no other queens and it is the most influential (after the king) and dependent actor on your chart, we can attribute the role of the queen to that specific actor. Remember, always check that your role attribution has a consistent logic in the overall game of actors.

Facilitation notes

We strongly recommend that you perform the MID as a physical, virtual or hybrid workshop, as it ensures the highest quality of the outputs. The MID workshop can be very time-consuming: a physical, virtual or hybrid workshop to complete a MID table usually takes between 4 and 6 hours depending on the number of actors that you are considering and the experience you have with this type of exercise.

In the case study used at Step 4, the system of study Sudan 2027, the Actors File from the structural analysis contained 24 actors, which allowed the facilitators to build a 24 actors × 24 actors MID and analyse 576 directions of influence. The exercise was run as a hybrid workshop that lasted 1 week and required 6 hours of group discussion and voting.

If the group selected for the MID workshop cannot (or does not want to) dedicate this much time to a long group discussion, it is possible to perform Step 1 and Step 2 on a short virtual call, then ask all participants to complete the MID table (Step 3) individually and combine the results yourself. You should then host a second call for the interpretation and discussion in Step 4.

Virtual workshop

You can run a virtual MID workshop using the approach outlined in the 'How to do it' section by hosting a long video conference where you facilitate the discussion in the same way as you would in person. However, this can be very challenging to get people to commit to and to participate in without distractions. If you want to run a MID virtually, we recommend holding a virtual workshop in two parts, in between which the participants complete their MID independently and you process the final results.

A toolkit for humanitarian action   161

Part 1

Preparation

i. You must ensure that participants are properly informed and pre-pared. As in Step 1 you should share the introduction, the summary of the Actors File and a list of the participants ahead the call. You should allow at least 1 week for people to read the material. Then prepare your MID table as in Step 1.

Virtual call 1: Fulfilling the MID spreadsheet (45–60 minutes)

ii. To start the call, you should remind the participants of your defini-tion of your system of study and the purpose of the MID exercise. You can skip the introduction of the participants (but ask that they be on camera if possible and make their names visible). (10 minutes)
iii. After the introduction you should launch a quick quiz to check that your participants understand the strategy that the actors are imple-menting or intend to implement in your system of study. This can be done either through discussion (i.e. you ask them to explain what the agenda of a particular actor is) or by using a polling platform onto which you can load a series of multiple-choice questions. The purpose of this is to ensure that they are clear on the actors that you will be analysing. (15 minutes)
iv. Then share the MID table and explain how to fill the Actor × Actor cells, making clear the 0 to 4 scale which they will be using and ensuring that they understand the direction of influence (actor in the row over actor in the column) of each question. You should allow for a 10-minute question-and-answer session. (20 minutes)
v. Once you are sure the exercise is well understood, share the MID spread-sheet template (into which you should embed a little reminder on the level of influence and the relative values) and fix a deadline by which all participants must return the completed spreadsheets. (5 minutes)
vi. Conclude by offering an optional 30-minute call during the week for a question-and-answer session if necessary (set a date and time if there is interest).

Follow-up

vii. Once you have received the individual completed spreadsheets, com-bine the input from each participant in a new MID table and fill all the Actor × Actor cells with a formula calculating the mode of all

162 *A toolkit for humanitarian action*

the values that were individually expressed. This operation can take more or less time depending on the software you are using and your familiarity with it. Then plot the final MID chart with the combined game of actors analysis as explained at the end of Step 3 and in Step 4.

Part 2

Preparation

viii. You should have your completed MID table and chart ready to present for the next call. In addition, you should prepare a few slides to explain how to interpret the MID chart (use the figures in Step 4).

Virtual call 2: MID interpretation (1–1.5 hours)

ix. After welcoming the participants, you can take the chance to run a brief survey asking them for their feedback on the exercise (this can be done using an online polling software). (15 minutes)
x. Share your presentation. Start by showing the combined MID and its chart without the actor analysis layered on top. Once you have presented their combined work you should allow for a 10-minute question-and-answer session. (15–20 minutes)
xi. Continue your presentation using your prepared slides on the interpretation and then present their final MID chart with the interpretation layered on top. (15 minutes)
xii. Open the floor for a discussion on the interpretation of the actors analysis, as demonstrated at the end of Step 6, to conclude the call. (15–20 minutes)

Follow-up

xiii. Distribute the combined MID table and final chart with the actors analysis, and create and share a file with all the documents, records and slides.

Resources: presentation; survey or pre-prepared polls to assess participants knowledge of the actors in your system loaded on an accessible online platform; survey or pre-prepared polls to gather feedback on the process loaded on an accessible online platform (optional); MID table in a sharable format

Between the preparatory work and the group workshop (or the alternative individual contribution version), a virtual MID workshop will take between 2 and 3 weeks to be finalised.

A toolkit for humanitarian action 163

WRITING SCENARIOS

Scenario thinking (meaning the whole process of analysis to the point of writing scenarios) has origins in many different places and times including a 16th century Jesuit scholar in Spain, Herman Khan at the RAND institute in the 1950s and Betrand de Jouvenel in 1960s France (JiSC 2013). Ultimately, the goal of all scenario approaches is to produce an analytical product which summarises analyses of complex systems and posits different ways they may evolve over time to support organisations to plan for the long term. While this is often in the form of written reports or presentations, there are also ways to represent scenarios experientially (Candy and Dunagan 2017). Writing scenarios has been a foundational part of organisational and business strategy for decades.

Writing a scenario report provides you with an effective and efficient way to communicate all the analyses that you have undertaken as part of your study. The way in which you present the information and insights that you have gathered through this process is critical if your outputs are to be used and translated into decision-making. As such, writing your scenarios is an incredibly important step. When they are well constructed, scenarios can stimulate the imagination, give everyone in the discussion the same language to speak, build a shared understanding about what obstacles and opportunities the future could present, and help to develop a shared vision. In short, scenarios are a critical communications document.

Prerequisites

To write your scenarios you will need to first to complete either a Morphological or Matrix Scenario exercise.

How to do it

Step 1 Introduction

If you are using the morphological approach to scenarios you will use the hypotheses grid as the outline of your scenarios. When creating the hypotheses grid, you will have selected one hypothesis from each of your critical drivers; these can now be used as bullet points from which to begin writing your scenarios.

If you are using a matrix approach you will have the bullet points, summary and scenario names from the Matrix Scenario exercise. The

164   *A toolkit for humanitarian action*

process of converting your hypotheses and bullet points is the same for both approaches to scenario development.

Step 2 Structure your report

Structure your scenario report by giving a brief introduction to your system of study. Without this context your scenarios will be difficult to use.

Step 3 List your assumptions

List your assumptions before you begin to write your scenarios. It is absolutely necessary for the validity of your study to be clear about what assumptions you have made about your context. These should be pulled from your work at the outset of your project (Scoping Workshop, pp. 82–93) and if there are any others you want to add from the heavy trends section of your MIU (MIU, pp. 107–116).

Step 4 Write the narrative

Write a half- to one-and-a-half-page narrative setting out the details of each scenario. Building from the framework that you have created (either morphological or matrix). The narrative should focus on

- The interplay of the drivers you have identified
- How the confluence of the dynamics you are exploring will shape the future
- How the other drivers which were identified but not selected to frame the scenarios may evolve in the future you are developing
- How the role of most influential actors (identified in your MID; see pp. 146–162) would unfold in this future; it is vital to reintegrate your actor analysis when writing your scenarios

Step 5 Draft the scenarios

Your scenarios should always be written in the present tense or as if what you are describing has already happened. You are writing your scenarios as if you are already at the end of your outlook, looking back to describe how you got to where you are and what the world around you looks like in this future. You should not include words which suggest that there is uncertainty in what you are describing, e.g. using 'might', 'may' or 'could'. This is because you are trying to produce a compelling image

A toolkit for humanitarian action 165

of the future to transport the reader into that new environment so that they can most effectively consider the ramifications of what that new reality would be. The fact that there are multiple versions of this future presented in your report already includes the dimension of uncertainty that using words such as 'may' or 'might' connote. For example, when writing a set of scenarios with an outlook to 2025, instead of writing 'The conflict will continue and may cause increased displacement by 2025' phrase it as 'The conflict continued and in 2025 there is increased displacement across the region'.

The following extract is from a set of scenarios written in 2020 looking at the impact of the COVID-19 pandemic with an outlook to 2022 (IARAN 2020, p. 3):

> Until the middle of 2021, most countries alternate between suppression tactics to control the virus (social distancing, and national or regional confinement) and a resumption of near normal economic and social activities. This strategy allows them to contain the spread and make strides towards developing herd immunity, while limiting social and economic disruption as much as possible. Although many people return to work (even if it is repeatedly disrupted at the local level), all countries are suffering from the impact of the global recession. By the summer 2021, most countries hit first, finally manage to contain it.
>
> Lack of coordination delays various clinical trials (Recovery, Discovery, COLCORONA, etc.) and a vaccine is not available before the second wave hits. Technical advances in COVID-19 testing allows for the tests to be systematically rolled out in developed countries from late summer 2020. These tests make it possible to prepare more effectively for the second wave, which strikes the northern hemisphere before a vaccine is made widely available in 2021. Prior to the release of the vaccine, where health systems can scale up widespread testing to the general public, the resurgence of the virus is kept in check as new cases are quickly identified and contained. However, hotspots have recurrent periods of imposed reduced movement or lockdown.

Step 6 Consolidate the scenarios

When you have drafted your scenarios, you should consider how you can increase their relevance for your audience. There are several ways to do this depending on the kind of audience that you are targeting

166 *A toolkit for humanitarian action*

and the kind of system you are studying. One example of how to help people embed the scenarios into their thinking is through presenting the implications of the scenarios for either the context or an actor beneath each one. By doing this you can help to concretise how the dynamics you have explored translate into changes on the ground. Some examples of how to do this include:

- Identifying the humanitarian consequences (sometimes organised in thematic sectors) and considering where the added vulnerability for populations of concern are in each future. For example, if you are looking at a scenario which includes increased levels of conflict, what does that mean for education.
- Highlighting the challenges and opportunities for different actors in each future. You can do this from multiple different perspectives as you should consider the fact that challenges and opportunities are unlikely to be the same for each actor in your system. As a result, you must be clear when describing the challenges and opportunities, and which perspective you are representing.

Scenarios for a study with an organisational viewpoint

- It is at this point that if you created an architecture with an organisational viewpoint, you can reintroduce the components from your specific system. One of the ways to do this is to conduct a stren gths/weaknesses/opportunities/threats analysis (SWOT) using the factors that you listed in your Architecture for each future. Consider how the organisation would perform in that particular future, what their particular strengths and weaknesses would be, and where the dynamics you are describing present either opportunities or threats for your organisation to achieve its mission.

Including a section on implications after each of your scenarios can help the audience to consider what these scenarios mean for them and begin to provoke discussions of how they can use them.

Step 7 Create indicators for each scenario

As with writing indicators for your drivers in your Driver Files (see pp. 137–140), you should create indicators for each one of your scenarios. Indicators for scenarios are the primary way of avoiding surprises, as they prepare you and your audience to recognise changes in your context and ensure that your scenarios are constantly challenged and kept current.

A toolkit for humanitarian action 167

Table 4.12 Examples of indicators for the sample scenario in Step 5

	Indicator	Definition	Source
	Limitations to travel to and from developed countries	There are restrictions on the ease of travel to and from many OECD countries. These could take the form of denials of visas, flight bans and forced quarantine.	Various media and government sources
Walking the tightrope	COVID-19 vaccine	There is a COVID-19 vaccine (above 70% efficacy) that is at least moderately accessible in most developed countries.	World Health Organisation, 'R&D Blueprint' (World Health Organisation n.d.)
	Global unemployment rises	"Unemployment refers to the share of the labor force that is without work but available for and seeking employment".	World Bank, 'Unemployment, total (% of total labor force) (modeled ILO estimate)' (World Bank, 2021)

Good indicators for scenarios are only applicable to one scenario. If an indicator could be relevant for all of your scenarios, it will not be useful in identifying how your context is evolving. In addition, it must be a highly likely factor. If your indicator is unlikely to manifest itself over the course of your outlook then monitoring, it will not help you to identify shifts in your environment. Finally, you must be able to observe the indicator over time. Indicators for scenarios serve a purpose, and if you cannot track the changes which you have identified as being significant, then you will not be able to use your indicators as intended. In order to be of use, indicators should be consistently monitored and reported on. See Table 4.12 for indicators written for the sample scenario in Step 5.

Note: Pitfalls in writing scenarios:

- Scenarios must be relevant
- You must ensure that your scenarios are coherent and there should be no inconsistencies in the internal logic of each scenario

168   *A toolkit for humanitarian action*

- You must be transparent about how you came to these scenarios, clearly stating your assumptions and be able to present all your preparatory work to demonstrate the process you engaged in
- Do not present your work in a way which encourages people to choose one scenario and disregard the others

Step 8 Reviewing

Validate your scenarios. Once you have a draft of your scenario report, you should share it with reviewers to seek their comments and feedback.

Frequently asked questions

What if my scenarios are too long?

While we do not advise using scenarios that are over one-and-a-half pages in length, if you feel that the detail you have provided will be useful to your audience, then this is your editorial choice. The guidance on length is to ensure the usability of the final product, but this is, of course, a decision that should be dependent on who is going to read your report and how they are going to use them.

Does it have to be a written in prose?

There are instances where scenarios are written as bullet points, and while this can be useful for sections such as thinking through the humanitarian consequences of each future, we would advise that the main body of your scenarios are written as a consistent narrative. Writing your scenarios as a story with a good flow can help to transport the reader into that future.

Do all my scenarios have to follow the same structure?

This is an editorial decision but for the sake of readability we would suggest that all your scenarios are written in the same format and the same tone. This allows the reader to more easily distinguish the differences between them and helps them to jump back and forth as they are considering what the implications of each future is.

Facilitation notes

The writing of scenarios is usually led by a single person. If more than one person is part of the writing process, you should ensure that the tone

A toolkit for humanitarian action 169

and structure of each scenario is similar so that they can be used as a set. As with each step of your analysis, you should endeavour to validate the scenarios with as many experts as you can. The review process usually takes at least 2 weeks.

170   *A toolkit for humanitarian action*

THE STRATEGY TREE

The Strategy Tree is a fundamental tool for strategy development purposes. This tool is predominantly a combination of the causal analysis tool (also called situational analysis, problem analysis or just a problem tree) and an objectives analysis tool used in project planning approaches. The Strategy Tree is used as an additional layer of analysis for each of the scenarios in a foresight study, enabling you to design a specific strategy for each potential future.

The Strategy Tree gives you the structure to outline the cause–effect relationship between factors in your scenario in a succinct and easily digestible way while not losing the complexity of your system. It is an analytical tool which will enable you to map out the anatomy of the cause–effect dynamics between interconnected and even contradictory factors and identify a hierarchy of objectives, including win–win solutions, strategic options and finally a holistic strategy for your scenario.

A Strategy Tree is an iterative process of analysis on three levels:

Causal analysis: your scenario's factors are categorised into problems and opportunities, which are then reframed in a diagram of causality according to a cause–effect and time sequence logic.

Objectives analysis: problems are converted into objectives, cause–effect links are transformed to means–end relations and the diagram of causality becomes a diagram of objectives, illustrating a hierarchy of the objectives.

Strategy analysis: the hierarchy of the objectives is analysed, strategic options and unrealistic objectives are identified, and finally a draft strategy is outlined.

The three levels of analysis outlined correspond respectively to Step 2 (problem analysis), 3 (objective analysis) and 4 (strategy analysis) in the analysis stage of the Logical Framework Approach (LFA), when LFA is applied to the identification phase in Project Cycle Management (EuropeAid 2004, p. 60).

Prerequisites

Building a Strategy Tree should be structured as a participative workshop to prompt a discussion with experts and stakeholders. Before you begin to plan your Strategy Tree workshop, you should have already completed writing your scenarios (founded on a process of structural analysis) or have obtained quality scenarios from an external source which you are able to exploit.

A toolkit for humanitarian action 171

You cannot conduct a Strategy Tree workshop without a set of scenarios. Each scenario is the foundation that will allow you to outline a specific strategy tailored to that potential future, and while in the end you will chose 'a strategy', having already considered the alternatives will enable you to have backup strategies ready in case your reality shifts towards another possible future, thereby mitigating some of the concerns about the uncertainty of your system.

The Strategy Tree workshop

To start, invite a group of participants to join the workshop. To identify them, you need to consider the viewpoint of your system of study:

For an organisational study: you will engage with the senior leadership team of the organisation. They will constitute three-fifths of the panel and they should identify the other two-fifths of participants from the stakeholders.

For a contextual study: you will engage with a choice of internal and/or external experts (by experts you should first consider people affected by crises), with a high level of understanding of the geography and/or thematic area and an interest in building a collaborative vision.

The quality of the participants is critical not only for the validity of your strategy, but also for getting buy-in and building consensus and consistency around the overall strategy development process.

How to do it

Each scenario needs a specific Strategy Tree and dedicated workshop, i.e. if you have four scenarios you need to split the participants in four subgroups (making sure you have a good mix of participants in each subgroup) and run four parallel exercises.

The **causal analysis (level 1)** establishes the cause-and-effect relationships between the problems and opportunities in your specific scenario. You should act as if the image of the future presented in the scenario you are working on is your present-day reality.

Step 1 Preparation

Assign each subgroup a scenario. In order for the participants to be fully versed on the scenario on which they will be working, you can ask them

172 *A toolkit for humanitarian action*

to complete one of the uptake exercises explored in Chapter 2 (see pp. 20–46).

After you are confident that the participants understand the dynamics of the scenario they will be working on, ask each subgroup to identify the problems and the opportunities created in each future, i.e. problems and opportunities for the organisation (for an organisational study), and problems and opportunities for stakeholders (for a contextual study). Participants should use coloured Post-it notes on a whiteboard/wall, e.g. orange for the problems and green for the opportunities. One consideration that is very important is that the problems should be expressed as negative statements of the specific factor (lack of, denied/decreased access to, risk of, etc.) and the opportunities as positive statements of a specific factor (surplus of, access to, innovations in, etc.)

Step 2 Diagram of causality

Once the list of problems and opportunities is complete for each scenario, ask each subgroup to position problems and opportunities according to a logic of cause and effect. They can start to position rooted/structural causes (problems or opportunities) at the bottom and, building on them, identify the effects of these problems or effects of each opportunity. They should proceed until all the problems and opportunities are placed on the board, connecting each entry with cause–effect arrows

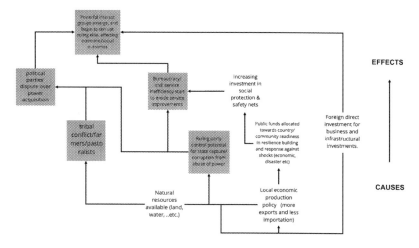

Figure 4.24 Example of diagram of causality (problems are in grey textboxes)

showing the linkages between them. The guiding question should be: What causes this problem/opportunity or what are the effects of this problem/opportunity?

At the end of the exercise, the subgroup should have built a *diagram of causality*, similar to a tree, as in Figure 4.24.

To finalise this step, ask each group to review the diagrams of the others and verify their rationality and comprehensiveness. Ask each subgroup if there are any other problems or opportunities to consider and allow them to add/modify the diagrams' components.

The **objectives analysis (level 2)** describes the process of turning each problem into a solution and converting the relationship of cause–effect into means–end links. The solutions to the problems you have identified and the pre-existing opportunities from your causality diagram become objectives linked and ordered according to a logic of means–end.

Step 3 From problems to objectives

Once the diagram of causality is reviewed and finalised, ask each subgroup to focus on the problems and convert them into solutions, expressed as positive achievements. For example, the problem 'the harvest is destroyed' is converted in the solution 'preconditions for agricultural production are re-established'. Once you have turned all the problems from your diagram of causality into solutions, you should review the pre-existing links of cause and effect which you had established. You must verify if the links that were established still make sense under a logic of means–end, and erase the linkages that are in place which do not.

Step 4 The diagram of objectives

In the means–end logic the guiding question is, What are the means (lower-level solutions/opportunities) for that end (higher-level solutions)? Some of the pre-existing cause–effect links will turn into means–end logics; others will disappear because the solution of a problem or an eventual opportunity is an end to itself, no longer connecting to a high-level solution. If you think that the link between the solutions/ opportunities are still valid but that it is no longer coherently represented, you can always revise the formulation of the solution (though always to be expressed as positive achievements).

Once the conversion is done, all these interlinked new solutions and pre-existing opportunities are objectives and are presented in a *diagram of objectives* showing a means–end hierarchy. Because of the process of

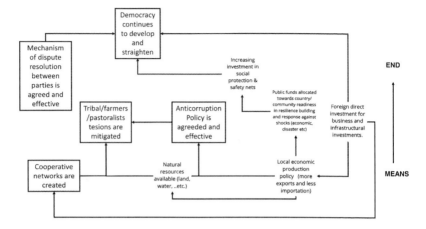

Figure 4.25 Example of diagram of objectives

transformation, the diagram of objectives may change form compared to the diagram of causality, as in Figure 4.25.

Step 5 Reviewing

To finalise it, review the diagram and verify its rationality and comprehensiveness. Ask the subgroup if there are any complementary solutions to consider and ask them to add new objectives that are achievable and suitable if they are relevant and necessary to achieve the objective at the next higher level. Finally, delete objectives that are unrealistic, but ensure that you're still being sufficiently ambitious and innovative in what you contribute to.

The **strategy analysis (level 3)** studies the hierarchies of the objectives and helps you to identify your strategic options. The strategy analysis outlines the draft strategy for your specific scenario.

Step 6 Identifying strategic options

Once the diagram of objectives is reviewed and finalised, ask each subgroup to highlight all the objectives which are the end–objectives of a minimum of two objectives at the lower level. Only the objectives that have two or more points of connection with lower-level objectives or opportunities on the diagram can be considered to be a strategic option (see examples in the black boxes in Figure 4.26).

A toolkit for humanitarian action 175

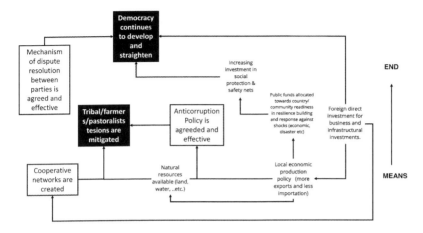

Figure 4.26 Example of diagram of objectives with strategic options (in black textboxes)

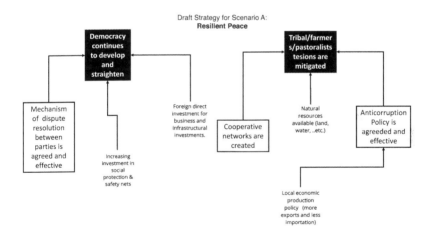

Figure 4.27 Example of outlined strategy draft

A strategic option can be a potential programme (with many projects) or a potential project (with many outcomes) (see Chapter 3 for more information on these concepts, pp. 47–78). A diagram of objectives contains many strategic options and their combination outlines a draft strategy. Using our example, a draft strategy could look like Figure 4.27.

176   *A toolkit for humanitarian action*

Step 7 Draft scenario strategies

After the combination of the general objectives (as in the black boxes of Figure 4.27), each draft strategy should be named by the subgroup. In Figure 4.27, the draft strategy for scenario A was named 'Resilient Peace'. The 'Resilient Peace' draft strategy is constituted of two general objectives (programmes) underpinned by three specific objectives (projects) and supported by the unchanged opportunities outlined in our diagram of causality.

Frequently asked questions

How many people can participate in a Strategy Tree workshop?

The number of participants has an impact on the performance of the workshop. It depends on the number of scenarios you have; try to limit your participants to a maximum of 6 per subgroup, which means an overall maximum of 24 if you have four scenarios, 30 if you have five scenarios, etc.

What you do when the executive is reluctant to include communities in the panel?

Stakeholders are the cornerstone of the strategy itself. Try to convince your leaders that without the contribution of people affected by crises, all the strategies that are designed have a risk of failure because they may not be an accurate representation of the problems that need to be addressed and the extant capacities of the communities or the opportunities they have outside of the formal humanitarian system. It is critical that you have a minimum representation or a channel of participation during the process.

Can I work from someone else's scenarios?

If you haven't got the time to go through a foresight exercise yourself, you can decide to work on scenarios built and provided by external sources. In this case, during the imprinting in Step 1 spend time ensuring that the participants understand the dynamics at play in each future and the consequences of them.

Facilitation notes

The Strategy Tree workshop is a collaborative exercise that can be performed physically or virtually. If performed physically, make sure you have a nominated leader that you have briefed on the exercise to support each subgroup. Regardless of if the workshop is physical or virtual you should rotate among the subgroups to ensure that they are able to complete the exercise.

With either format of workshop, you need to pay particular attention to the scenario uptake in Step 1: the subgroups of participants needs to really dive into the specificity of the scenario and act as if it was not a possible future but their reality. Also, the three levels of analysis need to be framed in three unique periods.

Level 1 (Steps 1 and 2) can be quite time-consuming and you should pay particular attention to the list of problems and opportunities and how they are formulated. Do not hesitate to remind people that problems are formulated as negative statements, whereas opportunities are formulated as positive potential changes.

Note: If the participants are the same group that have gone through the structural analysis and the scenarios writing, you can also suggest a tip. They can be inspired by the factors in the middle and high important areas of the MIU to begin to identify their problems and their opportunities.

Steps 3, 4, and 5 in Level 2 can be quick, but the process can difficult for some participants, particularly when it comes to questioning the logic of causality and transforming it to a means–end logic. It is important that you ensure each subgroup verifies whether all their pre-existing links are still valid under the means–end logic. The fact that a link of causality disappears doesn't mean that the resultant problem or opportunity disappears. For a problem to disappear, all the underlying causes need to be solved. Second, you should consider the time sequence: only if the achievement of the underlying solutions solve a resultant problem immediately could you consider erasing it. Usually the inertia in your system of study and its complexity means that there is always some delay between those actions.

In Step 6 you need to pay attention to the identification of the strategic options. A strategic option is an end–objective with a minimum of two lower-level objectives connecting to it. Sometimes, if there are lots of connections, the participants might become confused. You should remind them that only the objectives that have two or more points of connection with lower-level objectives or opportunities on the diagram can be considered to be a strategic option. A simple way to make this exercise of identification easier is to use the structure of a triangle and depict its tip as a strategic option: only if the triangle has a tip at the top do you have a strategic option (Figure 4.28).

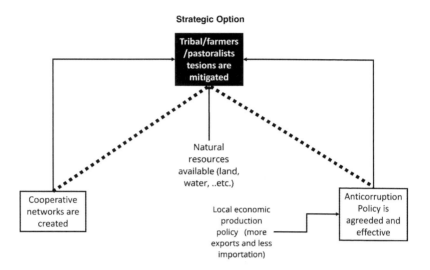

Figure 4.28 Use of a triangle tip to identify a strategic option

You should allow some group discussion for Step 7. It is important that the group visualise the combination of strategic options and name the strategy themselves with very limited facilitation.

A physical Strategy Tree workshop with 24 people, 4 scenarios, 1 facilitator and 4 assistants/support can be performed in 5 hours.

Virtual facilitation notes (3.5–6 hours, with no breaks)

You can run a Strategy Tree workshop virtually, following the same steps as those outlined above, using a virtual whiteboard. Here is some guidance on how to adapt the steps above to an online setting.

Preparation

i. Circulate all the scenarios to all participants prior to the workshop.
ii. Before the workshop, prepare your virtual whiteboard with as many fields or subareas as you have scenarios (one field for each scenario). In each field, list the title of the scenario and some visuals recalling the main descriptive elements of it. On each field, place an orange and green Post-it note, orange for problems and green for opportunities.

A *toolkit for humanitarian action*   179

iii. Prepare a short presentation to explain the overall process to the participants for Step v and an explanation for Step x.
iv. Prepare your class and breakrooms by splitting the participants in as many subgroups as the number of the scenarios.

Workshop

v. Open the workshop with an introduction to the exercise (using your presentation) and ensure that all participants are confident in being able to manipulate the software. (15 minutes)
vi. Begin with Step 1, asking each subgroup to list the problems on the orange Post-it and the opportunities on the green Post-it. Insist that the problems should expressed as negative statements and the opportunities as positive statements. If you are the only facilitator, rotate among the groups supporting them in the process of optimising their input, synthesising their problems/opportunities, removing duplicate notes and grouping those entries which are very similar. (30–60 minutes)
vii. Once the list of problems and opportunities is complete for each scenario, continue with Step 2 by asking each subgroup to position and link the orange Post-its (problems) and the green Post-its (opportunities) according to a logic of cause and effect. If you are the only facilitator, rotate among the groups supporting them to position root causes (problems or opportunities) at the bottom and building on them. They should proceed until all the problems and opportunities are placed on the board and interlinked. (60–90 minutes)
viii. When the diagrams of causality are completed, bring all the participants back together and provide the space for 10–15 minutes of debriefing on the exercise and a question-and-answer session. At this point you need to allow for a break so that you can prepare the whiteboard for the next level. During the break, duplicate each diagram of causality and reduce the size of the copy moving it to the side of the field and locking its position so that it cannot be modified. You should also make a digital copy of the diagram of causality for your records. (15 minutes)
ix. After your break, you can start Step 3 by asking each subgroup to focus on the orange Post-it notes (problems) and converting them into solutions, expressed as positive achievements. Once they have done this they should change the colour of the Post-it note to green. After all the notes on the diagram are green, ask each group to review the pre-existing links of cause and effect between the new

180 *A toolkit for humanitarian action*

solutions and the opportunities, and then transform them to means–end links according to the instructions in Step 3. If you are the only facilitator, rotate among the groups supporting them in the process of turning pre-existing cause–effect links into means–end logics, and eventually erasing links and pre-existing problems according to the instructions in Step 3. Continue with Steps 4 and 5. (30–60 minutes)

x. Once the diagrams of objectives are completed, ask the participants for their feedback on the process and respond to any questions they may have. Then introduce the concept of 'strategic option', as explained in Step 6, and use the triangle tip (see preceding 'Facilitation notes') in your presentation to help the participants identify the strategic options in their subgroups. (20–30 minutes)

xi. Return to the virtual whiteboard for Step 6 asking each subgroup to identify their strategic options by placing red squares around the green Post-it notes depicting the end–objective and to list on their field on the virtual board the combination of end–objectives and their specific lower-level objectives, thereby outlining their draft scenario strategy. Finally ask them to put a name to their draft scenario strategy. (60–90 minutes)

Resources: a set of scenarios, a preloaded virtual whiteboard and an explanatory presentation.

A toolkit for humanitarian action   181

ACTOR/OBJECTIVE MATRIX (MAO)

The MAO is the second part of the MACTOR method. It builds from you MID (MID, pp. 146–162) and is used to assess your strategy through the lens of the most influential actors in your system.

The MAO is used to build on the Strategy Tree workshop, enabling you to refine your draft scenarios strategies by testing your strategic options against the game of actors analysis (MID). Your strategic options are tested against the game of actors in your system of study to identify potential stratagems where they are useful and refine your draft scenario strategy.

We use the term 'stratagem' to mean an unconventional tactic to manipulate the lower-level objectives in your strategic options to make them more achievable using misdirection. A stratagem is an unconventional approach which you apply to gain an advantage in your game of actors. Often in humanitarian action you do not need to exploit stratagems to achieve your strategy as your strategy can be implemented in a transparent manner. However, particularly in campaigning, advocacy and lobbying some misdirection is needed.

Prerequisites

The MAO requires a participative workshop to prompt a discussion with experts and stakeholders. In order to conduct the MAO, it is necessary to first have a set of scenarios for your system (either developed yourself using a process of structural analysis or provided by an outside source), a completed MID (or a preselected group of the most influential actors in your system with some basic analysis from an external source) and a set of draft scenario strategies which have been developed for each of the futures you are considering using the Strategy Tree tool.

The MAO workshop

To start, build a coherent group where all the participants have the background information to contribute to the workshop. For this you need to select the workshop participants according to the viewpoint of your system of study.

For an organisational study: you will engage with the senior leadership team of the organisation. They will constitute three-fifths of the panel and they should identify the other two-fifths of participants from the stakeholders.

182 *A toolkit for humanitarian action*

For a contextual study: you will engage with a choice of internal and/or external experts (by experts you should first consider people affected by crises), with a high level of understanding of the geography and/or thematics and an interest in building a collaborative vision.

The quality of the participants is critical not only for the validity of your MAO workshop, but also for getting buy-in and building consensus and consistency around the overall strategy development process. If you are building your MAO workshop on the foundation of your structural analysis and strategy development exercises, we recommend you to use the same group you built for the MID workshop.

How to do it

At the end of your Strategy Tree exercise, each scenario has been shaped into a draft strategy defined by the compilation of strategic options. These draft scenario strategies are a combination of the high-level objectives you identified which are underpinned by lower ones. If you have worked on four scenarios you are going to have a set of four draft scenario strategies that need to be refined. For the MAO workshop, you need to begin by splitting the participants in four subgroups (making sure you have a good mix of participants in each subgroup) and run four parallel exercises to conduct the MAO.

The purpose of the MAO is to consider each of the strategic options of your draft scenario strategy to identify an effective combination that fits the dynamics of the game of actors in your system of study.

Step 1 Preparation

The participants need to read some light preparatory work before attending the workshop, particularly if they haven't contributed to the structural analysis or strategy development. You should share your MID chart, a summary of the scenarios and the Strategy Trees (the draft scenario strategies with the underpinning strategic options) with all participants. When doing so, you should include a brief introduction, where you explain the purpose of the MAO workshop.

Step 2 Set the MAO table

Review your MID chart and select only the most influential actors: the kings (or knights in absence of kings), bishops and queens. You should also select the pawns above the line of control, starting from a reasonable

A toolkit for humanitarian action 183

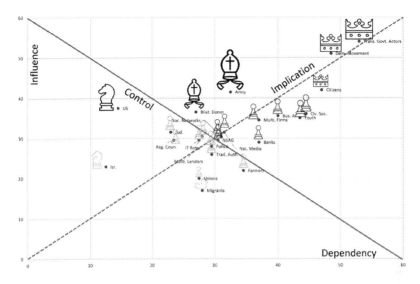

Figure 4.29 Case study for MID chart Sudan 2027, with actors selection (bolded icons)

level of influence. Figure 4.29 is a case study on Sudan 2027 shown in the MID guide (MID, pp. 146–162) as an example.

In this case, we have selected the most influential knight (because there are no kings), then all the pawns above the line of control with an influence value greater than 30 (we have considered that criteria of influence reasonable for this grid), then the bishops and the queens.

Note: When you are selecting your influential actors from your MID, make sure that you have no more than 15 actors. You can also use this limit to fix your reasonable level of influence for selecting pawns (i.e. it should not be so low that you need to take more than 15 actors).

Once you have selected your actors, prepare a MAO table by building an Actor × Objective grid in a spreadsheet (one for each scenario), using your selected actors from your MID and the objectives from your draft scenario strategy (the general objectives).

Then build an implication column and row at the end of your table, which will be filled by a formula summing the absolute values of each column and each row of the Actor × Objective table. Finally build two supplementary rows, one summing all the positive values of each column

184 *A toolkit for humanitarian action*

(the agreements) and the second summing all the negative values of each column (disagreements). See Table 4.13 as an example.

This spreadsheet will be used as a base for your workshop; the cells need to be filled in during the group discussion.

Step 3 Workshop

At the beginning of the workshop, after a short introduction of the participants, you will split them into their groups (you need the same number of groups as scenario strategies) and assign each group a draft scenario strategy to work on. Then, share the relevant MAO table with each group. You should assume that all the participants have done their homework and they have a good knowledge of the MID chart and all the Strategy Trees. However, it can be useful to provide a copy of the MID chart and the specific Strategy Tree to each subgroup for reference during the session.

Then, you will instruct them on the purpose of the MAO workshop and explain, in detail, how the MAO table will be filled by a swift subgroup discussion and vote. Particular attention needs to be paid to how you will define the values in the empty cells. Each cell represents your analysis of the relationship between an actor and an objective: the nature of the implication of an actor over an objective and the level of implication of an objective over an actor.

First, the group will be tasked with assigning the nature of the relationship between an actor and an objective by using a mathematical sign (positive, negative or zero) according to the following scale:

- If the actor is neutral (i.e. they have no position) on an objective, you place a 0 in the cell
- If the actor agrees with (i.e. supports it) an objective, you place a '+' sign in the cell
- If the actor disagrees with (i.e. does not support it) an objective, you place a '−' sign in the cell

This is demonstrated in the example in Table 4.14 by the black arrows analysing the relationship between actor 2 and objective 2 (the 'actor2 x obj2' cell).

Table 4.13 Empty MAO table

	Objective 1	Objective 2	Objective ..	Objective N		Implication Absolute S
Actor 1	actor1 x obj1	actor1 x obj2	actor1 x obj..	actor1 x objN		=sum(abs (actor1 x obj1; actor1 x obj2; actor1 x obj..; actor1 x objN)
Actor 2	actor2 x obj1	actor2 x obj2	actor2 x obj..	actor2 x objN		etc.
Actor 3	actor3 x obj1	actor3 x obj2	actor3 x obj..	actor3 x objN		etc.
Actor ..	actor.. x obj1	actor.. x obj2	actor.. x obj..	actor.. x objN		etc.
Actor N	actorN x obj1	actorN x obj2	actorN x obj..	actorN x objN		etc.
Implication AbsoluteS	=sum(abs (actor1 x obj1; actor2 x obj1; actor.. x obj1; actor1 x objN)	etc.	etc.	etc.		S
Agreements S (+)	=sum(+)	etc.	etc.	etc.		
Desagrements S (-)	=sum(-)	etc.	etc.	etc.		

Table 4.14 Example of a MAO table with cells filled with relevant signs, figures and sense of the analysis

	Objective 1	Objective 2	Objective ..	Objective N		Implication Absolute S
Actor 1	*actor1 x obj1*	*actor1 x obj2*	*actor1 x obj..*	*actor1 x objN*		=sum(abs (actor1 x obj1; actor1 x obj2; actor1 x obj..; actor1 x objN)
Actor 2	*actor2 x obj1*	*actor2 x obj2*	*actor2 x obj..*	*actor2 x objN*		etc.
Actor 3	*actor3 x obj1*	*actor3 x obj2*	*actor3 x obj..*	*actor3 x objN*		etc.
Actor ..	*actor.. x obj1*	*actor.. x obj2*	*actor.. x obj..*	*actor.. x objN*		etc.
Actor N	*actorN x obj1*	*actorN x obj2*	*actorN x obj..*	*actorN x objN*		etc.
Implication Absolute S	=sum(abs (actor1 x obj1; actor2 x obj1; actor.. x obj1; actor1 x objN)	etc.	etc.	etc.		S
Agreements S (+)	=sum(+)	etc.	etc.	etc.		
Desagrements S (-)	=sum(-)	etc.	etc.	etc.		

If the sign selected is not 0, then the group will be tasked with assessing the degree to which the objective has an influence on the actor. You assess the value of the relationship between the objective and the actor by assigning a numerical value (0 to 4) according to the following scale:

- If the objective has no influence on an actor, you must replace the sign in that cell with 0
- If the objective has an influence on (or jeopardises) the operations of the actor, you would place a 1 in the cell
- If the objective has an influence on (or jeopardises) the tactics of the actor, you would place a 2 in the cell
- If the objective has an influence on (or jeopardises) the strategy of the actor, you would place a 3 in the cell
- If the objective has an influence on (or jeopardises) the existence of the actor, you would place a 4 in the cell

This relationship is illustrated by the grey arrows in the actor 2 and objective 2 analysis represented in Table 4.14.

Once you have explained how to fill the empty cells of the MAO table, it is important to ask participants if they are familiar with the meaning of 'strategy', 'tactic' and 'operations' and their differences. A good enough collective understanding of these terms is critical for the success of the exercise. If you need to explain these concepts further, you will find more explanation in Chapter 3 (p. 52).

The implication column and row will be automatically computed as the exercise progresses as the sum of the absolute values in the Actor x Objective cells of the MAO table (the actor's implication is the sum of each row, the objective's implication as the sum of each column).

The disagreements and agreements rows will be automatically computed as well, respectively as the sum of the negative value and the sum of the positive value Actor x Objective cells of the MAO table.

Step 4 Filling the MAO table

After you have introduced the workshop, explained the mechanics of how to fill the table and responded to any questions, it's time for the exercise to start. First, you want to fix some facilitation rules:

Voting and timekeeping. Apart from the facilitator, all the participants vote by expressing first a sign (+, −, 0) according to the level of implication of an actor over an objective (see Step 3) and if the winning vote is different from 0, then a value from 0 to 4 according to the level

188 *A toolkit for humanitarian action*

of implication of one objective over an actor (see Step 3). If the sign is − or +, to fill the relative Actor x Objective value, the facilitator will input the mathematical mode or modal value which is the value expressed most often by the votes of the participants. For example, if eight participants vote, respectively 0, 0, 1, 3, 1, 0, 0, 0, then the facilitator will input 0. In case of a tie, e.g. 0, 0, 1, 1, 1, 1, 0, 0, the facilitator will allow a discussion of no more than 5 minutes where each side (in this example those who voted 1 vs. those who voted 0) will present their rationale and then run a new voting session to see if anyone has changed their minds. In case of a tie that cannot be broken through discussion, the facilitator will cast the deciding vote. Remember, if the level of implication of one objective over an actor is 0, it overwrites the eventual − or + vote and is replaced with a 0.

The *role of the facilitator* should rotate among the attendees. Each attendee should complete at least one complete row (i.e. the inputs for one actor). During their time as facilitator, the facilitator is the timekeeper, the mediator in case of a tie and the tie-breaking vote if necessary. The facilitator manages the input into the MAO spreadsheet and fills it in according to the outcome of the voting. If your group is different from the one that has performed the MID workshop, you should start with the first row or two to show an example of how the facilitation works and then you can hand it over to another member of the group to take forward, switching facilitators every row or every other row.

Once your Actor x Objective cells are filled, the implication column and row will be computed (usually your spreadsheet can be formatted as a formula so this is automatic) as the sum of the absolute values of the Actor x Objective cells, and you should obtain a value for each actor and for each objective.

Step 5 MAO interpretation

After all the MAO tables are completed, it is time to share the MAO interpretation. You can do this directly on the table with filled cells like in Table 4.15.

The most involved actors. In the implication column each cell represents the sum of the absolute implication values for each actor. The highest value identifies the actors most implicated with your draft scenario strategy. By this, we mean the ones that are most intensely in concurrence or disagreement with the objectives in your scenario strategy.

A toolkit for humanitarian action 189

Table 4.15 Example of a MAO table with filled in cells and interpretation

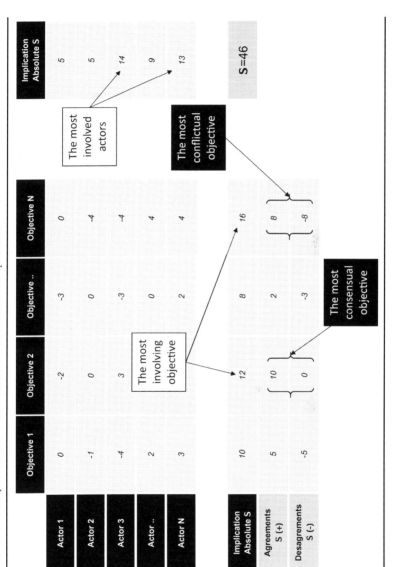

190 *A toolkit for humanitarian action*

The most involved objectives. In the implication row, each cell represents the sum of the absolute implication values for each objective. The highest value identifies the objective which has the most interest (either positive or negative) from the actors in your system.

The most consensual objective. In the agreement and disagreement rows, each cell represents the sum of the positive values for each objective and the sum of negative values for each objective. Respectively, if the arithmetic sum between an agreement and a disagreement cell results in the highest positive value, that indicates that it is the most consensual objective (see Table 4.15).

The most conflictual objective. If the arithmetic sum between an agreement and a disagreement cell results in 0 or the nearest value to 0, that indicates it is the most conflictual objective. If you have two equally conflictual objectives, you should focus on the one with the highest absolute sum (see Table 4.15).

Step 6 Design of stratagems

The MAO analysis is very useful for refining your draft scenario strategies. This process helps to ensure that the strategy is well designed to be effective in your game of actors. Where possible you want to choose the most consensual objectives and avoid the most conflictual ones. However, sometimes you cannot avoid the most conflictual objectives, as it is at the core of your purpose, or you might have many conflictual objectives and therefore need to take some forward.

In these cases, you can disarticulate the lower-level objectives from the conflictual higher-level objective of your strategic option and try to reconfigure them in your strategy to find a more advantageous approach. The disarticulation and rearticulation of lower-level objectives of strategic options to find a more advantageous approach is a tactical-level exercise which enables you to design stratagems.

The rearticulation of the lower-level objectives into alternative strategic options in your strategy can be a simple exercise, as you can follow the existing logic of means–end connections in your Strategy Tree. If necessary, you may need to force new means–end links by artificially creating new bonds with the lower-level objectives you intend to rearticulate, for example by changing the formulation of those objectives.

Once you have completed your MAO you can consider whether it is necessary to employ a strategy to achieve your objectives. If so, there are many stratagems where you can exploit your configuration of conflictual and consensual objectives to your advantage. Next we outline two examples.

The Trojan Horse. This applies when you have a consensual objective and a conflictual objective, both with a very high implication in your MAO. The Trojan Horse approach is when you hide the lower-level objectives of a conflictual strategic option within the most consensual one. The objectives underpinning the conflictual objective are disarticulated from it and embedded under the most consensual objective as new lower-level objectives or downgraded into the existing lower-level objective as outputs. This enables you to implement your conflictual objective in a more subtle and less confrontational way.

Divide and conquer. This approach applies when you have a set of conflictual objectives. By divide and conquer we mean exploiting the more conflictual objective to create divisions within the actors in your system and implementing an objective which is less conflictual directly or via a Trojan Horse while the actors are diverted by quarrelling or fighting. This stratagem is ultimately a diversionary tactic and works optimally when the conflictual objective involves all of the most influential actors.

The MAO workshop will allow each subgroup to refine their draft scenario strategies according to the game of actors. At the end of the exercise, all the subgroups will have produced a definitive combination of strategic options encapsulated in a refined scenario strategy with a title describing its core objectives.

Frequently asked questions

What is a reasonable level of influence when selecting the actors for the MAO?

It depends on the number of the actors you have in your MID chart: do not select more that 15 actors starting from the more influent at the top. The only exception to the rule of taking the most influent actors from your system is if you do not have a king you should prioritise including the knight of highest influence. For selecting pawns, do not include those that are under the line of control and focus on the ones concentrated in the centre of your chart and along the line of implication. Avoid the actors below the median line on the chart (to obtain its value divide the influence axis in two).

192 *A toolkit for humanitarian action*

***How do you rearticulate the specific objectives
underpinning a conflictual objective when there are
no existing links with other objectives?***

You should go back to the diagram of objectives in the Strategy Tree (end of Step 6 in the Strategy Tree guide) to see if the lower-level objectives of the strategic options have other means–end links with other lower-level objectives of alternative strategic options. It is rare that you end up identifying no links; in this case create intermediary objectives and related means–end links to another alternative strategic objective. Following those manipulations, your Strategy Tree will change form. Remember to save your previous version in case you require it as a reference if you need to design stratagems.

Facilitation notes

The MAO is a collaborative exercise that can be performed physically or virtually. If performed physically, make sure that for the MAO exercise you have a willing co-facilitator to support the subgroups. Whether the workshop is physical or virtual, you should rotate among the subgroups to ensure that they are able to complete the exercise.

We strongly recommend that you perform the MAO as a physical, virtual or hybrid workshop, as it ensures the highest quality of outputs. The MAO workshop is not as time-consuming as the MID, however a physical, virtual or hybrid workshop to complete an MAO table usually takes between 2 and 3 hours depending on the number of actors you are considering and the experience you have with the type of exercise.

If the group selected for the MAO workshop cannot (or won't) dedicate this much time to a group discussion, it is possible to perform Step 1 and Step 2 on a short virtual call, ask all participants to complete the MAO table (Step 3) individually and combine the results, and then host a second call for the interpretation and the stratagems in Step 4 and Step 5.

Virtual workshop

Though you can endeavour to run the full MAO workshop online, we recommend that if you are hosting the event virtually that you hold an introductory call and supplement that by asking each individual in each group to complete the MAO table on their own time before returning the completed sheets to you to compile. Then you should host a call to review the interpretation.

Preparation

i. You must ensure that participants are properly informed and prepared. As in Step 1, you must share your MID chart, a summary of the scenarios and the scenario strategies (draft strategies with the underpinning strategic options developed in your Strategy Tree). Include a brief introduction, in which you explain the purpose of the MAO and a list of the participants divided in as many subgroups as you have scenarios ahead the call, allowing 1 week for people to read the material. Then prepare your MAO table as in Step 1.
ii. You need to prepare a quiz to ensure that your participants understand the dynamics of the scenarios they are working on and the actor analysis that you shared.
iii. You need to prepare a series of live polls to gather feedback on the exercise.
iv. Prepare slides to explain how to interpret the MAO.

Virtual call 1: Introduction (40–60 minutes)

v. You should begin the call by explaining the purpose of the exercise. You can skip the introduction of the participants (but ask that they be visible if possible and put their name on the screen) if you are short on time. To complete the introduction of the session you should launch a quick quiz to check that the participants understand your actor analysis and the draft strategies produced in the Strategy Tree workshop. (15–30 minutes)
vi. Then share the MAO table, explaining how it is filled and give space for a question-and-answer session. As in Step 2, you need to explain how to fill the Actor × Objective cells, making sure to pay particular attention to the sequencing of the questions (first designating a sign and subsequently a number). (15 minutes)
vii. At the end of the call, share the MAO spreadsheet (embed in a little note on the level of implication and the relative sign, as well as the level of influence and the relative values) and fix a deadline (allow at least 1 week) to receive all the completed spreadsheets. (10 minutes)
viii. Offer an optional 30-minute call during the week for a question-and-answer session if necessary (set a date and time if there is interest).

Follow-up

194 *A toolkit for humanitarian action*

Once you have received the individual completed spreadsheets, combine them per subgroup in a master version, and in a new MAO table per subgroup fill all the Actor × Objective cells with a formula calculating the mode of all the values that were individually expressed. This operation can take more or less time depending on the software you are using and your familiarity with it. Prepare a few slides to explain how to interpret the MAO table (use the figures in Step 3).

Virtual call 2: MAO interpretation and stratagems design (1–1.5 hours)

ix. After welcoming the participants, launch a brief survey using your live polling platform to allow participants to express their individual feedback from the exercise. (15 minutes)
x. Share your presentation on the MAO interpretation. Start by showing the combined MAO per subgroup and reveal the MAO interpretation. Discuss if stratagems are necessary to achieve the scenario strategy and if so which stratagem would be most effective. (30–45 minutes)
xi. Open up discussion on the outcome of the MAO exercise. (15–30 minutes)
xii. At the end of the call fix a deadline (allow at least 3 days) to receive all the refined scenario strategies. (5 minutes)

Follow-up

Distribute the combined MAO table for each subgroup and final scenario strategies, and create and share a file with all the documents, records and slides.

Resources: presentation; survey or pre-prepared polls loaded on an accessible online platform; MAO table in a sharable format

Between the preparatory work, the MAO workshop (or the alternative individual contribution version) and the other tests, the Testing will take a maximum 2 weeks to be finalised.

TESTING

The robustness and relevancy tests explored in this guide were developed by Francois Bourse at Futuribles International in Paris.[3] They were developed to support decision makers in evaluating their strategies in a comprehensive and futures-focused way. These tools continue to be part of the Futuribles International training course.[4]

Testing is a succession of tools for strategy development purposes. By testing the robustness of your scenarios strategies against each of the possible futures that you have created and/or their relevance to an overarching strategy designed by an upper structure (e.g. alliance, federation, consortium, network), you can assess each scenario strategy that you have created.

Testing can also be used as a diagnostic tool. If you already have a strategy, you can use the testing tools outlined next to check your current strategy against new scenarios or to analyse your programme against a new overarching strategy.

Testing will perform two essential functions:

Robustness test: your scenarios strategies are tested against all the possible futures of your system of study to reveal how adaptable they are and support you in deciding which one to pursue

Relevancy test: your scenarios strategies are tested against an overarching strategy designed by an upper structure (e.g. alliance, federation, consortium, network) to judge the relevancy of your scenario strategies to wider goals to which you are committed to working and help you decide which one to pursue

Prerequisites

Each of the tools explored during the testing phase require a participative workshop to prompt a discussion between experts and stakeholders.

In order to conduct a robustness test, it is necessary to have a set of scenarios for your system (either developed yourself using a process of structural analysis or provided by an outside source) and a set of refined scenario strategies which have been developed for each of the futures you are considering using the Strategy Tree tool and the MAO workshop.

In order to conduct a relevancy test, it is necessary to have a set of refined scenario strategies which have been developed for each of the futures you are considering using the Strategy Tree tool, the MAO workshop, and the overarching strategy designed by an upper structure (e.g. alliance, federation, consortium, network) against which you want to compare your work.

The Testing workshop

To start, build a coherent group where all the participants have the background information to contribute to the appropriate workshop. For this you need to select the workshop participants according to the viewpoint of your system of study:

For an organisational study: you will engage with the senior leadership team of the organisation. They will constitute three-fifths of the panel and they should identify the other two-fifths of participants from the stakeholders.

For a contextual study: you will engage with a choice of internal and/or external experts (by experts you should consider first people affected by crises), with a high level of understanding of the geography and/or thematics and an interest in building a collaborative vision.

The quality of the participants is critical not only for the validity of your tests, but also for getting buy-in and building consensus and consistency around the overall strategy development process. If you are conducting your testing on the foundation of your strategy development process, we recommend you to use the same group you built for the MAO workshop.

How to do it

There are two parts to the testing workshop: the robustness test and the relevancy test.

Step 1 Preparation

To prepare the participants of your workshop in advance (especially if they have not been a part of the structural analysis, scenario development and strategy development processes) you should share the following documents: the scenario report, the refined scenario strategy for each scenario and the overarching strategy which you want to consider for your relevancy test. You should ask all participants to read and internalise the information contained in these documents before the workshop begins. If you have the time you can run one of the uptake exercises explored in Chapter 2 (pp. 20–46).

Step 2 Create the templates

Next you need to create the templates that you will use for the workshop itself. These can be constructed on a physical wall or a virtual whiteboard. To prepare for your robustness workshop, structure a Strategies × Scenarios table (as shown in Table 4.16) on a physical or virtual wall.

A toolkit for humanitarian action 197

Table 4.16 Example of robustness matrix, empty

	Scenario 1	Scenario 2	Scenario 3	Scenario 4
Strategy A				
Strategy B				
Strategy C				
Strategy D				

This matrix will be used as a basis for the robustness part of your workshop; the cells need to be filled in during the group discussion.

To prepare for your relevancy test, you first need to identify the global objectives from your overarching strategy that you will call 'overarching objectives' (or o. objectives), then plot a matrix of Scenario strategies × O. objectives on a physical or virtual wall (Table 4.17). Usually, the overarching objectives are easy to identify as they are defined as the goals of the organisation/structure.

Table 4.17 Example of Relevancy matrix, empty

	O. Objective 1	O. Objective 2	O. Objective 3	O. Objective 4
Strategy A				
Strategy B				
Strategy C				
Strategy D				

This matrix will be used as a base for your relevancy workshop; the cells need to be filled in during the group discussion.

Step 3 Workshop

When beginning your workshop, you should assume that all the attendees have a good knowledge of the scenarios, the strategies they have refined and the overarching strategy which you distributed before the workshop. However, it can be useful to provide a copy of all these documents for reference during the session as it is a significant amount of information for them to remember.

You should start by introducing the testing workshop, explaining that it will be made up of two tests, (the robustness test and the relevancy test), and then describe the difference between them and what the outcomes of each test will show you. You should inform participants that you will begin with the robustness test, so they should turn their attention to the scenarios and their corresponding strategies.

198 *A toolkit for humanitarian action*

You should then present the scenarios, talking through each of the potential futures that you have created. This will help the participants to engage more constructively with the tests as they progress through the workshop.

Step 4 Robustness test

Before you begin the robustness test you should reiterate its purpose: that it tests all your scenario strategies against each of the possible futures that you've created to give you an idea of how flexible your strategy is by assessing whether it can be effective in contexts (futures) it was not designed for. Then you must explain that the robustness template will be filled in by a vote.

The participants will be tasked with assessing the robustness of a strategy in each possible future (scenario) by assigning it a colour according to this scale: green/white = highly effective, yellow/grey = somewhat effective and orange/black = not at all effective.

The participants will be given grey, white and black Post-its, and they will vote individually by placing the Post-it of the appropriate colour on the board in the relevant square (i.e. in Table 4.18, if they believe that strategy would be effective in Scenario B they would place a green/white Post-it note in that square).

Table 4.18 Example of filled robustness matrix

	Scenario 1	Scenario 2	Scenario 3	Scenario 4
Strategy A				
Strategy B				
Strategy C				
Strategy D				

Step 5 Fill the robustness matrix

You should explain that you will complete the table by assessing the robustness of one strategy at a time. Take 5 minutes to outline the first

A *toolkit for humanitarian action* 199

strategy that you will be considering (e.g. Strategy A in Table 4.18) and ask participants to deliberate on how robust that strategy would be in the Scenarios 2, 3 and 4 – scenarios for which it was not designed. Give them 5 minutes to complete the first row (e.g. Strategy A in Table 4.18). Repeat the process with each of the remaining strategies until the matrix is complete.

Step 6 Discuss the robustness test outputs

Once the exercise is complete, you should have a discussion about the output that you have created. You can easily ascertain how robust each strategy options is: the lighter or greener the row, the more robust the specific strategy.

In Table 4.18, Strategy B seems to be the most robust across the four scenarios, while Strategy A is considered, by many in your group, to be ineffective in two of the four futures (Scenarios 3 and 4). This means that Strategy B could be riskier to pursue, as if your context shifts towards Strategy 3 and Strategy 4 you may quickly find you are working to a strategy that is not fit for purpose.

Next you move on to the relevancy test. You must first explain that the relevancy test tests all your scenario strategies against an overarching strategy determined by your global organisation, your alliance, your federation or your network. This test allows you to assess whether the scenario strategies you have designed are in line with the overarching strategy of your upper structure or another organisation with which you wish to work. Adhering to an overarching strategy can limit your strategic thinking and innovation and, by primarily basing your strategy on a global organisational strategy, it can create a one-size-fits-all approach that is not well adapted to the context in which you are working. This is why the relevancy test is usually done last. It is necessary to ensure your strategy's relevancy and effectiveness, not adherence, to an overarching strategy drive your thinking.

Step 7 Introduce the relevancy test

After you have explained why the relevancy test is being conducted, you should take 10 minutes to present the overarching strategy and the overarching objectives that you will be using to ensure they are clear to everyone. By this point, you can assume that participants are familiar with the refined scenario strategies that you are assessing. You then need to explain how the matrix will be filled in by a vote, in a similar fashion to the robustness test. As for the robustness test, the group will be tasked

200 *A toolkit for humanitarian action*

with assigning the fit of a scenario strategy against each of the overarching objectives with a colour according to the following scale: green/white = aligns well, yellow/grey = some alignment and orange/black = no alignment.

Step 8 Fill the relevancy table

The participants will then be given Post-its and they will vote individually using the appropriate colour to express their opinion of the relevancy of each strategy. You can choose to approach this test in a similar fashion to the robustness test or you can instruct participants to complete the whole table at once. As they are now more familiar with the process and the specific strategies that they are working on and they are likely already somewhat well versed in the overarching objectives, it is not too overwhelming for them to consider the table as a whole.

Step 9 Discuss the relevancy test outputs

Have a discussion to interpret your relevancy test; you can easily read the visualisation. The lighter or greener the row is, the better the scenario strategy fits with the global strategy. As is demonstrated in Table 4.19, Strategy A seems to fit the best for the overarching strategy, while Strategy C has the most significant clash with O. objective 4.

Table 4.19 Example of filled relevancy matrix

	O. Objective 1	O. Objective 2	O. Objective 3	O. Objective 4
Strategy A				
Strategy B				
Strategy C				
Strategy D				

The robustness and the relevancy test are useful tools to provide some additional analysis for deciding which strategy to pursue. However, when the time comes to make a decision on which scenario strategy to implement, it is necessary that the testing remains an aid for decision-making and does not replace it. It is important that you, as the facilitator, steer your group to understand that no matter the outcomes of the testing exercise, they are free to choose the strategy they want to pursue. If they are ready to invest and take a risk on a less flexible or less relevant strategy because they think it will be more effective or they want to achieve it, they are free to do so. The power of strong leadership and consensus among a group of implementers should override the outcomes of the testing exercise.

Frequently asked questions

In the robustness test, why are some Strategy × Scenario cells all white or green?

These cells are preset. As the scenario strategies have been designed for that specific scenario via the Strategy Tree, they are assumed to be effective. For example, in Table 4.18, Strategy A was designed to be effective in Scenario 1 and as a result their corresponding cell is pre-filled to be fully white.

Why is the relevancy test not used to assess the strategic options of each scenario strategy before it is finalised?

The relevancy test can be used before, at the stage of refining your scenario strategy in the subgroups, or after you have conducted the MAO. This approach might be suitable for a very hierarchical organisation, where the space for deviation from the overarching strategy is limited or non-existent. However, we strongly recommend that you avoid doing it at the earlier stage when possible and apply the relevancy test only at the end to the refined draft scenario strategy because this way you guarantee the maximum degree of freedom for innovation within your organisation and also creativity among the participants. If you want to apply the relevancy test in the subgroups at the strategic options level, make sure that all the subgroups perform this test in the same way. The final scenario strategies need to be balanced in terms of innovation (or lack of it) to perform the robustness test.

Facilitation notes

We strongly recommend that you perform the testing as a physical, virtual or hybrid workshop, as it ensures the highest quality of the outputs.

202 *A toolkit for humanitarian action*

The Testing workshop is not time-consuming; a physical, virtual or hybrid workshop to complete the robustness and relevancy tables usually takes between 1 and 2 hours.

If the group selected for the testing workshop cannot (or won't) dedicate this much time to a group discussion, it is possible to perform the exercise as a survey and subsequently compile the results.

Virtual workshop

If you are conducting your testing workshop virtually you should invite participants to join you on a 1–2 hour call on a virtual whiteboard.

Preparation

i. You must ensure that participants are properly informed and prepared. As in Step 1, you should share the scenarios, the refined scenario strategies, and the overarching strategy of your upper structure before the workshop. With this preparatory material you should include a brief introduction, in which you explain the purpose of the testing exercise and a list of the participants.

ii. Create a short quiz on the dynamics of your scenarios, their applicable strategies and the organisation's overarching strategy to ensure that participants are well versed on the analysis before your workshop begins.

iii. Prepare your virtual whiteboard using the figures in Step 2 of the robustness test and the Relevancy test as your frames. Next to each table load a Post-it note for each colour on the scale that you will be using (white, grey and black; or green, yellow and orange) so you can use them as an example.

iv. For the robustness test, preset the cases in white or green for the scenario/scenario strategy correspondences.

Tip: As you would usually conduct the robustness test first, it can be useful to hide the relevancy table and reveal it only when you are ready to conduct the relevancy exercise. Otherwise, you may find participants getting confused between the two tables.

Virtual workshop (2–2.5 hours)

v. To begin the exercise, after the participants have introduced themselves, launch your quick quiz to check that they understand the scenarios, the scenarios strategies, and the overarching strategy of your upper structure. As in Step 3, you should also reiterate the purpose of the testing exercise, ensure that everyone can access the virtual whiteboard and allow some time for questions. (20 minutes)

vi. Explain that you will first focus on the robustness test, then share the virtual board demonstrating how to vote with the Post-it notes. As in Step 4, you need to explain how to fill the cells, insisting on the significance of the colour scale. Then complete the table by assessing the robustness of one strategy at a time as in Steps 5 and 6. (30–40 minutes)

vii. Facilitate a short discussion to reflect on the outcome of your robustness test as in Step 7. You could ask participants if they are surprised by any of the outcomes and what the results of the robustness test say to them as decision makers. (10–20 minutes)

viii. Repeat Steps ii and iii with the relevancy test as in Steps 8, 9 and 10. (30 minutes)

ix. When you are concluding the exercise, make sure that you stress that the test should be used to support, not replace, their decision-making. Insist that despite the test results, the choice of which strategy to implement belongs to them. (15 minutes)

Follow-up

Once the tests are performed, suggest that the decision makers meet and discuss all the outputs from the test in more detail. Then recommend that they make a decision on which specific strategy they wish to implement. Reassure them that despite the fact that they need to choose one strategy, the others will be always available if they need to shift between them because of a change in the situation (scenario or overarching strategy).

Resources: presentation, quiz, tests frames and Post-it notes on a virtual board

Notes

1 This question is adapted from the definition of uncertainty "an individuals perceived inability to predict something accurately" (Millken, 1987)

2 Mactor method has been developed by François Bourse and Michel Godet in 1989. A free software is available (in English and French) to help the user to easily obtain the results of the calculus treatments. MACTOR Software is available on http://www.laprospective.fr/methodes-de-prospective.html

3 Durance, P., Monti, R. and Bourse, F., 2014. La prospective stratégique en action. Paris: Odile Jacob, Chapitre 18.

4 Futuribles. 2021. Pratiques de la prospective stratégique. [online] Available at: <https://www.futuribles.com/fr/formation/methodes-et-outils-de-la-prospective-str_0/> [Accessed 27 February 2021].

204 *A toolkit for humanitarian action*

References

Aguilar, F (1967) *Scanning the Business Environment*, New York, MacMillan.

Brown J L and Agnew N M (1982) Corporate agility, *Business Horizons*, 25(2), pp. 29–33, ISSN 0007-6813, https://doi.org/10.1016/0007-6813(82)90101-X.

Candy, S and Dunagan, J, (2017) Designing an experiential scenario: the people who vanished, *Futures*, 86, pp.136–153. DOI: https://doi.org/10.1016/j.futures.2016 .05.006

Durance, P, Monti, R and Bourse, F (2014) *La prospective stratégique en action*, Paris, Odile Jacob.

Europaid (2004) *Project Cycle Management Guidelines: Aid Delivery Methods*, Vol.1, Bruxelles, accessed on 19/03/2021, https://europa.eu/capacity4dev/iesf/docu ments/aid-delivery-methods-project-cycle-management-guidelines-europaid -2004

European Parliament (2014) *The Impact of Remittances on Developing Countries*, Brussels, Policy Department, DG for External Policies

Futuribles (2021) Pratiques de la prospective stratégique, accessed on: 27/02/2021, https://www.futuribles.com/fr/formation/methodes-et-outils-de-la-prospective -str_0/>

Gladwell, Malcolm (2005) *Blink: The Power of Thinking Without Thinking* (18th ed.), New York, Little, Brown and Co. Harvard.

Godet, M (1994) *From Anticipation to Action: A Handbook of Strategic Prospective*, Paris, France, UNESCO Publishing.

Heuer, Richard (2014) *Structured Analytic Techniques for Intelligence Analysis*, Washington D.C., CQ Press.

Inter-Agency Research and Analysis Network (2016) *Future of Aid: INGOs in 2030*, London, IARAN, accessed on: 11/02/2021, https://www.iaran.org/future-of-aid

Inter-Agency Research and Analysis Network (2018) *Voices to Choices: Expanding Crisis-affected People's Influence Over Aid Decisions: An Outlook to 2040*, IARAN, accessed on: 15/03/2021, https://www.iaran.org/voices-to-choices

Inter-Agency Research and Analysis Network (2020) *COVID 19 Preliminary Scenarios for the Humanitarian Ecosystem*, London, IARAN, accessed on: 20/02/2021, https ://static1.squarespace.com/static/593eb9e7b8a79bc4102fd8aa/t/5ed8dcb21 5a38f0504cbd294/1591270588418/COVID+19+humanitarian+scenarios_Upd ate_June4th.pdf

International Labour Organisation (n.d.) *ILO Glossary Index Unemployment Rate*, International Labour Organisation, accessed on: 28/08/2020, https://ilostat.ilo. org/glossary/unemployment-rate/

International Maize and Wheat Improvement Center (CIMMYT) (2021) 2025: Agri-food systems in a plus COVID-19 world: Global Perspective, Unpublished.

JiSC (2013) Scenario planning: a guide to using this strategic planning tool for making flexible long-term plans, accessed on: 29/08/2020, https://www.jisc.ac. uk/guides/scenario-planning

Lamblin, Victoria (2017) The driver report, in *The Prospective and Strategic Foresight Toolkit*, Paris, Futuribles.

Milliken, F (1987) Three types of perceived uncertainty about the environment: state, effect, and response uncertainty, *The Academy of Management Review*, 12(1), pp.133–143. page 136, DOI: https://doi.org/10.5465/amr.1987.4306502

Organization for Economic Cooperation and Development (OECD) (n.d.) *OECD Member Countries*, OECD, accessed on: 7/08/2020, http://www.oecd.org/about/

Ritchey, T (2018) General morphological analysis as a basic scientific modelling method, *Technological Forecasting and Social Change*, 126, pp.81–91. DOI: http://dx.doi.org/10.1016/j.techfore.2017.05.027

Schwartz, Peter (1996) *The Art of the Long View*, Toronto, Doubleday.

World Bank (2021) Unemployment, total (% of total labor force) (modeled ILO estimate), World Bank, accessed on: 20/02/2021, https://data.worldbank.org/indicator/SL.UEM.TOTL.ZS

World Bank (n.d. a) *Metadata Glossary GDP Annual %*, The World Bank, accessed on: 1/08/2020, https://databank.worldbank.org/metadataglossary/jobs/series/NY.GDP.MKTP.KD.ZG#:~:text=GDP%20is%20the%20sum%20of,the%20value%20of%20the%20products.&text=Each%20industry's%20contribution%20to%20growth,in%20the%20industry's%20value%20added

World Bank (n.d. b) *Metadata Poverty Headcount Ratio at National Poverty Lines (% of Population)*, The World Bank, accessed on: 1/08/2020, https://databank.worldbank.org/metadataglossary/millennium-development-goals/series/SI.POV.NAHC

World Health Organisation (n.d.) *R&D Blueprint and COVID-19*, World Health Organisation, accessed: 29/08/2020, https://www.who.int/teams/blueprint/covid-19

Annex 1
Glossary

accountability "The process of using power responsibly, taking account of, and being held accountable by, different stakeholders, and primarily those who are affected by the exercise of such power" (CHS 2015, p. 37).

actor An actor is a person, a group, a movement, an organisation, an enterprise or an institution with a role in your system of study.

agility "The capacity to react quickly to rapidly changing circumstances" (Brown and Agnew 1982, p. 29).

decomposition and externalisation "Decomposition means breaking a problem down into its component parts. Externalization means getting the problem out of our heads and into some visible form that we can work with" (Heuer 1999, p. 85).

driver A driver is a factor or a combination of factors that drive a process. In foresight, critical drivers are the most important and uncertain factors in your system of study. They are used as the basis of your scenarios.

factor The dynamics, phenomena and events both natural and man-made which exist in your system of study.

foresight Foresight is not a prediction. It is a process of looking forward in time and using collective intelligence and imagination to consider a range of possible futures. It is the first phase in strategic foresight (definition derived from Lustig 2017).

foresight base A set of analytical outputs created during the structural analysis stage which is the foundation of your strategic foresight study and represents all the research you have done and information you have gathered.

formal humanitarian actors Actors for whom humanitarian work is their primary purpose, who have had a role in shaping the institutions that govern and structure international humanitarian action, and, finally, who subscribe to traditional humanitarian principles.

208　*Glossary*

These actors include the United Nations (UN), international non-governmental organisations (INGOs), the International Red Cross and Red Crescent Movement, and traditional donor governments such as those in the OECD Development Assistance Committee (adapted from IARAN 2016, p. 6).

formal humanitarian system The system composed of formal humanitarian actors, their economy, the Western rules and norms that govern their actions and the dynamics of power and influence.

futures studies "The study of systems and methodologies directed toward foreseeing, managing and creating the future" (Jensen 2012, p. 1).

humanitarian action All activities which are undertaken to improve the human condition (covering the spectrum of the humanitarian–development–peace nexus).

humanitarian ecosystem "All actors who participate in and contribute to humanitarian action (those who are part of the formal humanitarian sector and those who are not), the dynamics of the relationships between them and the factors that impact their operation" (IARAN 2018, p. 5).

local actors "Local actors includes civil society organizations engaged in relief and recovery in their own country (LNGOs, NNGOs and National Red Cross/Red Crescent Societies), local and national level state authorities of an affected country that are engaged in relief and recovery, and private-sector (for-profit) entities engaged in relief and recovery in their own country" (IARAN 2018, p. 5).

mission The mission is how the actor is going to reach its destination; it is the actor's path for its journey towards a possible future.

non-formal humanitarian actors Actors who have been operating on the periphery of the formal humanitarian sector but are gaining in influence and importance, including people affected by crises, local authorities, national governments in areas of humanitarian operations, military actors, private sector actors, local NGOs and new donors (adapted from IARAN 2016, p. 6).

non-formal humanitarian system The system composed of non-formal humanitarian actors, their economy, the culture of humanitarian action indigenous to each area, Western rules and norms, and the dynamics of power and influence.

operational dimension Lowest level of strategic thinking referencing to operations.

operations Operations are the activities to implement to produce outputs or outcomes to accomplish a strategy.

people affected by crises "The totality of people with different needs, vulnerabilities and capacities who are affected by disasters, conflict, or other crises at a specific location. For the purposes of this report, this includes people directly affected and indirectly affected, as well as members of communities who are hosting displaced affected people" (IARAN 2018, p. 5).

planning A process to translate a strategy into an effective plan to implement, identifying the activities and the outputs necessary to achieve a strategy. It is the third phase in strategic foresight.

programme A programme is a combination of many projects contributing to an overall objective or general objective.

project A project is an intervention with one specific objective or goal to achieve.

purpose The purpose is why the actor adds value to what it aspires achieve; it is the actor's vehicle for its journey towards a possible future.

quality Quality is determined by three elements: effectiveness, efficiency and relevance.

scenarios Scenarios are images of possible futures. They are narratives created to explore how the dynamics of a system could change over a given time period. Building scenarios is the second stage of foresight.

stakeholder An actor concerned by a strategy for your system of study.[1]

stratagem A stratagem is an alternative subset of a strategy used to lower-level objectives of strategic options to find a more advantageous approach. create misdirection. To build a stratagem is a tactical-level exercise consisting in disarticulating and rearticulating

strategic development Strategic development is a process which articulates possible futures with a strategy. Through this process actors identify objectives and their hierarchy, evaluate options, consider choices, and decide which strategy to implement. It is the second phase in strategic foresight.

strategic dimension Highest level of strategic thinking referring to strategy.

strategic foresight A process that enables actors to use collective intelligence to build their understanding of possible futures and identify pathways to achieve their vision. This process includes three phases: foresight, strategic development and planning.

strategic options Groups of objectives where you can distinguish one higher objective at the top and a chain of connected lower objectives below.

strategy A strategy defines an overall objective or mission, and its underpinning hierarchy of objectives; it is a journey towards a possible future.

210　*Glossary*

structural analysis　Structural analysis is a combination of tools that helps you to gather information, categorise the information that you have collected, analyse the complexity in your system, consider the way in which your system will evolve and synthesise the outputs so that they are digestible and easy to engage with. It is the first stage of foresight.

system　"A set of elements or parts that is coherently organised and interconnected in a pattern or structure" (Meadows 2008, p. 188).

system of study　The frame/parameters you have set to define the system that you will be studying in your strategic foresight project. Your system of study is defined by your topic, viewpoint and time horizon.

tactical dimension　Medium level of strategic thinking referring to tactics.

tactics　Tactics define the ordered combination of outputs or outcomes to accomplish a strategy.

time horizon　The length of the outlook of your study, e.g. 2 years, 5 years, 10 years.

topic　The issue or question that you would like to explore.

uncertainty　"An individual's perceived inability to predict something accurately" (Milliken 1987, p. 136).

value chain　The value chain is the sequence of strategic activities of an organisation (adapted from Kaplinsky 2001).

viewpoint　The perspective from which you explore a system. Your viewpoint can be either organisational (the structure and dynamics of your organisation are part of the system that you are exploring) or contextual (your organisation will be considered as an actor among the other actors of the system you are exploring and the focus will be on the evolution of the context).

vision　The vision defines the horizon of a journey towards a possible future, what the actor aspires to be and/or what the actor will achieve in the future; it's the actor's destination.

worldview　"The culture, values, beliefs and language that frame how a system operates" (IARAN 2018, p. 5).

Note

1 This is a larger definition than that used by the European Commission (EC) Project Cycle Management (PCM) Guidelines: "Any individuals, groups of people, institutions or firms that may have a significant interest in the success or failure of a project (either as implementers, facilitators, beneficiaries or adversaries) are defined as 'stakeholders'" (EuropeAid 2004, p. 61).

References

CHS Alliance, The Sphere Project, Groupe URD (2015) *CHS Guidance Notes and Indicators*, accessed on: 19/03/2021, available at: https://corehumanitarianstandard.org/resources/chs-guidance-notes-and-indicators

Brown J L and Agnew N M (1982) Corporate agility, *Business Horizons*, 25(2), pp. 29–33, ISSN 0007-6813, https://doi.org/10.1016/0007-6813(82)90101-X

EuropeAid (2004) *Project Cycle Management Guidelines: Aid Delivery Methods*, Vol.1, Brussels, accessed on 19 March 2021, available at: https://europa.eu/capacity4dev/iesf/documents/aid-delivery-methods-project-cycle-management-guidelines-europeaid-2004

Harrison, K (2019) What is value chain analysis?, *Business News Daily*, accessed on: 14/04/21, available at: https://www.businessnewsdaily.com/5678-value-chain-analysis.html#sthash.FawTepyB.dpuf

Heuer, Richard (1999) *Psychology of Intelligence Analysis*, Virginia, Centre for the Study of Intelligence, CIA.

IARAN (2016) *Future of Aid: INGOs in 2030*, London, IARAN, accessed on: 11/02/2021, available at: https://www.iaran.org/future-of-aid

IARAN (2018) *Voices to Choices: Expanding Crisis-affected People's Influence over Aid Decisions: An Outlook to 2040*, IARAN, accessed on: 15/03/2021, available at: https://www.iaran.org/voices-to-choices

Jensen, C J (2012) Beyond the tea leaves II: Integrating futures research into intelligence analysis, in Understanding and Improving Intelligence Analysis: Learning from Other Disciplines Conference, London, 12–13 July 2012, accessed on: 10/04/2021, available at: https://www.scribd.com/document/103632822/Futures-Research-and-Intelligence-Jensen

Kaplinsky, R and Morris, M (2001) *A Handbook for Value Chain Research*, Brighton, UK, Institute of Development Studies, University of Sussex.

Lustig, Patricia (2017) *Strategic Foresight: Learning from the Future*, Axminster, Triarchy Press.

Meadows, D and Wright, D (2008) *Thinking in Systems: A Primer*, London: Chelsea Green Publishing.

Milliken, F (1987) Three types of perceived uncertainty about the environment: state, effect, and response uncertainty, *The Academy of Management Review*, 12(1), pp. 133–143. pg136, DOI: https://doi.org/10.5465/amr.1987.4306502

Mintzberg, H (1987) The strategy concept I: five Ps for strategy, *California Management Review*, 30(1), pp. 11–24. DOI: 10.2307/41165263

Annex 2
Platforms for virtual facilitation/engagement

Even if you are able to run the majority of your strategic foresight processes in person, you may find that by integrating some virtual elements you are able to increase the diversity of those participating, opening the process to many more people, and reduce the costs of the exercise by creating a hybrid approach.

In addition to the specific kinds of platforms outlined next, if you are running a strategic foresight project with a group of stakeholders who will participate throughout the process it can also be useful to have a place where the group can communicate, share resources and coordinate. In the past we have often used Slack (www.slack.com) or Microsoft Teams (www.microsoft.com/en-gb/microsoft-teams/group-chat-soft ware), though we tend to prefer to use Slack as it is easier to access for those without Microsoft accounts and less trouble to integrate participants external to an organisation.

There are a multitude of options from which you can choose, depending on how much you will use each platform and how much money you have to dedicate to such software. We elected not to put specific recommendations of platforms into the facilitation notes of each tool. The number and functionality of platforms can change very quickly over time, and as a result we did not want the processes we outlined to become antiquated too quickly. Nevertheless, we felt it may be useful to include a few recommendations (as relevant and available at the time of writing) to help you explore how to use virtual facilitation in your foresight and strategy development processes. While you may already have online platforms which you are happy to use, following are a few examples of the software that we have regularly exploited in our work.

Polling platforms such as Slido (www.slido.com). A polling platform is one which allows you to conduct live polls, surveys, quizzes and manage audience questions. While Slido is by no means the only platform of its kind (others include Kahoot (www.kahoot.com) and Poll Everywhere

Platforms for virtual facilitation 213

(www.polleverywhere.com)), we have found the ease of its functionality, the ability to personalise the type of questions and the interface through which you engage participants as particularly helpful. What is essential is that whatever platform you choose is easy to moderate alone during a workshop. We have also found that platforms which are free for users and easy to access without an account or any sign-up increases the likelihood of participants engaging.

We use polling platforms (usually Slido) to ask ice-breaking questions, facilitate workshops (such as the MIU workshop), and seek feedback through open text questions, for example during the generation of hypotheses (for both Matrix and Morphological Scenarios) and when presenting draft scenarios.

The use of poling platforms during your research process can be a critical tool for engagement. Participants of events are more likely to be engaged and stay engaged if they can share their input in an easy, user-friendly (and, occasionally important, anonymous) way. Stakeholders who are short on time can communicate a lot of information through a short session using a polling platform, which can be key to ensuring high-level buy-in. Polling platforms also allow you to include a significant number of participants. We have previously run seminars to gather input from over 300 people in one session, an experience which not only opened up the foresight process to more participants but also acted as a way to ensure that the strategic design process was integrating feedback from a greater diversity of stakeholders.

Virtual whiteboards such as Miro (www.miro.com) or Mural (www.mural.com). These are open workspace platforms which gives all participants the chance to edit a shared workboard on which you can set up exercises and workshops. As with Slido, there are other, similar platforms which give you the same functionality, but we find Miro and Mural to be flexible and easy to use.

We use whiteboard platforms (usually Miro) for workshops such as the Scoping workshop, building an Architecture, to solicit feedback from experts on what we are missing from a set of draft scenarios, to do group work on the Strategy Tree or even as an open space to gather ideas throughout the process. The ability to provide an online space for live group work can be indispensable, particularly if you have to run the full foresight and strategy design processes by distance. This virtual whiteboard allows you to simulate the same kind of interaction (the creation of and moving of Post-it notes for example) that you can achieve in a physical workshop.

While we feel that these are both fairly intuitive to use, there is a certain amount of practice that is required to becoming fully confident on

214 *Platforms for virtual facilitation*

the platform. As such, if you are going to use one, we recommend that you ensure that the first few exercises are simple and more limited in how much of the platform's functionality you are asking participants to use. You can lock parts of your board to stop them from being inadvertently moved around and also hide particular frames to keep people's attention on the exercise at hand. As a facilitator using any kind of virtual whiteboard, you need to ensure that you set out the ground rules before allowing people into the space and that you feel confident to clean up as you go.

Dynamic presentations such as Prezi (www.prezi.com) or Haiku Deck (www.haikudeck.com). Being able to create presentations that are easy to share online and can be used by multiple different stakeholders can be a very useful communications tool. While of course it is possible to create a slide deck using other software, we have found that the dynamism of a presentation on a platform such as Prezi can increase the interest of your audience.

We find that this type of presentation can be especially useful when trying to share the overall foresight and strategic design process with the participants at the outset of the project and as a way to wrap up and communicate your findings. It is also useful if you can structure the presentation so that it is easy to share, for others to cascade the output to the interested stakeholders who may not have been able to be part of the process.

In addition to how much use you will get from any particular platform and the cost (some are free but often you will not get the full functionality of the system on a free account), you should consider whether the bandwidth each platform requires will be a problem for any of the stakeholders that you are seeking to include. The purpose of these virtual tools is to be able to be inclusive of different perspectives which will improve the quality of your analysis and generate buy-in. If you create a process which is inaccessible to many people due to their limited or potentially cost-prohibitive internet access, then you will not achieve these goals. While we have used these tools to run projects and workshops with colleagues from across the world in many different contexts with limited interruption or problems, it is something that you should consider before finalising your approach. Where limited internet is a constraint, you can often fall back to using spreadsheets and surveys (such as Survey Monkey (www.surveymonkey.com), among others), which are easier for people to manage though less interactive.

We do not seek to promote or endorse any particular platform. However, we wanted to share our experience to support you in exploring how virtual platforms can support your foresight and planning exercises.

Index

accountability 6, 48, 207
actor: and actor analysis 40, 61–62,
111, 162, 164, 193; and agenda
141–142, 144, 147, 149; and business
sector actors 7, 9; as component
96–97; definition 94, 207; and
formal humanitarian system 4;
and humanitarian actors 1–3, 6–7,
10–15, 20–21, 36, 38, 44, 47–48,
50–52, 55–56, 72, 76–77, 79; and
hypotheses 41, 137; and importance
30–31, 111, 141; as influential 36–37,
63, 146, 149, 151, 181–183, 191;
and local actors 208; and military
actors 2; as participant 24, 137; and
power 10; and roles of 40, 141, 144,
146, 153, 156–157, 160; and short-
termism trap 47–48; and state actors
2, 5–7; and strategic foresight 8; and
workshops 135
actor game analysis 141, 145; *see also*
game of actors
Actor/Objective matrix (MAO) *see*
MAO (Actor/Objective Matrix)
actors and factors: and Architecture
100–102, 113; assessing as
components 26–30; and MIU
107–110, 113–115; and PESTLE 36,
94–98, 100
Actors File: agenda 141–142, 144–145,
149; and facilitation notes 145; and
foresight 24, 54; and frequently asked
questions 144–145; and importance
of actors 30–31, 141–142; and
power analysis 38; and prerequisites
141; role of the actor 142, 144;

and scenario building 31; as used in
MID 146–147, 149, 159–161; and
workshops 149, 161
'ages of humanitarianism' 4–6
agility 11, 49, 54, 70, 76–77, 207
alternative futures approach 43–44
anticipation, culture of 47–48, 50–51, 77
Architecture: and Actors Files 141–142,
144; and foresight 24; and Matrix
Scenarios 126–128; and MIU 107,
110, 113, 115; and Morphological
Scenarios 117; and prerequisites 100;
and system maps 27; and templates
100–102, 106; as used in MID 146;
as used in Writing Scenarios 166; and
workshops 105–106
assumptions 24, 90–91, 93, 111, 164

Barnett, M. 4–6
bias: and challenges to 14, 77;
and mental models 90–91; and
methodological bias 62; as obstacle
23, 91; and workshops 89, 153
bishops 156, 182–183; *see also* MID
(Influence/Dependency Matrix),
interpretation
Bourse, Francois 195
brainstorming 26–27, 31, 98, 125,
131–132
business sector 7, 9, 20, 48–49
buy-in 20, 45, 84, 171, 182, 196

Candy, Stuart 39, 163
case studies: in East Africa and the Horn
34–35; and MAO 62–69; and Matrix
Scenarios 32–33; and Morphological

216 *Index*

Scenarios 34–35; in South Sudan 57–69, 71–72; and Strategy Tree 57–61; and Sudan 2027 (MID) 157, 160, 182; and Testing 71–72
causal analysis 55, 170–171
causality, diagram of 56; *see also* Strategy Tree
Causal Layered Analysis (Inayatullah) 42–43
cause-effect *see* Strategy Tree
changes: critical changes 22, 82, 84–93; and grouping of changes 92; important 89, 90; moderate 90; *see also* Scoping Workshop
classical actor mapping 61
Clausewitz, Carl von 10–11
collaboration: and case studies 33, 71–72; and the importance of 56, 69–70, 73; and MAO 192; and Scoping Workshop as 91; and short-termism 49; and strategic development 76–77, 176; and toolkit tools 79; in vision 147, 182
communication tools 21–22, 37–38, 40, 45, 163
complexity: and analysis of 117; and Architecture 100; and Matrix and Morphological Scenarios 126; and reducing 27–29; and scenarios 32, 123; and the Strategy Tree 170, 177; and structural analysis 24, 26; and system complexity 24, 26
conflictual and consensual objectives 62, 190–191; *see also* MAO (Actor/Objective Matrix), interpretation
contextual study *see* viewpoint
control, line of 153, 182–183
COVID-19 pandemic 12, 15, 32, 80, 165

decision-making: and bias 14; and evaluating strategies 195, 203; and MACTOR method 146; and money 7; and participation in 69–70; and PESTLE 94; and power 2–3, 7–8; and Project Cycle Management (PCM) systems 48, 50; and scenarios 21–22, 31–32, 35, 39–40, 163; and strategic development tools 76, 146; and strategic foresight 11–12, 14–15, 17, 20–21, 35, 38, 45; and SWOT

analysis 41; and testing strategies 70–72, 201; and uptake 39–42, 45
decomposition 26, 207
'Dictatorship and Dinka Dominance' 57–58, 60, 63, 67–68, 71
dimensions: operational dimension 208; strategic dimension 209; tactical dimension 62, 210
disarticulation and rearticulation 190–192
disaster risk reduction (DRR) funding 48; *see also* money
diversionary tactics *see* tactics
donors 2–3, 6–7, 38, 48–50
draft strategy: and assessment of 62; and case studies 58–61, 63, 67–69, 71–72; and game of actors analysis 61, 63; and refining of 181, 191; and the Strategy Tree 56–57, 61, 170, 176; and utility of 70
driver: and CLA 42–43; and critical drivers 21, 28–35, 110–112, 117–119; definition of 207; and hypotheses 119–121, 123, 131–132, 163–164; and Matrix Scenarios 126–136; and MIU 107; and Morphological Scenarios 117–119, 124–125; and Writing Scenarios 164, 166; *see also* Driver Files
Driver Files: and complexity 140; and drivers 30–31, 137–139; and foresight 24; and game analysis 145; and hypotheses 131, 139; and important factors 137; and indicators 139, 166; and Matrix Scenarios 126, 130–131, 135–136; and MID 146; and Morphological Scenarios 117, 119, 121, 124–125, 131; and prerequisites 137; and workshops 135; *see also* driver

early warning 21
economy 2–3, 7, 14, 38; *see also* money
ecosystem *see* humanitarian ecosystem
emergency responses *see* humanitarian and emergency response
EuropeAid 49, 51–52, 54–56, 72–73, 170
European Commission (EC) 49, 51–52

facilitation notes for workshops: and Actors File 145; and Architecture

105–106; and Driver Files 140; and Matrix Scenarios 134–136; and MID 152, 154, 160–162; and MIU 113–116; and Morphological Scenarios 124–125; and PESTLE 98–99; and Scoping Workshop 91–93; and Strategy Tree 176–180; and Writing Scenarios 168–169

factor: as component 95–97; and critical factors 29; definition of 94–95, 207; and Driver Files 138; and impact of 36; and influence of 28; and Matrix Scenarios 126, 134; and MIU grouping 110–111, 117–119; and morphological analysis 117; and strategic development 56; and the Strategy Tree 170, 173

factors and actors *see* actors and factors

finances *see* money

foresight: and analysis 20, 35, 37–39, 44; and assumptions 91; and decision making 35, 38, 45; definition of 207; and foresight studies 12, 22, 34–35, 45, 57, 91, 101, 170; and hypotheses 119; and PCM systems 51; as phase 8–10, 61–62; and power 9; and projects 34, 44–45; and scenarios 35, 39, 124, 176; and stages of 21, 24; and strategy 73; and tools 26, 79; *see also* strategic foresight

foresight base: and creation of 74; definition of 207; and strategic development 54–55, 57, 61, 63, 91; and structural analysis 24, 31

formal humanitarian actors: and bureaucratisation 6–7; definition of 2, 207–208; and funding 3, 12, 48; and power 3–4, 7–8; and short-termism 48; and standards development 6; and strategic development 55–57; and strategic foresight 13–14, 38; and strategy 6–7, 11, 76; *see also* case studies

formal humanitarian system 4–8, 13–14, 23, 176, 208

frequently asked questions and workshops: and Actors File 144–145; and Architecture 105; and Driver Files 140; and Matrix Scenarios 134; and MIU 113; and Morphological

Scenarios 124; and PESTLE 97; and Scoping Workshop 91; and Strategy Tree 176; and Writing Scenarios 168

funding *see* money

fundraising 13; *see also* money

futures: and actors 35, 37; and alternate futures 23, 43–44; and assumptions 91; and being futures-focused 17, 21, 37–39, 44, 48, 55, 195; and brainstorming 26; and CLA 42–43; and decision making 41, 70; and evolution of 9; and experiential futures 39; and generic futures 43–44; and Matrix Scenarios 133–134; and Morphological Scenarios 34; and scenarios 31–32, 35, 38–40, 62, 124, 164, 171, 176–177; and strategic development 56; and strategic foresight 13; and strategy 52, 54; and Writing Scenarios 164–166

futures studies 9, 45, 117, 137, 208

game of actors: and MAO 74; and MID 30, 146, 153, 157–160, 162, 181; and structural analysis 61–63, 111

general (higher) objectives (GO): and case studies 58, 61, 67–69; and draft strategies 176, 182; and strategic development 61; and strategy 73, 190; *see also* objectives

Geneva Conventions 4–6

'Global governance and international aid' 128, 130

goals: and long-term goals 49–50, 73; and Sustainable Development Goals (SDGs) 3, 12, 44; and testing 197

Godet, M. 9, 47, 117

Grand Bargain (2016) 8

Heuer, Richard 139, 207

higher objectives *see* general (higher) objectives (GO)

humanitarian action: definition of 1–2, 208; evolution of 7; and power 12; and quality of 6–8, 44; and stratagems 181; and strategic foresight 12–14, 52; and strategy 11; and systems thinking 37, 44

humanitarian and emergency response 1

218 *Index*

humanitarian ecosystem: and
Architecture 101–102, 105, 107;
and collaboration 56; and culture of
reactivity 47; definition of 2, 208;
and LFA 48; and money 2–3; and
power 3–4; and strategic foresight 12,
14–15
humanitarianism 4, 8
hypothesis: and actor relationships
159; and creating them 119–121,
134–135; definition of 119–120,
131; and Driver Files 135, 137, 140;
as historical hypothesis 120; and
hypothesis grid 121, 124–125, 163;
and LFA 49; and Matrix Scenarios
130–134; and Morphological
Scenarios 34–35, 37, 119, 139;
and scenarios 40, 121, 123–124;
as situational hypothesis 120; as
theoretical hypothesis 120; and trend
hypothesis 119, 131; and uncertainty
119–120, 137

IARAN (Inter-Agency Research and
Analysis Network): as author 2, 29,
128, 165, 208–210; as programme
15; and the Strategy Tree 55
impact and readiness 88–90, 92–93
impactfulness *see* importance and
uncertainty
Impact/Uncertainty Matrix *see* MIU
(Importance/Uncertainty Matrix)
imperial humanitarianism *see* 'ages of
humanitarianism'
implication: and implication line 153,
156, 191; and MAO 183–184,
187–188, 190–191; and scenarios
132, 135, 166, 168
importance and uncertainty: and actors
62, 141–142, 144–145; and actors
and factors 27; and factors 110–112,
118, 134, 137; and heavy trends
110–111; in Matrix Scenarios 126,
128, 134; and MIU 29, 107, 110; and
scenario drivers 118–119, 126, 128;
and workshop participants 113–115;
see also uncertainty
Importance/Uncertainty Matrix (MIU)
see MIU (Importance/Uncertainty
Matrix)

Inayatullah, Sohail 42
influence: of actors and factors 27; and
MID chart 61, 149, 157, 161, 164,
183, 191; and objectives 187
influence and dependency 28–29,
146, 149, 157, 159; *see also* MID
(Influence/Dependency Matrix)
Influence/Dependency Matrix (MID)
see MID (Influence/Dependency
Matrix)
international non-governmental
organizations (INGOs) 2–7, 34
International Red Cross and Red
Crescent Movement 2–3, 5–6

Jouvenel, Bertrand de 163

kings 153, 182–183, 191; *see also* MID
(Influence/Dependency Matrix),
interpretation
knights 157, 182–183, 191; *see also* MID
(Influence/Dependency Matrix),
interpretation

LFA (Logical Framework Approach)
48–51, 54–56, 61, 72–73, 76, 170
liberal humanitarianism *see* 'ages of
humanitarianism'
line of control 153, 182–183
lower objectives *see* specific (or lower)
objectives (SO)

MACTOR method 146, 181; *see also*
MAO (Actor/Objective Matrix);
MID (Influence/Dependency
Matrix)
Maietta, M. 4, 6
'Malnutrition and morbidity are
addressed among the most vulnerable
population in case of emergency'
67–68
MAO (Actor/Objective Matrix): and
Actor x Objective grid 183–184,
187–188, 190, 193; and assessing
strategy 181; divide and conquer
191; and draft strategy 61–67, 71,
74; and frequently asked questions
191–192; and implication 183–184,
187–188, 190–191, 193; and
interpretation 188, 190, 192; and

MACTOR method 146; and the
MAO table 183–184, 187–188,
192–194; and the MAO test 182;
and MID chart 191–193; and
relevancy tests 201; and stratagem
design 190–192, 194; and strategic
development 54; and Trojan Horse
approach 191; and workshops
181–182, 184, 187–188,
190–194, 196
maps and mapping 27, 31, 61, 102
matrix, temporal 49
matrix approach 31–32, 163–164
Matrix Scenarios: as communication
tool 37; and creating a scenario
matrix 132; and Driver Files 130;
and drivers 126–131; and foresight
24; and hypotheses 130–131; and
PESTLE 128–130; and scenarios
32–37, 133–134, 163; and workshops
126, 134–136
means-end *see* Strategy Tree
MICMAC (Matrix-Based
Multiplication Applied to a
Classification) 28, 30–31, 34
MID (Influence/Dependency Matrix):
and actors 30, 146, 149, 153,
156–160, 162, 181; and Actors File
159; and Actor x Actor table (MID
table) 147, 149, 151, 153, 159,
161–162; and facilitation notes 152,
154, 160–162; and foresight 24, 54;
and interpretation 153, 156–157;
and MID chart 61–63, 67, 151,
153, 156–157, 162, 182, 184; and
output 61, 164, 181, 183; and power
analysis 38; and prerequisites 146; and
robustness 30, 146; and viewpoint
147; and workshops 36, 146–147,
149, 151, 159–162, 182, 188, 192; *see
also* influence and dependency
military 2, 9–11, 21, 49
misdirection 11, 62, 67, 181
MIU (Importance/Uncertainty Matrix):
and Actors File 141–142, 144–145;
and Architecture 107, 108, 113, 115;
and drivers 31, 34, 36, 124, 134, 137;
facilitation notes 113–116; and factor
structure 117–118; and foresight 24;
frequently asked questions 112; and

interpretation 110–111; and Matrix
Scenarios 126, 130, 132–135; and
MID 146–147; and Morphological
Scenarios 117; and outputs 111,
164, 177; and PESTLE 107; and
prerequisites 107; and reducing
complexity 28–29; workshops
113–116
models: and economic models 7, 14,
38; and mental models 23–24, 45,
90–91; and quantitative modeling 21
money 2–3, 5–6, 12–13, 20, 47–50
monitoring 24, 110–111, 114, 119,
137, 167
morphological as approach 31–32, 117,
125, 134, 163–164
Morphological Scenarios: and Driver
Files 119, 126, 137; and drivers 111,
117–121, 123–124; and foresight 24;
and hypotheses 37, 119–124, 131,
139; and Matrix Scenarios 131; and
MIU 117, 124; and prerequisites
117; and scenarios 32, 34, 121–123;
and workshops 123–125; and writing
scenarios 35, 163

neo-humanitarianism *see* 'ages of
humanitarianism'
non-formal humanitarian actors 2, 6–8,
14, 38, 55, 76, 208
non-formal humanitarian system 208
non-governmental organizations
(NGOs) 3, 5
no-regret actions 41

objective analysis 55, 61, 170, 173
objectives: and case studies 58–61,
67–69; as conflictual and consensual
62, 190–192; and core objectives
191; and critical objectives 73–74;
and diagram of 56; and disarticulation
and rearticulation of 190–192;
and general objectives 52, 58–61,
67–69, 73, 176, 182–183, 190;
and hierarchy of 52, 56–57, 170;
and ideal consensual objectives 67;
and means-end objectives 56; and
overarching (o.) objectives 197; and
solutions and opportunities 173; and
specific objectives 56, 58–61, 67–69,

220 *Index*

73, 176–177, 180–182, 190–192; and stratagems 62; and strategic development 73; and strategic objectives 146; and tactical objectives 146; *see also* MAO (Actor/Objective Matrix); Strategy Tree

ODA (official development assistance) 2–4, 6–7, 48–49

online platforms *see* virtual platforms and tools

online workshops *see* workshops

operational dimension 208

operations 13, 52, 141, 208

optimisation 73–74, 91, 98

organisational study *see* viewpoint

outlook: and Actors File 30; and draft strategy 70; and drivers 111, 119, 138–139, 167; and heavy trends 110; and hypotheses 119, 121; and strategy implementation 62; and system of study 23, 30; and uncertainty 37; and Writing Scenarios 164–165, 167; *see also* time horizon

'out of game' 157

outputs: and analytical outputs 54; and Architecture 27, 36; and foresight base 24; and MAO 62, 74; and MICMAC 28; and MID 38, 61; and MIU 28, 107, 111, 113; and morphological analysis 117; and PCM 62; and PESTLE 27; and quality of 76; and Scoping Workshop 82; and strategic development 30, 52; and Strategy Tree tool 56–57; of structural analysis 31, 74; and toolkit 54, 79

overarching (o.) objectives 197, 200; *see also* objectives

overarching strategy 199–200, 202

participants in workshops 83–84, 176, 182, 196; *see also* workshops

path dependence 14, 20

path of action 50

pawns 156, 182–183, 191; *see also* MID (Influence/Dependency Matrix), interpretation

PCM (Project Cycle Management) 48–52, 54–56, 61–62, 72–73, 76–77, 170; *see also* LFA (Logical Framework Approach); ToC (theory of change)

people affected by crises: and actors 1–2, 8, 13, 47–48; definition of 208–209; and funding 3; and strategy development 7, 50, 76, 171, 176, 182, 196

persuasion 11

PESTLE (political, economic, social, technological, legal and environmental dimensions): and actors and factors 95–96, 106, 108; and Actors Files 141–142; and assumptions 94; and brainstorming 26–27; and Driver Files 138; and foresight 24, 36, 91; and frequently asked questions 97; and Matrix Scenarios 128–130; and MID 146; and output 94; and PESTLE table 95, 100–102, 109; and prerequisites 94, 100; and workshops 98–99

plan 52, 142

planning: and foresight 21, 209; and LFA 54–55, 72–73; and PCM systems 54–55; and scenarios 32, 37; and short-termism 48–49; and strategic foresight 38; and strategic planning 52, 57, 107; and ToC 49, 72

polling: and polling platforms 212–213; and seminars with live polling 113–115; and workshops 113–115, 193–194

poverty 7, 12, 96

power 2–4, 7–10, 12, 38

preparedness 22, 47–48, 87–88, 90

prerequisites for workshops: and Actors File 141; and Architecture 100; and Matrix Scenarios 126; and MID 146; and MIU 107; and Morphological Scenarios 117; and PESTLE 94; and Scoping Workshop 82–83; and Strategy Tree 170–171; and Writing Scenarios 163

problem analysis in LFA 170

programme: and agendas 142; and analysis 195; and case studies 69; definition of 52, 209; and design 56, 76; and integrative programming approaches 44; and objectives 61, 69, 73, 176; and operational research programme (IARAN) 15; and theory 49

Index   221

programming 13
project: and case studies 33–34, 69; definition 52, 209; and design 56, 69; and objectives 61, 69, 73, 176; as plan 52; and planning approaches 170; and scenarios 31; and strategic foresight 80; and strategic options 174
purpose 209

quality 48, 159, 209
queens 156, 182–183; *see also* MID (Influence/Dependency Matrix), interpretation

reactivity, culture of 47
readiness *see* Scoping Workshop
relevancy test 71
resilience 1, 7, 12, 47, 56
robustness 30, 34–35, 70–72, 74, 113, 117
roles and actors 40, 141, 144, 146, 153, 156–157, 160

scenarios: and Actor x Objective grids 183; and alternative futures 43–44; and analysis of 20, 41, 111; and archiving 72; as 'base case' or 'trend' 123; and building and construction of 9, 21–22, 24, 28, 30–32, 34–37, 39, 42–44, 51, 54–55, 57, 126, 146; and case studies 58–60; and CLA 42–43; and creating scenarios 17, 74, 124–125; and creating strategies 38, 112; and definition of 209; and development of 196; and draft strategies 62, 174; and explanatory scenarios 15, 17; exploratory scenarios 32, 74; and foresight 9, 21, 24, 124, 170; and game of actors 61; and generic futures 43; and hypotheses 121, 123–124, 132; and hypothetical scenarios 31–32; and indicators 166–167; and MAO 181–182, 192–194; and Matrix Scenarios 126, 132–136; and MID 159; and morphological analysis 117; and normative scenarios 31; and PCM systems 51; and predictive scenarios 31; and robustness test 195; and scenario thinking 163; and strategic

development 39, 58, 62, 69, 170–172; and strategy 183–184, 190, 195, 198–202; and Strategy Tree 56, 170–171, 176, 181; and systemic strategy 55; and system of study 164; and Testing 71, 198–199; and uptake of analysis 39–41, 45, 172, 177, 196; and workshops 178–179, 197; and writing scenarios 24, 29, 35, 37, 163–169, 177; *see also* case studies
Scoping Workshop: and assumptions 90–91, 93; and changes 22, 82, 84–88, 90–93; and collaboration 91; and facilitation notes 91–93; and frequently asked questions 91; and Impact/Readiness matrix 88–90; and prerequisites 82–83; and readiness 87–88, 90, 93; and system of study 90, 93; and Writing Scenarios 164
specific (or lower) objectives (SO): and case studies 58–61, 67–69; and draft strategies 58, 176; and strategic development 73; and strategic options 177, 181–182, 190–192; *see also* objectives
stakeholder: and buy-in 20; and collaboration 15; definition of 209; and planning 49; and simulated meetings 40; and strategic development 54–55, 61, 176; and strategic foresight tools 15, 24, 26–27; and uptake of foresight analysis 37; and virtual platforms 212–214; and workshops 36–37, 79, 170, 172, 181, 195
stratagem: definition of 62, 181, 209; design of 67, 190; divide and conquer 191; and identification of 181; and implementation of 74; and Trojan Horse stratagem 67, 191
strategic development: and actor analysis 61–62; as collaborative 55–56, 69–72; definition 209; and foresight 10, 30, 35, 52–53, 74; and futures 55; as futures-focused 76; and game of actors analysis 61; and integration of 73; and MID output 61; and participants 171; and PCM systems 50–52, 54; as process 182, 196; and scenarios 39, 41, 46; and

222 Index

short-termism 48; and strategy 52, 69–74; and the Strategy Tree 57–61, 170–171; and tools 74, 76, 79; and uptake of scenarios 41–42; *see also* strategic foresight

strategic dimension *see* dimensions

strategic foresight: and components 94; and decision making 38; and definition of 1, 8, 209; and humanitarian action 20, 52; and MACTOR method 146; and MID charts 157; and parameters of 23; and PCM systems 50–51; and planning 8, 13–14; and preparedness 76, 90; and projects 45, 80; and short-termism 48; and strategic development 8, 10–12, 15, 17; and systems-based approaches 22–23; and tools 1, 13–15, 17, 21, 24; and workshops 80; *see also* strategic development

strategic options: definition of 209; and game of actors analysis 181; and objectives 56, 170, 177, 181–182, 190–192; and projects 174; and relevancy tests 201; and scenario strategy 191; and the Strategy Tree 170, 174–175, 177–178, 180, 182, 192; and the Trojan Horse approach 191

strategy: and Actors File 141; and agenda 141, 147; and Arabic schools of 11; as concept 10–11, 209; and critical change 91; definition of 10–11, 52, 209; design and development of 6–7, 10, 15, 17, 20, 28, 50–51, 54, 62, 111, 146, 170, 176, 196; and exit strategy 13; and foresight study 91; and futures 11, 38, 170–171; global strategy 71, 200; and grass-roots 77; and implementation 62, 72–73; and LFA analysis 170; and MAO 62, 181; and misdirection 62; and objectives 73; and optimisation 73–74; and refining 74, 197; as robust 70, 74; and scenarios 31, 38, 69, 171, 181–182; and strategic activities 7, 13; and strategic development 52, 69–70; and systemic strategy 55, 79; and testing 70–72, 74

Strategy Tree: and case studies 57–61; and causal analysis 55, 170–171;

and causality 56, 170, 172–174, 176–177, 179; and cause-and-effect 56, 170–173, 179–180; and draft strategy 57–58, 170, 174–176, 180, 182; and end-objectives 174, 177; and frequently asked questions 176; and futures 171, 195; and holistic strategy 170; in MAO 181–184, 190; and means-end 56, 170, 173, 177, 180, 192; and objectives 56–61, 170, 173–174, 176, 179–180, 183; and objectives analysis 55, 170, 173; and prerequisites 170–171; and problems 170–173, 177, 179; and scenarios 170–171, 177, 182, 201; and solutions 170, 173–174; and strategic options 56, 170, 174–175, 177–178, 180, 182, 192; and strategy analysis 170, 174; and time sequence logic 170, 177; and workshops 170–180, 193

structural analysis: and Actors File 160; and Architecture 27; and brainstorming 26–27; and CLA 42–43; and complexity 24, 26–29; and deconstruction 55; definition 210; and foresight 9, 21, 24, 26, 28–29, 54; and game of actors analysis 61, 111; and MAO 182; and Matrix Scenarios 134–135; and mental models 23; and MID 62, 160; in PCM systems 51; and scenarios 31–32, 74, 134, 170, 181, 195; and the Strategy Tree 177; and system of study 55, 141; and testing 182, 186; and time constraints 36

structure 12, 14

Sun, Tzu 10–11, 62

surveys: and agendas 144; and perspective 24; and workshops 98, 113–114, 162, 194, 202, 214

sustainable development 3, 12, 44, 48

Sustainable Development Goals (SDGs) *see* goals

SWOT analysis (strengths, weaknesses, opportunities, and threats) 41, 166

system: definition of 23, 210; and formal humanitarian system 4–8, 13–14, 47, 176; and non-formal humanitarian system 208; and path

Index   223

dependence 14; and systems thinking 11; and understanding of 9–10, 13
system maps 27, 31, 102
system of study: and actors 96–97, 141–142, 144; and agendas 144, 147; and alternative futures 43–44; and assumptions 91; and bias 91; and CLA 42–43; and complexity 27–29, 100, 107, 123, 126, 170, 177; and components 31, 94–95, 100–102, 107, 108; and deconstruction 55; definition of 23, 210; and drivers 111, 118–119, 137; and evolution 55, 76, 108, 111; and factors and actors 96–97; and foresight 74; and game of actors 157, 182; and refining 90, 93; and scenarios 32, 35–36, 74, 117, 164, 195; and strategic development 54–56, 61, 76; and Strategy Tree 56; and structural analysis 21, 36, 61–62; and uncertainty 118, 123, 171; and viewpoints of 100, 181–182, 196
systems-thinking 1, 21, 37, 44

tactical dimension *see* dimensions
tactics: and adapting 62; and agenda 141; definition of 52, 210; and diversionary tactics 191; and humanitarians 14; and objectives 146, 181; and tactical-level exercise 190
terms (short and long): in case studies 32–33; as long-term 47, 49–50, 55, 73, 76; and scenario building 37; and short-termism 45, 47–49, 55, 76
testing: and case studies 71–72; and decision making 201; as a diagnostic tool 70, 195; and frequently asked questions 201; and objectives 197; and prerequisites 195; and relevancy test 71, 195–197, 199–203; and robustness and relevance tables 202; and robustness test 70–71, 74, 195–203; and strategic development 54; and Strategies x Scenarios table 196–197, 201; and templates 196; and workshops 194, 196–203
time horizon: and actors 144; and alternate futures 44; definition of 23, 83, 210; and drivers 138; as parameter 83, 90, 94; and short time horizons 36; and strategy 74; *see also* outlook
ToC (theory of change) 48–51, 54–55, 72–73, 76
trends: and brainstorming 26; and Driver Files 138–139; and heavy trends 34, 110, 112, 114, 134, 164

UN (United Nations) 2, 5, 7, 48
uncertainty: as array 9; and components 28, 107; and decision makers 40; definition of 210; and degree of 9; and drivers 30, 117–118, 137–139; and hypotheses 119, 131; and managing it 13, 50, 80, 137; and scenarios 32, 34, 37, 40, 117, 123; and system of study 117, 171; *see also* importance and uncertainty

value chain 7, 13–14, 210
viewpoint: as contextual 23, 74, 82–84, 88, 100–102, 107, 147; and contextual study 41, 83–84, 101, 105, 126, 128, 130, 147, 171–172, 182, 196; definition of 210; as organisational 23, 74, 82–84, 88, 100–102, 105, 107, 147, 166; and organisational study 41, 83–84, 101, 126, 130, 133, 147, 171–172, 181, 196; as parameter 90, 94, 171, 181, 196
virtual platforms and tools 212–214
virtual whiteboard *see* whiteboard, virtual
vision: and alternative futures 43–44; and collaborative vision 147, 182; as common or shared 22, 27, 34, 82, 163; definition of 210; and organisational vision 38; and strategic development 11; and strategic foresight 8, 11, 14; and strategy 17
visualisation 14, 27, 157, 178, 200
vulnerability 12, 38, 44, 47, 73, 166

war and warfare 11
whiteboard, virtual 92–93, 105–106, 135, 178–179, 202–203, 213–214
'white savior' complex 14

224   *Index*

workshops: and Architecture 105–106; and live polling 113–115, 193–194; and Matrix Scenarios 126, 134–136; and MID 36, 146–147, 149, 151, 159–162; and MIU 113–116; and Morphological Scenarios 123–125; as part of toolkit 79–80; and PESTLE 98–99; and Scoping Workshop 22–23, 82–93, 164; and Strategy Tree 170–180; and uptake of foresight analysis 39, 45–46; virtual workshops 79, 92–93, 98, 113–116, 124–125, 160, 176–178, 192–194, 201–203; *see also* surveys

worldview 1, 14, 210

writing scenarios: and actors 37; and decision making 35; and factors 29; as foresight tool 24, 163–169, 177

Printed in the United States
by Baker & Taylor Publisher Services